New Directions in Book History

Series Editors
Shafquat Towheed
Faculty of Arts
Open University
Milton Keynes, UK

Jonathan Rose
Department of History
Drew University
Madison, NJ, USA

As a vital field of scholarship, book history has now reached a stage of maturity where its early work can be reassessed and built upon. That is the goal of New Directions in Book History. This series will publish monographs in English that employ advanced methods and open up new frontiers in research, written by younger, mid-career, and senior scholars. Its scope is global, extending to the Western and non-Western worlds and to all historical periods from antiquity to the twenty-first century, including studies of script, print, and post-print cultures. New Directions in Book History, then, will be broadly inclusive but always in the vanguard. It will experiment with inventive methodologies, explore unexplored archives, debate overlooked issues, challenge prevailing theories, study neglected subjects, and demonstrate the relevance of book history to other academic fields. Every title in this series will address the evolution of the historiography of the book, and every one will point to new directions in book scholarship. New Directions in Book History will be published in three formats: single-author monographs; edited collections of essays in single or multiple volumes; and shorter works produced through Palgrave's e-book (EPUB2) 'Pivot' stream. Book proposals should emphasize the innovative aspects of the work, and should be sent to either of the two series editors.

Editorial Board:
Marcia Abreu, University of Campinas, Brazil
Cynthia Brokaw, Brown University, USA
Matt Cohen, University of Texas at Austin, USA
Archie Dick, University of Pretoria, South Africa
Martyn Lyons, University of New South Wales, Australia.

* * *

More information about this series at
http://www.palgrave.com/gp/series/14749

Ross K. Tangedal

The Preface

American Authorship in the Twentieth Century

palgrave
macmillan

Ross K. Tangedal
Department of English
University of Wisconsin–Stevens Point
Stevens Point, WI, USA

ISSN 2634-6117   ISSN 2634-6125   (electronic)
New Directions in Book History
ISBN 978-3-030-85153-8   ISBN 978-3-030-85151-4   (eBook)
https://doi.org/10.1007/978-3-030-85151-4

This Palgrave Macmillan imprint is published by the registered company Springer Nature Switzerland AG.
The registered company address is: Gewerbestrasse 11, 6330 Cham, Switzerland

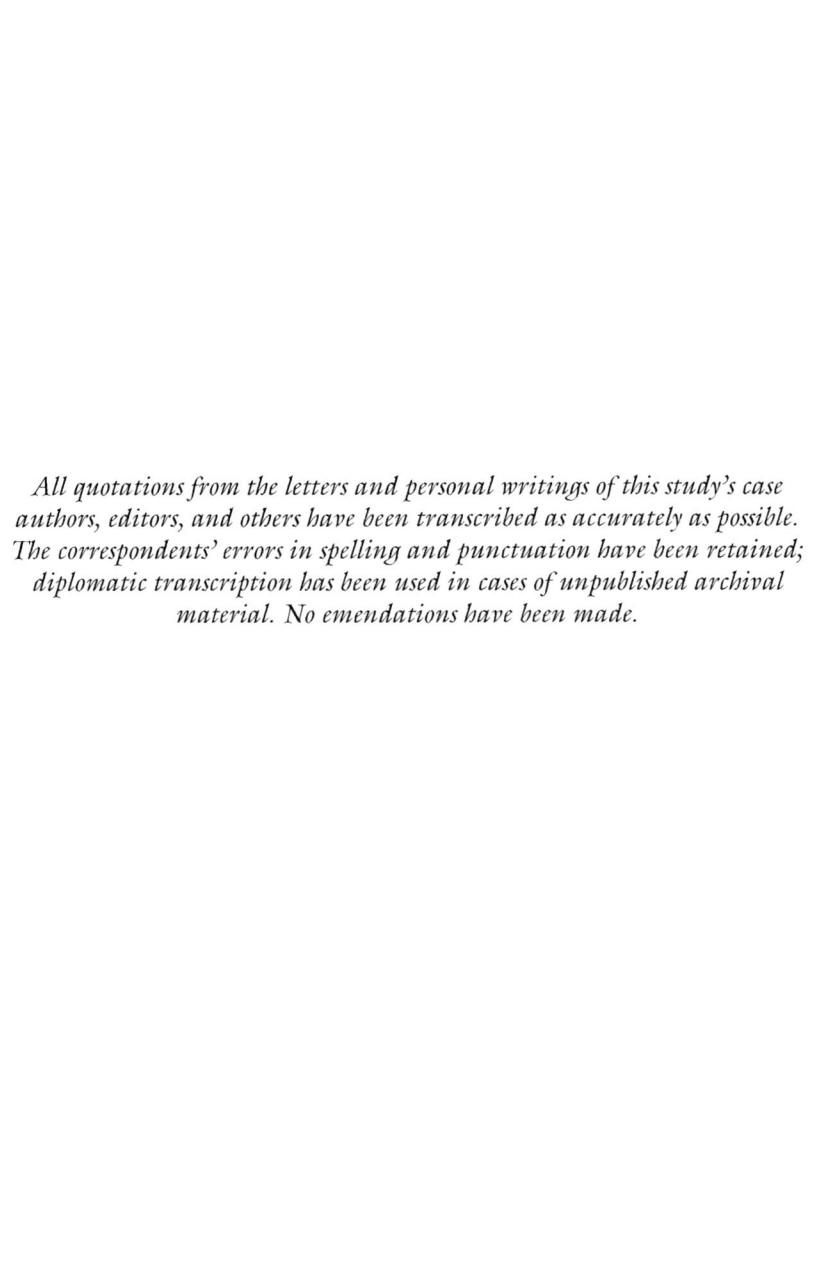

All quotations from the letters and personal writings of this study's case authors, editors, and others have been transcribed as accurately as possible. The correspondents' errors in spelling and punctuation have been retained; diplomatic transcription has been used in cases of unpublished archival material. No emendations have been made.

To my wife and daughters:
CJ, Adeline, and Hazel Tangedal.

ACKNOWLEDGMENTS

From 1925 to 1988, my great-grandfather William "Bill" Willard went from "printer's devil" to print manager and typesetter for the *Plentywood Herald*, a local northeast Montana newspaper. He learned how to set type by hand in the small basement press office on Main Street, and he went on to operate the paper's two Mergenthaler Linotype machines, as well as its small printing press, for well over forty years after that. I did not know this about my Grandpa Bill until I began working on print culture studies and bibliography. In many ways, my research is an extension of his commitment to putting together thousands of papers for the better part of his adult life. As the last Linotype operator in the state of Montana, Bill Willard dedicated his life to print. I am proud to do the same, and this book is my initial investigation into the business of printed works and their creators.

I am indebted to a number of individuals who made this book possible. My work would not be what it is without the mentorship, guidance, and trust of Robert W. Trogdon. He challenges me to be better, to work smarter, and to get it right, and he taught me how to be a scholar and a bookman. He is generous and passionate about doing the work, and through his friendship he continues to teach me. When I call with a question he answers, and when I have an idea he listens. For that I am forever grateful. Wesley Raabe made me a better writer and a more patient editor, and he asked difficult questions that needed answers. James L. W. West III gave excellent feedback on the manuscript and offered critical suggestions that made the book better. These three leading editorial scholars of American literature elevated my appreciation of and commitment to textual studies. They inspire me with their intellects, editorial expertise, and work ethic.

The English Department faculties at Montana State University and Kent State University gave me the tools to write this book. I thank all of my professors, in particular Amy Thomas, Marvin Lansverk, Greg Keeler, Robert Bennett, Kirk Branch, Linda Karell, Philip Gaines, and Lisa Eckert from Montana State, and, with Robert W. Trogdon and Wesley Raabe above, Tammy Clewell, the late Kevin Floyd, and the late Claire Culleton from Kent State. The English Department faculty at Mercyhurst University, especially Brian Reed, Christina Riley-Brown, and Jeffrey Roessner, gave me my first academic job and welcomed me into their program with such grace and enthusiasm. Without them I would not be where I am.

A number of colleagues and friends were generous with their time as this book was completed. Andy Oler read every version of the proposal that became this book, and I am grateful for his honesty, good humor, and friendship. Sara Kosiba, Marc Seals, and Doug Sheldon are good friends who get me through the highs and lows of Midwestern life. Joshua Murray has been my friend since our doctoral days at Kent State, and his goodness knows no bounds. I speak with the five of them weekly, and I am glad they're my friends. Thank you, also, to Dave Arnold, Kirk Curnutt, Scott Emmert, Verna Kale, Adam McKee, Jennifer Nolan, Andy Oler, and Marc Seals for reviewing chapter drafts. The Ernest Hemingway Society, the F. Scott Fitzgerald Society, and the Society for the Study of Midwestern Literature are my scholarly families. I share in the good work of these societies with many of the friends and colleagues listed above, but additionally I would like to thank Jeanne Alexander, Marilyn Atlas, Robert Beasecker, Susan Beegel, Tom Bevilacqua, Jackson Bryer, Bonnie Jo Campbell, Michelle Campbell, Mark Cirino, the late Michael DuBose, Lisa DuRose, Carl Eby, Kayla Forrest, Joe Fruscione, Suzanne del Gizzo, Larry Grimes, Ryan Hediger, Gary Holcomb, Laura Julier, Hilary K. Justice, Kevin Maier, Miriam Mandel, Martina Mastandrea, Debra Moddelmog, Patricia Oman, Scott Ortolano, Rachael Price, David A. Rennie, Gail Sinclair, Sandra Spanier, Kim Suhr, Jeff Swenson, Steven Trout, Lisa Tyler, and Michael Von Cannon.

The Department of English at the University of Wisconsin–Stevens Point (UWSP) deserves special mention for their enthusiastic support of my work: Jeff Snowbarger, for his friendship and integrity; Michael Williams and Rebecca Stephens, for their guidance and care; Mary Bowman, for her mentorship; and Dave Arnold, Mark Balhorn, James

Berry, W. John Coletta, Pat Dyjak, Lauren Gantz, Pat Gott, Tomoko Kuribayashi, Dejan Kuzmanovic, Lynn Ludwig, Wade Mahon, Larry Morgan, Samantha Pech, Erica Ringelspaugh, David Roloff, Robert Sirabian, Michael Steffes, Jill Stukenberg, Julie Tharp, and Chris Williams, for their support. I also wish to thank former Dean Eric Yonke and Dean Joshua Hagan of the College of Letters and Science, along with Tobias Barske, Assistant Dean of the School of Humanities and Global Studies, and Shanny Luft, Associate Dean of General Education and Honors, for their support of my work during my time at UWSP.

My Kent State cohort listened to my questions and shared their expertise; thank you Seth Johnson, Chris McCracken, Heather McCracken, Dan Miller, Melissa Pompili, and Rebekah Taylor-Wiseman. My Montana State cohort was a supportive, tight-knit group; thank you Katie Davison, Lauren Degraffenreid, Beth Forslund, Alsu Gilmetdinova, Aspen Haugen, Danette Long, Rachel Sarkar, and Micaela Young. My more recent editorial and print culture colleagues have added new angles to my research; thank you Noelle Baker, Kathryn Tomasek, Andrew Kopec, Caleb Milligan, and Jonathan Senchyne for modeling strong research and leadership in these fields. I'd also like to thank my good friends Chris Benson, Ryan Brensdal, Brandon Overland, and Edward Yperman for their two decades of friendship. I have been lucky to have had the support of these wonderful friends and colleagues.

I wish to thank the following for granting me access to archival materials: Susan Wrynn, past curator, and Hilary K. Justice, curator, of the Ernest Hemingway Collection at the John F. Kennedy Library in Boston, MA; Don C. Skemer, curator of manuscripts in the Department of Rare Books and Special Collections at Princeton University Library; Timothy Young, curator of Modern Books and Manuscripts, and Matthew Rowe, Library Services Assistant, at the Beinecke Rare Book & Manuscript Library of Yale University; and Alison Hinderliter, Lloyd Lewis Curator of Modern Manuscripts at the Newberry Library in Chicago, IL. *The Complete Letters of Willa Cather*, an ongoing digital project, is available to the public thanks to the Willa Cather Archive, which is freely distributed by the Center for Digital Research in the Humanities at the University of Nebraska–Lincoln. Thank you to project editors Andrew Jewell and Janis P. Stout, as well as to the entire editorial team, for their exceptional work.

I owe a great debt to the following organizations for awarding me research funding crucial to the completion of this book: the Ernest Hemingway Foundation & Society for twice awarding me the

Lewis-Smith-Reynolds Founders Fellowship; the John F. Kennedy Library for awarding me the Ernest Hemingway Research Grant; the Department of English at Kent State University for awarding me the Kenneth R. Pringle Dissertation Fellowship; the Graduate Student Senate of Kent State University for awarding me a Dissertation Research Grant for work at Princeton University Library; Mercyhurst University for awarding me a Thomas Merton Postdoctoral Fellowship; and the University of Wisconsin–Stevens Point for awarding me the University Scholar Award. Finally, I wish to thank Carrie Kline (circulation) and Rebecca Wisniewski (Interlibrary Loan), as well as the front desk staff, at the UWSP Albertson Learning Resources Center (Library) for their assistance in securing dozens of volumes and research materials for me.

Palgrave Macmillan believed in this book from the outset. Allie Troyanos, Rachel Jacobe, Emily Wood, Brian Halm, and the editorial staff have been astute editors and champions of this project from acquisition to publication. Two anonymous readers provided me with additional direction and encouragement, as did series editors Jonathan Rose and Shafquat Towheed. I am also grateful to the editors and peer reviewers of *Authorship*, the *F. Scott Fitzgerald Review*, and the *Hemingway Review*, journals where parts of Chaps. 3, 4, and 5 originally appeared in different versions. Thank you to Ghent University, the Pennsylvania State University Press, and the Ernest Hemingway Foundation & Society for permission to include revised portions of those essays in this book.

My parents, Jerry and Kathy Tangedal, taught me how to work hard at work worth doing. They bought me a complete *Encyclopedia Britannica* when I was five years old, knowing I would read every volume. They worked hard so my siblings and I could be successful. My mother's courage and tenacity, and my father's integrity and passion, are gifts. I'm glad they're my parents. Reanne and Ryan are great siblings, and Jordan and Logan are great cousins. I'm lucky to have them in my life. My in-laws, Rich and Cheryl Boberg, have always supported me, as have my wife's siblings, Christina and Bill. My parents and in-laws gave me a couple of precious writing weeks in April 2021, agreeing to spend time with their granddaughters while I worked on my book manuscript. They'll never know how much that meant to me. On the day he passed away, my grandfather Kurt Ueland was reading Hemingway's *For Whom the Bell Tolls* because I told him it was good. He and my late grandmother Adeline never shied away from a conversation with me about anything, nor from loving and supporting me. They taught me how to dance, how to tell stories, and how to love your family. They were good people, and I miss them and their goodness every day. My grandmother Yvonne Tangedal gave me a deep love of history. She took me to Washington, D.C., when I was eight, indulging my obsession with Abraham Lincoln and the Civil War. Her father was Bill Willard, which may explain her guiding hand over the years.

The most profound thanks belongs to my wife, CJ Tangedal, to whom this book is dedicated. We met in 2009, and since then she has supported me during my time as a graduate student, as a grill cook and irrigation repairman, as a postdoctoral fellow, and, finally, as a professor. She did this in the beginning by working long hours and longer weekends, and by cultivating the special moments for us to hold on to when we were young. She does it today by patterning for our two girls a deep sense of family, work ethic, and love. She makes sure that when I say I have writing to do I write, and she lets me know when it is time to be done for the day. Her sacrifices are part of this book, as there were days and nights when I'd emerge from my office knowing that she had taken care of things. Though we take great pride in sharing the parental and household duties, my wife holds it all together. She is my best friend, and the steady link to the happiness in my life. That happiness is reflected in this book's other dedicatees, our two daughters, Adeline and Hazel. Their intelligence, kindness, love, humor, and capacity for wonder are immeasurable gifts. I am proud of all three of them, who give me more than I deserve every day. This book is for them.

Praise for *The Preface*

"In *The Preface*, Ross K. Tangedal examines an often-overlooked textual element in literature: an opening commentary (either current or in retrospect) by an author about a particular work of fiction. The author addresses the reader directly to recall the creation of the work, to reply to critics, and to assert authority over interpretation. Tangedal's approach in this excellent new monograph yields a great many fresh and valuable insights, both critical and biographical."
—James L. W. West III, Sparks Professor of English, Emeritus,
Pennsylvania State University, USA, Author of *American Authors
and the Literary Marketplace since 1900*

"Ross K. Tangedal's *The Preface: American Authorship in the Twentieth Century* offers an expansive, inclusive take on a textual tradition that most readers consider the print equivalent of a hello. Tangedal's multi-level discussion of this device demonstrates how integral it is to theories of authorship, and how major novelists from Willa Cather to Toni Morrison, and now-overlooked writers like Ring Lardner, employed it to fashion their personae for public consumption. From F. Scott Fitzgerald's early self-deprecation (which did not serve him well) to Ernest Hemingway's pugilistic professionalism to Robert Penn Warren's obsession with historical motive, Tangedal reveals the range writers display and the risks they undertake in this textual space."
—Kirk Curnutt, Professor of English, *Troy University, USA*,
Editor of *American Literature in Transition, 1970–1980*

"Engaging, theoretically sophisticated, and well written, with fresh insights on every page, *The Preface* is much more than a study of prefaces. In the hands of Tangedal, this topic becomes a fascinating study of how the business of writing and publishing and the need for writers to construct and wield authority over their texts and authorial identities shaped the canon of twentieth-century American literature."
—Carl P. Eby, Professor of English, *Appalachian State University, USA*, Author
of *Hemingway's Fetishism: Psychoanalysis and the Mirror of Manhood*

"Through this *tour de force* of intellectual curiosity, Ross K. Tangedal reveals fascinating new dimensions to texts we thought we knew. Beyond that, he presents

profound ideas about writing and reading as a solemn, holy act. This book is inventive, assertive, generous, and impeccably researched. It is literary scholarship at its finest."
—Mark Cirino, Melvin M. Peterson Endowed Chair in Literature, *University of Evansville, USA*, Author of *Ernest Hemingway: Thought in Action*

"In this well-researched book, Ross K. Tangedal shows how American authors responded to the emergence of new literary institutions in the twentieth century. From literary clubs to reprint editions such as the Modern Library and paperbacks, the publishing landscape encouraged the rise of the authorial preface as a way to target specific audiences and markets. Tangedal sheds new light on the connections between authors and writers, mediated by a rapidly changing publishing industry."
—Lise Jaillant, Associate Professor of English and Digital Humanities, *Loughborough University, UK*, Author of *Modernism, Middlebrow and the Literary Canon: The Modern Library Series, 1917–1955*

"Ross K. Tangedal's fine study of the preface explores the changing face of American authorship and book publishing from Modernism to Toni Morrison. His discussion of prefaces by, among others, Willa Cather, F. Scott Fitzgerald, Ernest Hemingway, and Robert Penn Warren offers more than a mere analysis of a literary marketing device. This exciting and original book explores the complex implications of any paratextual material that purports to speak for an author."
—Steven Trout, Professor of English, *University of Alabama, USA*, Author of *Memorial Fictions: Willa Cather and the First World War*

"Tangedal's study of the evolving nature of twentieth-century American authorship and the literary market, as expressed through the often neglected genre of the authorial preface, is expansive in scope and rich in detail. Readers interested in the many authors Tangedal examines, or book history and its related disciplines, will find much to learn from in these pages."
—John K. Young, Professor of English, *Marshall University, USA*, Author of *Black Writers, White Publishers*

"*The Preface* is the first to provide an in-depth analysis of the preface in twentieth-century American literature, interlacing literary history with an analysis of the commercial market and literary criticism. It will be useful to those who are approaching the subject for the first time, as well as those seeking to better understand the ways in which authors control and exert authority over their artistic works. A fascinating and important study."
—Michelle E. Moore, Professor of English, *College of DuPage, USA*, Author of *Chicago and the Making of American Modernism*

CONTENTS

CHAPTER 1

Introduction: An Influence on the Public

> *A piazza must be had.*
> —Herman Melville, "The Piazza"[1]

> *To arrest, for the space of a breath, the hands busy about the work of the earth,*
> *and compel men entranced by the sight of distant goals to glance for a*
> *moment at the surrounding vision of form and colour, of sunshine and*
> *shadows; to make them pause for a look, for a sigh, for a smile—such is the*
> *aim, difficult and evanescent, and reserved only for a very few to achieve.*
> —Joseph Conrad, Preface to *The Nigger of the 'Narcissus*[2]

> *Sacred altogether to memory, in short, such labours and such lights.*
> —Henry James, Preface to Volume XV of the New York Edition[3]

Authorial introductions, prefaces, and forewords have been part of literature for centuries, dating back to Rabelais's prologue to *Gargantua*
(1534), which instructs readers to drink and eat heartily while reading.
However, authorial prefaces are rarely the focus of analysis, and few readers recognize the space as more than secondary. The dominant field of
inquiry regarding all extratextual materials (not just prefaces) is narratol-
ogy, with Gerard Genette's *Paratexts: Thresholds of Interpretation* (1987;
trans. 1997) the standard survey of the field. Paratexts, as defined by
Genette, "'surround' and 'extend' a book, in order to *present* it, in the
usual sense of this verb but also in the strongest sense: to *make present*, to
ensure the text's presence in the world, its 'reception' and consumption in

© The Author(s), under exclusive license to Springer Nature
Switzerland AG 2021
R. K. Tangedal, *The Preface*, New Directions in Book History,
https://doi.org/10.1007/978-3-030-85151-4_1

the form (nowadays, at least) of a book."[4] Placement, date of publication, and structure are keys to understanding these pieces, as are the various publishing circumstances which call for their composition. Prefaces are windows into professional authorship, as the business of literature informs their existence. Authors and publishers recognized the space as more than secondary to their literary endeavors, resulting in pieces designed to make public a writer's agency. To borrow Genette's phrasing, writers and publishers wanted to ensure a text's presence in the world by creating a variety of paratexts, and none was more closely related to a writer's authority than the preface.

Prefaces frame the central text, alter meaning prior to reading the central text, and assist in the increased sales of books by appearing in later reprint editions. However, these pieces do not exist solely to promote the sale of books. Authorial prefaces promote and represent professional authorship, which was integral to the growth of authority in twentieth-century American literature. These pieces help us trace the careers of several writers not only biographically but also textually. Why were certain books given prefaces and others not? Why did authors choose to remove, replace, or revise prefaces in subsequent editions of specific texts? What can be said about an author's legacy in the context of his or her prefaces? How much direction is given in them, and where can that direction help or hinder certain readings of texts? Can the preface in production change the textual make-up of the given text, and can that text be permanently altered because of it? Do unpublished or unfinished/aborted prefaces say as much about an author's professional attributes as his/her published texts? These questions spark what follows, an investigation into the business of literature in America in the twentieth century.

However, Genette casts a wide net when defining "the prefatorial situation of communication," including "every type of introductory (preludial or postludial) text, authorial or allographic, consisting of a discourse produced on the subject of the text that follows or precedes it."[5] Genette differentiates between the original preface,[6] the later preface,[7] the delayed preface,[8] the allographic preface,[9] as well as other forms, including the postface (which comes at the end of a book). I am concerned with prefaces, forewords, and introductions (introductory essays or short pieces) written by authors for their books, though I also investigate particular prefaces that Ernest Hemingway wrote for other writers (allographic, or third person, pieces), and F. Scott Fitzgerald's unconventional table of contents to his collection *Tales of the Jazz Age* (1922), which is composed of individual mini-prefaces for each story. Other devices, such as the schemata that James Joyce gave to Carlo Linati and Stuart Gilbert as keys to his novel *Ulysses*, subsequently printed in various editions and studies of the novel since their inception,[10] or William Faulkner's famed appendix to *The Sound and the Fury*, "1699–1945 The Compsons," published first in Malcolm Cowley's *The Portable Faulkner* (1946)[11] and subsequently reprinted in other editions, fall just outside of the kinds of prefaces I choose to investigate. Though each has had a considerable impact on the writers and books they are associated with, and both would come under Genette's definition of preface/postface, my goal is to investigate those particular essay-style prefaces that occur prior to the central text. First, essay-style prefaces at the beginnings of books are most common, and many reprint editions tend to include them in some form. Second, while the preface is far from an American form, the prefaces under investigation interrogate professional authorship in America in the twentieth century, a time of great change in the industry, and writers and publishers took advantage of the space for commercial and commemorative reasons. And third, in taking up primarily canonical American writers, I argue that their prefaces complicate and enhance our understanding of their authority over their texts, readers, and careers in a shifting literary environment. Prefaces are not a decidedly American form, but American writers wrote dozens if not hundreds of prefaces in the twentieth century, begging the simple but obvious question: why?

Authorial Prefaces and the Literary Marketplace in America

Prefaces add value to a book as a marketing and advertising mechanism in order to, at times, sell the same work twice, but this time with added features which may be—from an authorial and publishing standpoint—attractive to prospective readers. Value is also added to the reader. Prefaces offer direct links between authors and readers, giving the latter assurance that they are reading the book correctly. They also provide authors with the opportunity to brand their work for market, aligning with William Charvat's terms of authorship as a professional trade. In deciding to write prefaces which provide a new or amplified reading of a book, writers choose to participate in a professional zone of commerce where writing "is produced with the hope of extended sale in the open market" and where "the problem of the professional writer is not identical with that of the literary artist; but when a literary artist is also a professional writer, he cannot solve the problems of the one function without reference to the other."[12] Therefore the authorial preface, much like book publication, represents a choice every writer must make when tasked with becoming a public author. Where private concerns once dominated in the form of writing what becomes a book, public personae take over to promote that work to readers. However, a more complex process unfolds once books are brought out, as books influence the creation of other books, and writers influence the work of other writers. Authors "are unique in that they are not just the authors of their own works," writes Michel Foucault. "They have produced something else: the possibilities and the rules for the formation of other texts."[13] The rules of the game are in a constant state of flux, though the goal—a published book—remains the primary objective. Yet the features of books follow specific fads, just like any other trend. The twentieth century was not the first to feature authorial prefaces, but due to the increased opportunity for writers to produce prefaces for their work, coupled with the growth of writing as a consistent craft for the "serious author"[14] to ply, the twentieth century saw prefaces take on a new significance to the professionals who placed them between the covers of their books.

All the same, publication as a business spreads control over several participants and generally leaves the author with the least amount of power. Joshua Kopperman Ratner argues that nineteenth-century authors promoted an "aggressive engagement of readers" through paratextual experimentation as a means of authorial survival, a factor which translated into the twentieth century.[15] The complicated relationship between authors and their authority/authorship in a burgeoning literary marketplace filled with both skilled and unskilled readers drove writers to intensify their individual paratextual expression. Genette notes that "the original assumptive authorial preface, which we will thus shorten to *original preface*, has as its chief function *to ensure that the text is read properly*."[16] Whether engaging in preface writing or not, an author's main goal is to be read; to augment Genette slightly, authorial *centrality* enhances the paratextual goal of public consumption. In any case, the spatial dynamics of the authorial preface require a degree of control. In the twentieth century many prefaces were excised prior to publication, which left books ripe for definition and direction.[17] Generally, authors chose to preface reprints and new editions of the same work years after initial publication, a practice crucial in asserting authorial control over printed material that was already available to the public. If a writer's control was compromised in the first edition, reprints allowed for a return to authorial centrality, and many writers achieved (or attempted to achieve) some level of textual control by using a variety of paratextual devices.

Writers were able to find spaces for authorial reconstitution, from titles and epigrams to epilogues and headings. Franco Moretti argues that "as the market expands, titles contract; as they do that, they learn to compress meaning; and as they do that, they develop special 'signals' to place books in the right market niche."[18] From the eighteenth century onward, authors, editors, and publishers utilized paratextual space as a key component of book marketing and reader engagement. The space also became a place for writers to discuss the new professionalism associated with authorship. According to Ratner, "Literary history has been content to declare the death of the author; we have not paid enough attention to the ways that this death excited and upset writers in the early United States. This is partially because we have not paid enough attention to what writers said about the subject of authorship in paratexts."[19] Writers like Nathaniel Hawthorne and Washington Irving, Ratner argues, used every part of the book to their advantage, though readers fail to see just how "absolutely enmeshed" paratexts and texts become if read properly.[20] Writing about authorship for readers provided each new edition of a work with a window into America's newest profession and gave writers the opportunity to inform and direct their readers. Though a book is the product of many hands, the writer who gave it life reaches out to connect with readers in surprising places, if only to survive to write another one.

Authors in the twentieth century felt many of the same needs as those in the nineteenth century, though the role was evolving. James L.W. West III defines the twentieth-century author as "simultaneously an artist and an impresario, an aesthete and an entertainer, a thinker and a businessman."[21] In order to function successfully within the literary marketplace, authors needed to encompass various roles. Pierre Bourdieu describes the literary field as "a *field of forces*, but it is also a *field of struggles* tending to transform or conserve this field of forces,"[22] just as Foucault defines the *author* as "the result of a complex operation that constructs a certain being of reason that we call 'author.'"[23] According to Bourdieu, "the fundamental stake in literary struggles is the monopoly of literary legitimacy, i.e., *inter alia*, the monopoly of the power to say with authority who are authorized to call themselves writers."[24] Writers were able to legitimize their authorship in prefaces by recounting the trials and tribulations of composition and publication. Ernest Hemingway and Toni Morrison catalogue their struggles in prefaces that redefine and ultimately authorize their existence as writers. They create an authority of resilience, integral to legacy building and reader engagement, while F. Scott Fitzgerald amplifies the integrity of his talent (and what he sees as the indifference of critics) in his late career prefaces, partially as a response to the youthful pose on display in his earlier work. He does not persevere; he laments what could have been and the effect that has on a writer. Robert Penn Warren grapples with facts and fictions, stories and origins, and the myth of Huey Long orbiting *All the King's Men* (1946), and Willa Cather subdues the character of Willa Cather in her revised introduction to *My Ántonia*, which actually amplifies her control, the disappearance into narrative complete and true. Of course Ring Lardner throws it all out the window—babies, bathwater, and all—with his prefaces for Charles Scribner's Sons. But he knew what a "real" writer was supposed to look like, how a "real" writer would instruct readers in a preface, and why "real" writers were too proud to admit that the market was built to chew them up. His legitimacy was his survival in spite of the overwhelming calls to evolve, something he never did. The tasks each of the previously mentioned writers undertook complicate authority further, much like how their literary ancestors of the previous century had used paratexts to cry out for control of their work.

Foucault recognizes that "these aspects of an individual which we designate as making him an author are only a projection ... of the operations we force texts to undergo, the connections we make, the traits we establish as pertinent, the continuities we recognize, or the exclusions we practice."[25] In order to establish a market niche, writers became authors because the projection, to borrow from Foucault, was enacted for a specific publication purpose; such projections continue to display the complicated web of literary creation integral to publication and market consumption. Rather than displaying literary production as a linear model, both Bourdieu and Foucault define authority in more complex terms. With his "communications circuit," Robert Darnton claimed that the cycle of publication "runs from the author to the publisher (if the bookseller does not assume the role), the printer, the shipper, the bookseller, and the reader. The reader completes the circuit because he influences the author before and after the act of publication."[26] Whether a struggle, a projection, or a circuit, the terms of authorship in the literary marketplace require explanation, for the force of book production results in compromises.

Writers and authors, both part of Bourdieu's "field of struggle" and Darnton's "communications circuit," are inhabited by a singular artistic mind. As a private figure the writer enacts the physical act of writing, while the public author is presented to a readership in the form of literary publication. Where these two functions meet (the text) forms a canvas of compromise. Over time the dynamics of the preface continued to confound critics and readers alike, as authors chose to either utilize the space fully or ignore the space altogether. Genette argues that "more than a boundary or a sealed border, the paratext is, rather, a *threshold*, or ... a 'vestibule' that offers the world at large the possibility of either stepping inside or turning back. ... [It is] a zone not only of transition, but also of *transaction*: a privileged place of pragmatics and a strategy, of an influence on the public."[27] The paratext "is at the service of a better reception for the text and a more pertinent reading of it (more pertinent, of course, in the eyes of its author and his allies)."[28] Consequently, authors of the twentieth century were given access to new markets in the wake of the reprint culture that had expanded the century prior. Meredith McGill chronicles the rampant effects of literary piracy which helped build—for better or worse—America's literary identity. She notes: "Antebellum struggles over the right to reprint domestic and foreign texts demonstrate that literary property is never simply or only a matter of individual property rights, but rather of systems of circulation in which persons, corporate bodies, and the state have complicated and often conflicting interests."[29] Publishers treated literary works as publicly owned rather than privately owned entities, reprinting works by Dickens, Poe, and Hawthorne while granting authors little to no control over their reprinted work. Essentially these reprints forged a uniquely public literary community in which texts flowed between publisher and reader. The centrality of the author was in conflict with the complicated "rights" of readers.

The losers in the game—the authors—pressed for stringent copyright restrictions, resulting in books as authorial property as opposed to a publicly owned good by the end of the nineteenth century. McGill argues that the reprint culture from 1837 to 1853 helped grow the national literature, for "in establishing a public sphere based on the general accessibility of printed texts but defined by the stutter of locally interrupted circulation, and in its disaggregating response to the challenges posed by economic development, the system of reprinting represents the Jacksonian form of national culture."[30] Access was paramount, and texts were readily available for readers to purchase at low prices. British texts were predominantly reprinted since no international copyright law restricted their reprinting. James J. Barnes notes that "as a country, nineteenth-century America was akin to a present-day underdeveloped nation which recognizes its dependence on those more commercially and technologically advanced, and desires the fruits of civilization in the cheapest and most convenient ways. Reprinting English literature seemed easy and inexpensive, and so America borrowed voraciously."[31] In doing so, the reprint policy "partook of a curious blend of protectionism and free trade: protection for American industry but not American authors; freedom to reprint British works but not to import them."[32] The phenomenon produced a decentralized literary market, in which "the mania for cheapness won out over the interests of the literary community."[33] Reprinting various texts produced an anti-authorial vacuum in which writers were separated from their texts, a separation fraught with antagonism between author, publisher, and reader.

Authorship shifted within the unregulated transatlantic reprint market, for "in rejecting authorship as a governing principle for the production and distribution of literary texts," argues McGill, "the culture of reprinting does not eliminate authors so much as suspend, reconfigure, and intensify their authority, placing a premium on texts that circulate with the names of authors attached."[34] The name of the author was important, not their interests, which echoes the splitting of private and public writing functions crucial to authorship. West notes that as professions in America became more identifiable than before, "American writers began to lose their sense of authority and audience, to retreat from society and to see themselves as alienated, misunderstood figures."[35] Instead of authorial control, McGill claims that authorial manipulation in the public reading sphere fueled "the fiercely competitive reprint publishers who pioneered American book marketing techniques, trumpeting the names and fortifying the reputations of authors as a means of distinguishing their editions from rival reprints."[36] Generally done without the input of the author, publishers separated an author from his or her work and effectively marginalized the creator from the creation while still using the name to sell the book. West argues that "part of the problem has been lack of public identity" for authors at the turn of the century,[37] and McGill concludes that "the antebellum culture of reprinting gives us access to a long history of American skepticism about tight controls over literary property."[38] What is the property: the writer or the book? Or both? McGill forecasts and West examines the intense attention to commercial interests that authors gave their work in the twentieth century. As Anglo-American copyright became law in 1891, the protection of authors and their properties hampered the reprint market, but authorship continued to professionalize as new markets developed. The twentieth century saw new forms of literary growth, predominantly in four forms: the formation of literary clubs (the Book-of-the-Month Club and the Literary Guild), the proliferation of affordable reprint series (such as the Modern Library), the paperback revolution, and new trade editions with prefaces written by the authors. Though the free-for-all reprint culture of the mid-nineteenth century ceased, a new reprint standard took shape in the twentieth century. Continued attention to audience fostered a new interest in authorial prefaces as a means of creating and expanding authorship in the new century, with writers and publishers taking advantage of this phenomenon to sell books and grow authority. While not a wholly unique moment in the history of books, the prefaces written by American writers in the twentieth century catalogue the shifting landscape of a more self-consciously professionalized trade—the American writer—fraught with tension and compromise, and informed by evolving reading publics.

HENRY JAMES AND JOSEPH CONRAD

Though the reprint and literary club boom served as a catalyst for the twentieth-century preface, at the turn of the century two literary icons turned to the authorial preface: Henry James and Joseph Conrad. The opportunity for prefacing came as part of the "collected edition" phenomenon, of which both writers took full advantage. Conrad's preface to *The Nigger of the 'Narcissus'* (1897, 1914)—retitled *The Children of the Sea* in the first American edition[39]—evoked clear authorial commitment, while James's prefaces to his twenty-four-volume *New York Edition of the Novels and Tales of Henry James* (1907–1909) forwarded a new Henry James, a public figure dedicated to art and creation, and to setting the record straight.[40] Their prefaces were professional and artistic. Michael Anesko argues that "in writing his prefaces James had one of the rarest opportunities ever afforded to an artist: the chance to supply the [kind] of intelligent criticism his work deserved, but which it had failed to elicit from contemporary readers or men of letters."[41] As James was nearing the end of his life, the author chose to redesign his legacy into what John H. Pearson labeled a "mosaic sarcophagus," blending criticism with intention, and art with reception.[42] Each preface to the New York edition, then, would "result in a reading of the prefaced text that is more richly suggestive and far more rewarding for inquiring minds than a reading of that novel or tale without such preparation."[43] However, when gathered and published as part of a collected edition, the prefaces take on lives of their own and essentially form complex essays on art and literature rather than prefaces for specific novels. Though originally published as individual prefaces for each new volume in the collection, James's prefaces were collected later as a standalone volume in *The Art of the Novel: Critical Prefaces* (1934) and later as part of the collected editions of James's work for the Library of America, where they are divorced from their original texts. Genette accounts for this change in location, as prefaces frequently become "essays" in a collection rather than paratextual pieces.[44] The transition from preface to essay is an important one. We ought not separate the preface from its original home, for in doing so we deny the textual influence of the preface as designed. Prefaces are not essays, though essays can be utilized as prefaces. The pieces are designed to accompany a text, and reading prefaces outside of their textual context denies functionality, the most integral component of prefatory statements. With this in mind, attention to intention is crucial in determining the value of authorial prefaces.

James's intentions were clear from the outset, with Vivienne Rundle noting that "James uses the New York Edition prefaces as a crucially important recuperative opportunity."[45] Concerning James's disastrous foray into the theater, Rundle argues further "that the prefaces afford their author a way to reassert mastery over his oeuvre; they constitute a textual site for the reclamation of authority and identity."[46] Anesko contends that the prefaces became added capital, for "to assist the public in its search and to satisfy its craving for novelty, James was eager to embellish his Edition with prefaces and frontispieces and to rework his earlier fictions. To captivate a publisher and the public, James was prepared to frame his artistic goals in distinctly marketable form."[47] For example, James's preface to *The American* discusses "the only *general* attribute of projected romance" in the following way:

> The balloon of experience is in fact of course tied to the earth, and under that necessity we swing, thanks to a rope of remarkable length, in the more or less commodious car of the imagination; but it is by the rope we know where we are, and from the moment that cable is cut we are at large and

unrelated: we only swing apart from the globe—though remaining as exhilarated, naturally, as we like, especially when all goes well.[48]

James's prefaces feature long, detailed descriptions, psychological detours, and rereadings of each novel. Though James gives the impression in his prefaces of having reread his novels (and therefore discovered new ideas), Rundle and Anesko both question the veracity of the prefaces, as writers tend to create narratives of labor and inception rather than report actual events.[49] For instance, James likened *The Tragic Muse* to "some aromatic bag of gathered herbs of which the string has never been loosed; or, better still, to some jar of potpourri, shaped and overfigured and polished, but of which the lid, never lifted, has provided for the intense accumulation of fragrance within."[50] *The Portrait of a Lady* was constructed with "artful patience" by piling "brick upon brick."[51]

Pearson argues that "James desired his readers to be conscious not only of the value of his art, but of the value of his aesthetic performance. We must always read novel and novelist, in other words." James pushed his texts and himself into the public sphere, advanced his authority, framed his oeuvre, and recast control over his work.[52] Many authors would follow his example as the twentieth century progressed, as the product and the performance of an author became increasingly intertwined. In many ways James's prefaces provide a base for authorial self-conception in the twentieth century. His preface to Volume XV denounces editorial prescriptiveness (specifically as it pertains to his short story "The Death of the Lion"), and he charts how stories like "The Death of the Lion" "deal all with the literary life, gathering their motive, in each case, from some extreme predicament, of the artist enamoured of perfection, ridden by his idea or paying for his sincerity." Nearly three decades later, F. Scott Fitzgerald wanted readers (and critics) to recognize his sincerity in a preface to the Modern Library Edition of *The Great Gatsby*, where he became his own best critic (like James). "I think [*Gatsby*] is an honest book," he insisted, "that is to say, that one used none of one's virtuosity to get an effect, and, to boast again, one soft-pedalled the emotional side to avoid the tears leaking from the socket of the left eye, or the large false face peering around the corner of a character's head."[53] He pays for his sincerity, to borrow from James, with *Gatsby*, *Tender Is the Night*, and *Taps at Reveille* falling far short of critical and commercial expectations. Further, for James, his stories "testify indeed, as they thus stand together, to no general intention—they minister only, I think, to an emphasized effect."[54] Similarly, in

Fitzgerald's aborted foreword to *Taps at Reveille*, the beleaguered writer notes that he too "tried for an arduous precision in trying to catch one character or one emotion or one adventure—which is all that one can do in the length of a short story."[55] The restrictions placed upon writers by genre, editorial frameworks, and critical reception lead to compromise, and while some find freedom in breaking the rules (James), others eventually buckle under the weight of the rules (Fitzgerald). James offered an inside view of a writer as an artist, and future writers now had frameworks by which they too could express what once felt inexpressible.

Similarly, Joseph Conrad's author's notes for his collected works serve the same function as James's prefaces. Conrad revered James, as his collected prefaces looked to emulate James's New York Edition. After receiving copies of the edition from James, he wrote back on 12 December 1908, "I sat for a long while with the closed volume in my hand going over the preface [to *The American*] in my mind and thinking—that's how it began, that's how it was done!"[56] He wrote J. B. Pinker in July 1917 concerning his own prefaces: "I wouldn't even expand them. Of course I can't rivalise with poor dear H[enry] J[ames] and I don't know that it would be wise even to try."[57] Just like James, Conrad sought to expand both his marketability and his critical reputation. A series of author's notes for the Heinemann edition of the *Collected Works of Joseph Conrad* were written largely between 1919 and 1922. While some were written prior to the collection, Conrad furnished each of his books with a preface, a commonplace practice for a collected edition.[58] However, one preface in particular stands apart from the others, partly for its attention to artistic precision and partly for its reputation among writers. Conrad's *The Nigger of the 'Narcissus'* is generally regarded as the author's first major work, a short novel concerning the life of a Black sailor (James Wait) and the conditions aboard the eponymous ship "Narcissus." The novel followed two other sea tales, *Almayer's Folly* and *Outcasts of the Island*, with *'Narcissus'* an evolution in the author's style and technique. Conrad sent a potential preface to friend Edward Garnett on 24 August 1897; the piece then went on a rather complicated, though not unique, publication journey. Initially Conrad hoped to include it in the first edition, published by Heinemann, but editor Sydney Pawling refused to publish the preface. However, W. E. Henley of the *New Review* opted to include the preface as an afterword in the final serial installment of the novel (December 1897).[59] The preface was then reprinted in 1905 as "The Art of Fiction" in *Harper's Weekly*, which resembled the text Conrad had originally written. It appeared for a third time—but for the first time as a preface—in the second American printing published by Doubleday, Page, & Co. (23 May 1914) but was preceded by another preface entitled "To My Readers in America." Heinemann then included the preface—as it appeared in the second American printing—as the preface to the novel for the Collected Works (1921).

The publishing history of Conrad's preface to 'Narcissus' is no outlier, and it would be nearly duplicated several decades later by Toni Morrison's *The Bluest Eye* (1970, 1993, 1999, 2007); the first edition had no preface, the Nobel Prize reprint featured a new afterword by the author, the next reprint featured the afterword and a foreword, and the collected edition ran the revised afterword as a foreword. Genette argues that prefaces must be analyzed in spatial, functional, and aesthetic terms, especially when reprints, new editions, and collected editions alter the effect of a preface. The crucial elements of Conrad's oft-cited preface are the representation of his literary authority, his attention to the senses, and how to make readers "see." In his note to American readers Conrad insisted that "almost without laying down the pen I wrote a preface, trying to express the spirit in which I was entering on the task of my new life," which the novel fueled.[60] On 5 December 1897, as the serial run came to an end, Conrad wrote Garnett: "Henley printed the preface at the end as an Author's note. It does not shine very much, but I am glad to see it in type."[61] When asked to include a preface for the second American printing, Conrad jumped at the chance to resubmit his original preface. On 27 March 1914 he wrote Alfred A. Knopf (then working for Doubleday): "In the matter of the preface: it was suppressed simply because the publisher here (Mr Heinemann) thought it would do no good to the book—I don't know on what grounds—and I simply took his opinion meekly. I was a very young author them [sic]—remember!"[62] Conrad explains the effect his preface is meant to have on readers and on his career, as he notes his age and inexperience when first confronted with its suppression. Conrad's preface illuminates many of the central tenets of prefatory structure and imagination that authors would continue to follow for decades.

Conrad chose the preface as the primary forum to illuminate his new artistic sensibility. Conrad's first two novels were considered middling efforts, and when placed alongside 'Narcissus' we understand the author's motivation to chart his new artistic course with a preface, which begins: "a work that aspires, however humbly, to the condition of art should carry its justification in every line. And art itself may be defined as a single-minded attempt to render the highest kind of justice to the visible universe, by bringing to light the truth, manifold and one, underlying its every aspect."[63] While James created a "heroic narrative" with his collected prefaces, Conrad created an introspective narrative, whose purpose was to showcase how one harnesses truth and the imagination to heighten readers' senses. Rundle argues that Conrad's prefaces "memorialize the borderline moments attendant upon the birth and death of the creative impulse. And yet Conrad's elegiac prefaces allow the reader to live and perform in a way that James's absolutely preclude."[64] The self-reflective James leaves readers overwhelmed with authorial direction (and misdirection), but for Conrad a writer's "appeal is less loud, more profound, less distinct, more stirring—and sooner forgotten. Yet its effect endures forever."[65] Conrad argues that "all art, therefore, appeals primarily to the senses, and the artistic aim when expressing itself in written words must also make its appeal through the senses, if its high desire is to reach the secret spring of responsive emotion."[66] Ultimately, Conrad's task is "by the power of the written word to make you hear, to make you feel—it is, before all, to make you *see*. That—and no more, and it is everything."[67]

Many writers were influenced by Conrad's preface. Fitzgerald called the preface "the greatest 'credo' in my life, ever since I decided that I would rather be an artist than a careerist,"[68] and Ernest Hemingway borrowed from the preface when writing his father: "you see I am trying in all my stories to get the feeling of the actual life across—not to just depict life—or criticize it—but to actually make it alive. So that when you have read something by me you actually experience the thing."[69] He mirrors Conrad, who writes: "If I succeed, you shall find there according to your deserts: encouragement, consolation, fear, charm—all you demand—and, perhaps, also that glimpse of truth for which you have forgotten to ask."[70] Willa Cather wrote a "Mr. Miller" that "there is one kind of story that ought to tell itself—the story of action. There is another story that ought to be told—I mean the emotional story, which tries to be much more like music than it tries to be like drama—the story that tries to evoke and leave merely a picture—a mood. That was what [Joseph] Conrad tried to do, and he did it well."[71] Cather's evocation of music echoes Conrad's insistence that art "must strenuously aspire to the plasticity of sculpture, to the colour of painting, and to the magic suggestiveness of music—which is the art of arts,"[72] and the act of submerging herself deep into *My Ántonia* gets at the effect that Conrad believes "endures forever." Toni Morrison also channeled Conrad's preface in her foreword to *Beloved* when she likened the effect of her novel to a feeling and a sense rather than just words:

> In trying to make the slave experience intimate, I hoped the sense of things being under control and out of control would be persuasive throughout; that the order and quietude of everyday life would be violently disrupted by the chaos of the needy dead; that the herculean effort to forget would be threatened by memory desperate to stay alive. To render enslavement as a personal experience, language must get out of the way.[73]

Conrad's attention to literary effect and a reader's senses aims at a dynamic artistic purpose, which many twentieth-century writers took up as a defining feature of the modern preface: by illuminating the process the authors illuminate the work, and by illuminating the work they illuminate their authority.

The call for truth in representation, rendering the visible and tangible effects of prose, and establishing literary authority, echoes fully in the twentieth century. Fitzgerald considered Conrad a major influence throughout his career.[74] He wrote his editor Maxwell Perkins regarding *The Great Gatsby*: "the happiest thought I have is my new novel—it is something really new in form, idea, structure—the model for the age that Joyce and Stein are searching for, that Conrad didn't find."[75] Showing the breadth of Conrad's influence, Fitzgerald wrote Kenneth Littauer fourteen years later regarding his novel in progress: "by making Cecilia at the moment of her telling the story, an intelligent and observant woman, I shall grant myself the privilege, as Conrad did, of letting her imagine the actions of the characters. Thus, I hope to get the verisimilitude of a first person narrative, combined with a Godlike knowledge of all events that happen to my characters."[76] He cited Conrad specifically in his 1934 introduction for the Modern Library reprint of *The Great Gatsby*:

> reading it over one can see how it could have been improved—yet without feeling guilty of any discrepancy from the truth, as far as I saw it; truth or rather the *equivalent* of the truth, the attempt at honesty of imagination. I had just re-read Conrad's preface [to '*Narcissus*'], and I had recently been kidded half haywire by critics who felt that my material was such as to preclude all dealing with mature persons in a mature world.[77]

Conrad's preface made its impression on Fitzgerald early, and other authors similarly fell under the influence of the piece. Hemingway concluded his foreword to *Green Hills of Africa* with a call to the senses through honest depiction, declaring that "the writer has attempted to write an absolutely true book to see whether the shape of a country and the pattern of a month's action can, if truly presented, compete with a work of the imagination."[78] "To snatch in a moment of courage, from the remorseless rush of time, a passing phase of life, is only the beginning of the task," explains Conrad; "the task approached in tenderness and faith is to hold up unquestionably, without choice and without fear, the rescued fragment before all eyes in the light of a sincere mood."[79] As justification for claims of effectiveness and influence, and following the lead of Henry James, Joseph Conrad—and his preface to *'Narcissus'*—provided the essential introduction to the purpose and potential of prefaces in the literary marketplace of the twentieth century.

THE AMERICAN REPRINT MARKET
AND THE AUTHORIAL PREFACE

The problem with publishing books has always been distribution, and as a publishing mechanism the authorial preface took on a new role during what Charles Madison dubs "the commercialization of literature" between 1900 and 1945.[80] Borrowing from the title of publisher Henry Holt's 1905 essay for *Atlantic Monthly*, Madison explains that "the peculiarity of publishing is that while it is and must of necessity remain a business, it tends to attract a fair percentage of men who seek from it a satisfaction that money alone cannot provide," and publishers of the period sought to combine the literary quality of the modernist period with popular novels and bestsellers.[81] "It is important to understand that publishers were both marketers of and a market for modernism," writes Catherine Turner in *Marketing Modernism between the Two World Wars*. "They had to be convinced that modernist manuscripts were worth buying for their firms. Just as consumers had to be convinced modernism might be good for them, publishers had to be convinced that modernism might be good for business."[82] Publishers combined several authors' apparent disinterestedness with savvy marketing and created new forms of advertising in order to sell difficult and less accessible modernist works. Turner's survey of literary advertising in the early twentieth century shows publishers striving to both highlight an author's literary merit and distance an author from claims to popularity. The industry, at this point, looked like Bourdieu's "field of struggles," as writers campaigned for legitimacy by pretending to care little for promotion or economic remuneration.[83] Consequently, as the market shifted to accommodate these new books and authors, a newly energized reprint market created another bridge between popularity and sales. Bennett Cerf and Donald Klopfer, founders of Random House, purchased the Modern Library from Horace Liveright (of Boni & Liveright) in July 1925; in doing so, the two built one of the most successful reprint series of the twentieth century, composed of cheap editions of both popular and highbrow literature. Madison notes that by 1941, the series had sold over 10,000,000 copies, with the series expanding to include longer books.[84] As the popularity of the series grew, Cerf and Klopfer sought out introductions for their reprints in order to differentiate them from rival editions. Writing a Modern Library introduction became a cottage industry unto itself.

Jay Satterfield refers to the Modern Library introductions as "attractions" and cites Cerf's inclination to protect his introductions rather than allow them to be reprinted in other books. When asked by Max Eastman for permission to do so, Cerf responded: "that introduction is the exclusive feature of the Modern Library edition of the book, and we wouldn't want to see it appear in any other format."[85] The series featured introductions written by critics, professors, and celebrities, but Cerf and Klopfer pressed authors for their own introductions when possible. Though Willa Cather, F. Scott Fitzgerald, Ernest Hemingway, and Robert Penn Warren all had titles appear on the Modern Library list, only Fitzgerald and Warren offered introductions for publication (*The Great Gatsby*, 1934; *All the King's Men*, 1953). Prior to *Gatsby*'s appearance in the Modern Library, Fitzgerald wrote Perkins:

> The people who buy the *Modern Library* are not at all the people who buy the new books. *Gatsby*—in its present form, not actually available in sight to book buyers, will only get a scattering sale as a result of the success of this book. I feel that every time your business department has taken a short-sighted view of our community of interest in this matter, which is my reputation, there has been no profit on your part and something less than that on mine.[86]

Fitzgerald differentiates the reading markets for his books and discusses the difference between Modern Library readers, paperback readers, and trade edition readers. The Modern Library's attention to price and accessibility weighed heavily on authors and publishers alike, as did the cheap creation and distribution of mass market paperback editions. Concerning Scribner's dealings with reprint giant Grosset & Dunlap, Perkins wrote Hemingway: "In a letter you pointed out the disappointing fact that books do not hold up as you had thought from year to year. We know that well enough. It is increasingly true. And the chief reason for it is the short-sightedness and avariciousness of publishers."[87] For authors like Fitzgerald, reprint series such as the Modern Library provided "continued distribution and an additional seal of critical appreciation for an already successful title" and offered authors a chance to reestablish their books, and their authorities, in a new form.[88] But not all writers were fond of the series. Willa Cather spent years fending off Cerf and Klopfer, who wanted to include her most popular works in the series. She finally relented in 1931, allowing the Modern Library to reprint *Death Comes for the Archbishop*, but she refused to renew the contract five years later, and the novel was removed from the series. Lise Jaillant explains that "Cather made little attempt to reach the academics that continued to admire her work," and though her contemporaries had cheap editions in series like the Modern Library, "she underestimated the importance of these series in canon making."[89] Cather maintained careful control over her work, and in doing so she passed on the opportunities that cheap reprint series provided writers looking to expand their reach. Other writers took the chance and ran with it, with many regarding the series favorably over time.[90]

Consequently, the advent and proliferation of cheap paperback editions forced publishers to reissue works with new prefaces, as they hoped to cash in on renewed exposure and the new shift to classroom editions. With already a large-scale distribution of paperbacks in a variety of new venues—including drug stores, grocery stores, and train stations—publishers sought out another venue for their authors' works. Scribner's began releasing the Scribner's Library trade editions in the 1950s, after they recognized the growth of one of the most important publishing venues of the mid-century: the classroom. West argues that "the demand for cheapness, utility, and wide circulation, together with the lure of a vast domestic market, had their effect on the publishing industry," which partly led to the paperback revolution.[91] Kenneth Davis notes that "the option of ignoring the paperback grew less viable as the reprint was increasingly viewed as a source of income. Reprint royalties were once thought of as icing on the cake of regular trade and book-club sales. But this income was beginning to mount as paperback sales grew, more titles were reprinted, and prices …

crept up to thirty-five cents."[92] And in tracing Willa Cather's relationship with the Modern Library, Jaillant concludes that "Cather's opposition to cheap reprints partly explains her declining critical reputation in the 1930s."[93] Reprints meant potential profits, both short-term and long-term visibility, and an increased likelihood that particular books would be in the hands of students. Though someone of Cather's stature felt compelled to resist the phenomenon, most writers knew what these reprints and editions meant for their legacies.

Fitzgerald asked Perkins several years before the Scribner's Library editions hit bookstores to consider creating an omnibus collection: "I think the novels should come first and, unless there are factors there you haven't told me about, I think it is a shame to put it off. It would not sell wildly at first but unless you make some gesture of confidence I see my reputation dieing on its feet from lack of nourishment."[94] Fitzgerald forecasted the firm's intentions, though in the 1930s Scribner's saw no need to create a vast reprint library. He reiterated his feelings to Perkins near the end of his life:

> Would the 25 cent press keep *Gatsby* in the public eye—or *is the book unpopular*. Has it *had* a chance? Would a popular reissue in that series with a preface *not* by me but by one of its admirers—I can pick one—make it a favorite with class rooms, profs, lovers of English prose—anybody. But to die, so completely and unjustly after having given so much. Even now there is little published in American fiction that doesn't slightly bare my stamp— in a *small* way I was an original.[95]

The previously mentioned Scribner's Library series would go on to feature the firm's eventual bestselling title: F. Scott Fitzgerald's *The Great Gatsby*. His longing to be remembered and repositioned is similar to Toni Morrison's forceful forewords to her canon for Vintage. Such a move has become commonplace, and authors are still eager to situate their work, regardless of their popularity.

While the Modern Library and paperback editions featured prominently in most professional authors' portfolios, the Book-of-the-Month Club (BOMC) also became a market force once established in 1923. Mail-order book clubs date back to the nineteenth century, whereby club members were sent books regularly selected by a committee or club group, but the critical and popular weight of the BOMC label assisted in sales and promotion more so than clubs of the past. Charles Madison notes that by the early 1960s, "the club had sent to its members a total of 183,000,000 books," as the club targeted middle-brow readers with a wide variety of books.[96] Janice Radway highlights club founder Henry Scherman's refusal "to perpetuate the distinction between two forms of value, one determined by the operations of particular interests in the market, the other understood to be fixed, universal, and transcendent."[97] In terms of readership, Radway argues that

> to look at the construction of middle-brow culture by the Book-of-the-Month Club and at the howls of rage its transgressive posture generated among its many critics is to begin to understand the crucial ideological work performed then, and even now, by a transcendent and idealized culture embodied in the literary classic, bound in vellum and treated with reverence and awe.[98]

The BOMC stamp of approval meant many things; in order to assuage publishers' fear of price-cutting, the club offered essential services—exposure, advertising, marketing—and promised to keep prices stable rather than below the net average. Along with these tenets came an attention to culture, and "the Book-of-the-Month Club, then, as it was initially envisioned in 1926," notes Radway, "promised not simply to treat cultural objects as commodities, but even more significantly, it promised to foster a widespread ability among the population to treat culture itself as a recognizable, highly liquid currency."[99] Blending cultural capital with savvy marketing, the BOMC flexed significant social muscle throughout the twentieth century.

The middle-brow culture strove to occupy the same cultural space as Hemingway, James Joyce, and others, while editors such as Max Perkins were reticent about the BOMC's power. After Hemingway's *For Whom the Bell Tolls* was made a featured selection by the BOMC in 1940, Perkins wrote F. Scott Fitzgerald: "I suppose you have heard of the good fortune that has befallen Ernest. 'For Whom the Bell Tolls' has been taken by the Book of the Month Club.—The stamp of bourgeois approval. He would hate to think of it that way, and yet it is a good thing, practically speaking."[100] Eight years prior Hemingway responded dismissively to Perkins when asked about the possibility of placing *Death in the Afternoon* in the BOMC:

if anyone so acts as to put themselves out as a book of the month they cannot insist in ramming the good word shit or the sound old word xxxx down
the throats of a lot of clubwomen but when a book is offered for sale no one
has to buy it that does not want to—and I will not have any pressure brought
to bear to make me emasculate a book to make anyone seven thousand dol-
lars, myself or anyone else.[101]

By 1940, Hemingway had changed his tune with regard to *For Whom the Bell Tolls.* Robert W. Trogdon argues that "Hemingway wrote the novel without using any of the obscene words he had fought to include in his previous works. In writing the novel, he gave in to commercial pressures, writing the novel in the way that he did to increase the chances of serial-izing it or of selling it to a book club."[102] This self-censorship flies in the face of his earlier criticism of the club's membership, as even Hemingway caved in the face of increased commercial prospects. Conversely, Fitzgerald pressed actively to place *Tender Is the Night* with the BOMC. He told Perkins that "it is to both our advantages to capitalize if possible such facts as that the editors of those book leagues might take a fancy to such a curi-ous idea that the author, Fitzgerald, actually wrote a book after all these years."[103] Books are commodities, goods to be sold at market, and whether the BOMC was seen as deleterious or positive, Scherman's "subtle under-standing of the ideological dilemma of the modern moment" and "his remarkable ability to address them through a particular, innovative orga-nization of the business of cultural goods production" positioned the club in the middle of the literary conversation in the twentieth century.[104]

AN INFLUENCE ON THE PUBLIC

American writers in the twentieth century frequently chose to introduce their own materials with prefaces to first editions, the Modern Library series, Book-of-the-Month Club editions, and authorized trade reprints. As outlined earlier, the culture of reprinting in the nineteenth century influenced the growing attention to professional authorship in American publishing in the twentieth century. Each chapter in this book examines specific prefaces written by representative professional authors as attempts to market, explain, and wield authority over published texts. Fredson Bowers argues passionately for the attention to an author's composition identity, for "a critic who becomes impatient at the bibliographer's con-cern to establish the exact form of a text in all its possible pre-publication states of variance is throwing away, almost wilfully, one of the best possible ways of understanding an author by following him step by step at work."[105] Bowers also highlights the importance of "the shaping development of idea" and the modification of textual expression through literary creation, as contexts and concepts matter.[106] G. Thomas Tanselle notes that "the insubstantial nature of language means that finished works must be searched for through the activity of mind," as textual evidence possesses "a tranquility that comes from their being outgrowths of life, distillations of experience."[107] Recognizing the value of authorial prefaces requires a measure of faith in textual study, as Bowers determines that "when one is working with a difference in degree, not in kind, the point at which one feels a need to defend the bridge is shifting and uncertain."[108] Readers can see in a preface both the private and public sides of authorship, a deeply human device writers used to situate, define, and defend themselves and their work. The authors under investigation offer narratives in this vein, with each attempting to "see" (as Conrad would have it) their texts, their readers, and themselves, in new and fascinating ways. Each chapter focuses on a different aspect of Genette's definition of prefaces: make certain a "text is read properly";[109] offer readers the possibility of "stepping inside or turning back"[110]; obstruct readers as "inhibiting signposts"[111]; promote the author's "will to control"[112]; show a writer remembering a text at "a safe distance"[113]; and "ensure the text's presence in the world."[114] Willa Cather, Ring Lardner, F. Scott Fitzgerald, Ernest Hemingway, Robert Penn Warren, and Toni Morrison used prefaces in different ways, and each case study complicates key components of American publishing in the twentieth century.

Chapter 2 examines the introduction to Willa Cather's *My Ántonia* (1918) and surveys the critical response to the revisions the author made to that introduction in 1926. The first edition featured an original preface (titled an introduction by Cather), and eight years later, Cather reworked her introduction for a revised printing (1926).[115] In the interim, a World War had raged, modernism had taken hold of the literary consciousness, and Cather had signed with a new publisher. The introductions are markedly different, with Cather's treatment of narrator Jim Burden the primary revision. But unlike many prefaces, Cather's introduction to *My Ántonia* has been the subject of scholarly focus. I investigate Cather as editor in control of her novel and the impact of the 1926 revisions to the introduction, as well as the ways in which critics and scholars have accounted for the revisions she made to the introduction. Though prefaces, as I stated earlier, are rarely the focus of scholarly interest, the two versions of the introduction to *My Ántonia* and the attention they have received prove, partially, the value of engaging with prefaces as zones of control.

Chapter 3 highlights Ring Lardner, a widely popular writer in his day who cared little for literary pretension, evidenced by his satirical prefaces for *How to Write Short Stories (with Samples)* (1924) and *The Love Nest and Other Stories* (1926) for Charles Scribner's Sons. Both pieces complicate the intended function of the preface—the most important of which, per Genette, "is to provide the author's interpretation of the text or, if you prefer, his statement of intent"[116]—by commenting indirectly on the business of literature through comedic misdirection. Lardner's editor, Maxwell Perkins, may well have intended for the prefaces to reposition Lardner in hopes of attracting new readers. However, it is clear that Lardner wanted to reinforce an already established authorial persona for an already established set of consumers. He refused to fix what wasn't broken. Though difficult to position because of his relative indifference to the literati, Lardner and his work for Perkins at Scribner's provides a sterling example of authorial resistance in the face of expected evolution. Ring Lardner altered the preface from a place of serious textual positioning to a space of textual resistance, resulting in biting commentaries on the "literary game" from the only perspective he knew: his own.

Chapter 4 maps the authorial anxiety that F. Scott Fitzgerald dealt with for most of his career. The table of contents to his story collection, *Tales of the Jazz Age* (1922), written as a series of mini-prefaces to each story in the collection, peddled the image of Scott the celebrity hobbyist rather than Fitzgerald the serious writer, while the introduction to the Modern Library edition of *The Great Gatsby* (1934) and an unpublished three-sentence foreword to *Taps at Reveille* (1935) suggest the degree to which his reputation had waned by the mid-1930s. Designed partially as apologies and correctives, the 1930s prefaces highlight Fitzgerald's desire to be recognized as a craftsman and his doubts that he ever would. The introduction to *The Great Gatsby* provides a cogent, insightful, and ultimately sad window into an author only fourteen years into his professional career. His unpublished foreword to *Taps at Reveille* reminds readers of the author's goal: to create fiction out of his own material and unique perspective, regardless of time, place, or circumstance. Scholars rarely discuss these pieces, or analyze them in sequence for how they illuminate Fitzgerald's glittering beginnings and career disappointments. The table of contents, the introduction, and the foreword amplify the anxiety of a writer at odds with himself, his artistic choices, and eventually, his own talent.

Chapter 5 investigates Ernest Hemingway's defense of writers and writing in the prefaces he wrote for himself and others. As a writers' writer, he often commented on the constraints put upon writers in the literary marketplace. With his prefaces to specific works, including *Green Hills of Africa* (1935) and *The Fifth Column and the First Forty-Nine Stories* (1938), and the works of others, including books by Kiki (Alice Prin), Elio Vittorini, and Jerome Bahr, Hemingway produced a deliberately controlled persona that enhanced his authority, granted him greater public exposure, and allowed him to defend his positions on good writers and writing while denouncing the critical community. The preface, one of many "instruments of authorial control,"[117] gave him the space to highlight the action of writing, similar to his letters for *Esquire* in the 1930s. However, his will to control went beyond persona. He cared deeply for writers, whom he favored over the critic. Writing meant action, while critiquing meant passivity; his prefaces reinforce this dictum.

Chapter 6 explores the introductions that Robert Penn Warren wrote for various American editions of his most famous novel, *All the King's Men* (1946), over a twenty-eight-year period (1953–1981). In prefaces for the Modern Library (1953), Time, Inc. (1963), the Franklin Library (1977), and the Book-of-the-Month Club (1981), Warren inhabits a number of personas: teacher, writer, critic, reader. Known as a renaissance man for his success in poetry, prose, and criticism, Warren displays the tools necessary to maintain a literary career *and* sustain a public for his book. In each introduction, Warren describes how and why he wrote the novel, and who and what inspired specific characters and scenes. However, the most important element of his introductions is the influence of Huey P. Long, populist Governor (1928–1932) and US Senator (1932–1935) from Louisiana, on Willie Stark, the fictional populist governor in the novel. Warren's view of Long and Stark (and earlier, Talos) forms the kind of interpretive exercise that Genette argues can only happen "at a safe distance"[118] from the original text, and Warren takes the many opportunities afforded him and his book to reflect on the intentions and integrity of his most celebrated novel. To get at Warren's introductions, I focus on his treatment of origins (both of the novel and of origins themselves), followed by a survey of Warren's "Huey," whose treatment drives, to a great extent, the success and staying power of the novel.

Chapter 7 examines the forewords that Toni Morrison wrote in her post-Nobel laureate years. Her forewords for a Vintage reprint series of her novels (2004–2014) stem from her desire to maintain a narrative project rooted in language, though the forewords complicate that project in various ways. Morrison searches for the language of legacy as much as a language "worthy of the culture,"[119] and her choices can be read as either significant supplements to her texts or textual deterrents. For a writer who referenced readers and reading regularly in her public lectures, interviews, and essays, Morrison uses her forewords as vehicles of explanation and interpretation, not unlike Henry James's prefaces for the New York edition. But the forewords elicit more questions than answers: Was the act of reading still her primary focus, or had the target shifted slightly in the wake of her increased profile due to her Nobel Prize win in the early 1990s and her exposure as part of Oprah's Book Club in the early 2000s? Are Morrison's forewords an extension of her lifelong "narrative project"[120] or a unique authorial act, connected perhaps, but not necessarily a continuation of that project? With particular focus on storytelling, language interrogation, and Black representation, this chapter evaluates Morrison's forewords in the context of her own mission. Are they worthy of the culture, and therefore, worthy of Toni Morrison?

Chapter 8 concludes the book with a sampling of mini-studies of prefaces written by Robert Frost, Arna Bontemps, Mary Karr, William Styron, William Faulkner, Philip Roth, Dave Eggers, and Katherine Anne Porter. With so many writers and so many books, the final chapter shows where we can take detailed research into prefaces if we are open to the concept. The goal of *The Preface: American Authorship in the Twentieth Century* was always to help readers see prefaces, actually see them, as part of the books written by writers. It is impossible for any study on what could include hundreds of possible case studies to approach anything resembling a definitive or complete treatment. Writers canonical and underground, academic and popular, have taken part in the phenomenon of the preface. As this book makes its way into the world, like the books under investigation herein, my sincere hope would be to see more studies of writers and their prefaces; studies on afterwords and epilogues, epigraphs and prologues, dedications and acknowledgments, author biographies and readers' guides. In my effort to blend bibliographic examination with the forgotten (or discounted) ephemera of major writers, I attempted to choose case studies that could serve as starting points for a field in need of one. With any luck, *The Preface* will be only the beginning, so to speak, of a more rigorous and complete investigation into the prefaces of books.

In discussing delayed prefaces (which many of the prefaces under investigation are), Genette notes that "an author's tastes or ideas evolve—indeed, undergo a sudden conversion. More generally, a middle-aged or elderly writer, when the time has come to compile his Complete Works, sees a delayed preface as an opportunity to express his thoughts, at a safe distance, about some past work."[121] Though I use "a safe distance" as the title for Chap. 6, the phrase defines the purpose of this book. Authors negotiate textual, artistic, and personal distance as their careers move forward, with each preceding text building upon the next. Authors' prefaces offer readers an opportunity to gauge an author's relationship to his or her text and offer textual evidence to support the lively interchange of ideas present in any given text. For a writer, a work is never truly finished; writing for publication presents the public with a compromised authority, and when writers choose to preface their experience with new material after time has passed, the result forever alters the text that follows. The preface was one of the most frequently used paratextual devices by American writers in the twentieth century, and by examining these prefaces in more detail, we grow our understanding of the complex and deeply personal business of professional authorship in America.

NOTES

1. Herman Melville, "The Piazza." *The Piazza Tales: and Other Prose Pieces, 1839–1860*, eds. Harrison Hayford, Alma A. MacDougall, and G. Thomas Tanselle (Evanston, IL: Northwestern University Press, 1987), 2.
2. Joseph Conrad, *The Nigger of the 'Narcissus'* (Garden City, NY: Doubleday, Page & Co., 1927), 16.
3. Henry James, "Volume XV," 1908. *Literary Criticism: French Writers, Other European Writers, The Prefaces to the New York Edition*, ed. Leon Edel (New York: Library of America, 1984), 1236.
4. Gerard Genette, *Paratexts: Thresholds of Interpretation*, 1987, trans. Jane Lewin (Cambridge: Cambridge University Press, 1997), 1.
5. Genette, *Paratexts*, 161.
6. Genette, *Paratexts*, 196.
7. Genette, *Paratexts*, 239.
8. Genette, *Paratexts*, 247.
9. Genette, *Paratexts*, 263.

10. The Linati and Gilbert Schemata have a complicated publication history. Neither were printed with the original 1922 text, though both had been circulated prior to and after publication of the first edition. The Gilbert Schema was printed first, appearing in Stuart Gilbert's *James Joyce's Ulysses: A Study* (New York: Alfred A. Knopf, 1930), while the Linati Schema was not printed until Richard Ellman included it *Ulysses on the Liffey* (New York: Oxford University Press, 1972). The schemata were published as appendices to *Ulysses: The 1922 Text* (2008). See James Joyce, "Appendix A: The Gilbert and Linati Schemata," *Ulysses: The 1922 Text*, ed. Jeri Johnson (Oxford, UK: Oxford University Press, 2008), 734–739. Bennett Cerf, publisher at Random House, wanted to include one of Joyce's schema as part of the first American edition (Random House, 1934). Joyce refused, but the *Saturday Review of Literature* published a two-page ad entitled "How to Enjoy James Joyce's Great Novel *Ulysses*," which coincided with the release of the first American edition. See Catherine Turner, *Marketing Modernism between the Two World Wars* (Amherst, MA: University of Massachusetts Press, 2003); and A. Nicholas Fargnoli and Michael Patrick Gillespie, *Critical Companion to James Joyce: A Literary Reference to His Life and Work* (New York: Facts On File, Inc., 2006), 280, 311, 349–350.

11. William Faulkner, "1699–1945 The Compsons," *The Portable Faulkner*, ed. Malcolm Cowley (New York: Viking, 1946), 325–343. Harold Bloom called the appendix Faulkner's "will-to-power over his own text," while Philip Cohen refers to the piece as "a kind of authorially sanctioned fifth section of *The Sound and the Fury*." See Harold Bloom, "Introduction," in *William Faulkner's* The Sound and the Fury, ed. Harold Bloom (New York: Infobase Publishing, 2008), 2; and Philip Cohen, "Faulkner by the Light of a Pale Fire: Postmodern Textual Scholarship and Faulkner Studies at the End of the Twentieth Century," in *Faulkner and Postmodernism*, eds. John N. Duvall and Ann J. Abadie (Jackson, MS: University Press of Mississippi, 2002), 177. Textual editor Noel Polk removed the appendix (which had circulated for some time as an introduction) in major reprints of *The Sound and the Fury*, though he included it in a 1992 Modern Library reprint edition as an appendix. See Cohen, "Faulkner by the Light," 177.

12. William Charvat, *The Profession of Authorship in America, 1800–1870*, 1968, ed. Matthew J. Bruccoli (New York: Columbia University Press, 1992), 3.

13. Michel Foucault, "What is an Author?" *Aesthetics, Method, and Epistemology*, ed. James D. Faubion (New York: The New Press, 1998), 217.

14. For a further discussion of writing in the twentieth century as a trade, see James L. W. West III, *American Authors and the Literary Marketplace since 1900* (Philadelphia: University of Pennsylvania Press, 1988), 7–22.

15. Joshua Kopperman Ratner, *American Paratexts: Experimentation and Anxiety in the Early United States*. Dissertations available from *ProQuest*. 2011. AAI3500774. https://repository.upenn.edu/dissertations/AAI3500774, vi.

16. Genette, *Paratexts*, 197.

17. For example, F. Scott Fitzgerald cut prefaces to *Tender Is the Night* (1934) and *Taps at Reveille* (1935), and he may have cut his preface to *This Side of Paradise* (1920); he also wished to revise a published introduction to the Modern Library edition of *The Great Gatsby* (1934), but poor sales prevented the revision. For more on Fitzgerald and the Modern Library, see Andrew Myers, "'I Am Used to Being Dunned': F. Scott Fitzgerald and the Modern Library," *Columbia Library Columns* 25 (February 1976): 28–39.

18. Franco Moretti, "Style, Inc. Reflections on Seven Thousand Titles (British Novels, 1740–1850)," *Critical Inquiry* 36, no. 1 (2009): 141.

19. Ratner, *American Paratexts*, 10.

20. Ratner, *American Paratexts*, 11.

21. West, *American Authors*, 5.

22. Pierre Bourdieu, "The Field of Cultural Production, or: The Economic World Reversed," 1993, in *The Broadview Reader in Book History*, eds. Michelle Levy and Tom Mole (Toronto, ON: Broadview Press, 2015), 337.

23. Foucault, "What is an Author?" 213.

24. Bourdieu, "The Field of Cultural Production," 343.

25. Foucault, "What is an Author?" 213–214.

26. Robert Darnton, "What is the History of Books?" 1990, in *The Broadview Reader in Book History*, eds. Michelle Levy and Tom Mole (Toronto, ON: Broadview Press, 2015), 233.

27. Genette, *Paratexts*, 2.

28. Genette, *Paratexts*, 2.

29. Meredith L. McGill, *American Literature and the Culture of Reprinting, 1834–1853* (Philadelphia, PA: University of Pennsylvania Press, 2002), 276.

30. McGill, *American Literature and the Culture of Reprinting*, 108.

31. James J. Barnes, *Authors, Publishers, and Politicians: The Quest for an Anglo-American Copyright Agreement, 1815–1854* (Columbus, OH: Ohio State University Press, 1974), 50.

32. Barnes, *Authors, Publishers, and Politicians*, 235.

33. Barnes, *Authors, Publishers, and Politicians*, 152.

34. McGill, *American Literature and the Culture of Reprinting*, 17.
35. West, *American Authors*, 19–20.
36. McGill, *American Literature and the Culture of Reprinting*, 17.
37. West, *American Authors*, 20.
38. McGill, *American Literature and the Culture of Reprinting*, 277.
39. Joseph Conrad, *The Children of the Sea* (New York: Dodd, Mead, and Company, 1897).
40. Michael Anesko refers to James's "Olympian" prefaces as an "heroic narrative" that self-fashions legacy and history. See Michael Anesko, *'Friction with the Market': Henry James and the Profession of Authorship* (New York: Oxford University Press, 1986), 4.
41. Anesko, *'Friction with the Market'*, 4.
42. John H. Pearson, *The Prefaces of Henry James: Framing the Modern Reader* (University Park, PA: Pennsylvania State University Press, 1997), 8. Pearson's study suggests that James created the modern reader by instructing them in his method with prefaces while creating a monument to his own life and work. Pearson points out the various anxieties inherent in James, noting that the author "would recall readers to an earlier time when his values were more in tune with the world about him, yet he would propel both his readers and his work into an uncertain future where he hoped to be canonized." James's prefaces still stand as a hallmark of craft, self-fashioning, and authorial control. See Pearson, *The Prefaces of Henry James*, 8.
43. Pearson, *The Prefaces of Henry James*, 16.
44. Genette, *Paratexts*, 173.
45. Vivienne Rundle, "Defining Frames: The Prefaces of Henry James and Joseph Conrad," *The Henry James Review* 16, no. 1 (1995): 68.
46. Rundle, "Defining Frames," 68.
47. Anesko, *'Friction with the Market'*, 144.
48. Henry James, "*The American*," 1907. *Literary Criticism: French Writers, Other European Writers, The Prefaces to the New York Edition*, 1064.
49. In many cases James rewrote large portions of his novels for the edition. James accounted for new directions in his prefaces.
50. Henry James, "*The Tragic Muse*," 1908. *Literary Criticism: French Writers, Other European Writers, The Prefaces to the New York Edition*, 1104.
51. Henry James, "*The Portrait of a Lady*," 1908. *Literary Criticism: French Writers, Other European Writers, The Prefaces to the New York Edition*, 1083.
52. The New York Edition was ultimately a significant financial failure for James and Charles Scribner's Sons, though his prefaces were a boon to his critical reputation.

53. The preface to the Modern Library edition is reprinted in F. Scott Fitzgerald, *The Great Gatsby*, 1925, ed. Matthew J. Bruccoli (New York: Cambridge University Press, 1991), 222–225.

54. Henry James, "Volume XV," 1227–1228.

55. F. Scott Fitzgerald, *Taps at Reveille*, 1935, ed. James L. W. West III (New York: Cambridge University Press, 2014), 402.

56. Frederick R. Karl and Laurence Davies, eds., *The Collected Letters of Joseph Conrad*. Volume 4: 1908–1911 (New York: Cambridge University Press, 1990), 162.

57. Laurence Davies, Frederick R. Karl, and Owen Knowles, eds., *The Collected Letters of Joseph Conrad*. Volume 6: 1917–1919 (New York: Cambridge University Press, 2002), 108.

58. Prefaces for *Youth, Lord Jim, Nostromo*, and *A Personal Record* were written in 1917.

59. The serialized version of the novel ran in five installments (August–December 1897). The review ceased publication altogether by 1898.

60. Conrad, *'Narcissus'*, 9–10.

61. Frederick R. Karl and Laurence Davies, eds., *The Collected Letters of Joseph Conrad*. Volume 1: 1861–1897 (New York: Cambridge University Press, 1983), 417.

62. Frederick R. Karl and Laurence Davies, eds., *The Collected Letters of Joseph Conrad*. Volume 5: 1912–1916 (New York: Cambridge University Press, 1996), 368.

63. Conrad, *'Narcissus'*, 11.

64. Rundle, "Defining Frames," 83.

65. Conrad, *'Narcissus'*, 12.

66. Conrad, *'Narcissus'*, 13.

67. Conrad, *'Narcissus'*, 14.

68. F. Scott Fitzgerald to H. L. Mencken. 23 April 1934. See Matthew J. Bruccoli, ed., *F. Scott Fitzgerald: A Life in Letters* (New York: Simon and Schuster, 1994), 256.

69. 20 March 1925. See Sandra Spanier, Robert W. Trogdon, and Albert Defazio III, eds., *The Letters of Ernest Hemingway (1923–1925)* (New York: Cambridge University Press, 2013), 256. Hemingway also wrote a eulogy of Conrad for the September 1924 *Transatlantic Review*. See Ernest Hemingway, "Conrad, Optimist and Moralist," *By-Line: Ernest Hemingway*, ed. William White (New York: Charles Scribner's Sons, 1967), 132–133.

70. Conrad, *'Narcissus'*, 14.

71. Willa Cather, "#0750: Willa Cather to Mr. Miller, October 24, 1924," in *The Complete Letters of Willa Cather*, eds. the Willa Cather Archive team. The Willa Cather Archive, 2018. Accessed April 6, 2021, https://cather.

unl.edu/writings/letters/let0750. Cather was responding to a reader ("Mr. Miller") who had written her regarding *My Antonia*.

72. Conrad, *'Narcissus'*, 13.
73. Toni Morrison, *Beloved*, 1987 (New York: Vintage International, 2004), xix.
74. Fitzgerald listed "the wide sultry heavens of Conrad" among his literary influences in a 1920 self-interview for Scribner's. See reproduction in Matthew J. Bruccoli, *Some Sort of Epic Grandeur: The Life of F. Scott Fitzgerald* (Columbia, SC: University of South Carolina Press, 2002), 137–138. Fitzgerald also told Perkins on 15 July 1928 that "Conrad has been the healthy influence on the technique of the novel." See John Kuehl and Jackson R. Bryer, eds., *Dear Scott/Dear Max: The Fitzgerald-Perkins Correspondence* (New York: Charles Scribner's Sons, 1971), 151.
75. 1 May 1925. See Kuehl and Bryer, *Dear Scott/Dear Max*, 104.
76. 29 September 1939. See Matthew J. Bruccoli and Margaret M. Duggan, eds., with the assistance of Susan Walker, *Correspondence of F. Scott Fitzgerald* (New York: Random House, 1980), 547. The novel was published posthumously as *The Last Tycoon* (1941).
77. F. Scott Fitzgerald, *The Great Gatsby*, 224.
78. Ernest Hemingway, *Green Hills of Africa* (New York: Charles Scribner's Sons, 1935), vii.
79. Conrad, *'Narcissus'*, 14.
80. Charles A. Madison, *Book Publishing in America* (New York: McGraw Hill, 1966), 155.
81. Madison, *Book Publishing in America*, 163.
82. Catherine Turner, *Marketing Modernism between the Two World Wars* (Amherst, MA: University of Massachusetts Press, 2003), 33.
83. Bourdieu, "The Field of Cultural Production," 337.
84. Madison, *Book Publishing in America*, 356.
85. Reprinted in Jay Satterfield, *The World's Best Books: Taste, Culture and the Modern Library* (Amherst, MA: University of Massachusetts Press, 2002), 85.
86. 23 September 1933. See Kuehl and Bryer, *Dear Scott/Dear Max*, 182. Fitzgerald hoped that releasing the Modern Library *Gatsby* prior to his long-awaited novel, *Tender Is the Night*, would bolster sales of both books. However, the edition did not sell its initial printing, and sales of *Tender* were disappointing.
87. 11 June 1931. Reprinted in Robert W. Trogdon, *The Lousy Racket: Hemingway, Scribners, and the Business of Literature* (Kent, OH: Kent State University Press, 2007), 94.
88. Satterfield, *The World's Best Books*, 131.

89. Lise Jaillant, "Canonical in the 1930s: Willa Cather's *Death Comes for the Archbishop* in the Modern Library Series," *Studies in the Novel* 45, no. 3 (2013), 476.

90. Hemingway was sad to see his connection to the Modern Library go under when Scribner's consolidated the author's reprint contracts in order to release their own editions in the 1950s. He wrote Bennett Cerf on 14 November 1952 lamenting the dissolution of their relationship, but he also offered his services as a partner in the Modern Library: "I really think I could be useful to you and that would handle the question of losing the damn name for the Library. I would be very happy to be on the masthead. You know we don't all get the Nobel prize." Hemingway would go on to win the Nobel Prize for Literature in 1954. See Ernest Hemingway, Letter to Bennett Cerf, 14 November 1952, Ernest Hemingway Collection, John F. Kennedy Library, Boston, MA.

91. West, *American Authors*, 45.

92. Kenneth C. Davis, *Two-Bit Culture: The Paperbacking of America* (Boston, MA: Houghton Mifflin Co., 1984), 145–146.

93. Jaillant, "Canonical in the 1930s," 491.

94. 24 December 1938. See Kuehl and Bryer, *Dear Scott/Dear Max*, 252.

95. 20 May 1940. See Kuehl and Bryer, *Dear Scott/Dear Max*, 261. Fitzgerald died in December 1940.

96. Madison, *Book Publishing in America*, 394.

97. Janice A. Radway, *A Feeling for Books: The Book-of-the-Month Club, Literary Taste and Middle-Class Desire* (Chapel Hill, NC: University of North Carolina Press, 1997), 153.

98. Radway, *A Feeling for Books*, 153.

99. Radway, *A Feeling for Books*, 173.

100. 19 September 1940. See Kuehl and Bryer, *Dear Scott/Dear Max*, 266.

101. Matthew J. Bruccoli, ed., with the assistance of Robert W. Trogdon, *The Only Thing That Counts: The Ernest Hemingway-Maxwell Perkins Correspondence* (Columbia, SC: University of South Carolina Press, 1996), 163.

102. Robert W. Trogdon, "Money and Marriage: Hemingway's Self-Censorship in *For Whom the Bell Tolls*," *Hemingway Review* 22, no. 2 (2003): 6.

103. 25 September 1933. See Kuehl and Bryer, *Dear Scott/Dear Max*, 181.

104. Radway, *A Feeling for Books*, 186.

105. Fredson Bowers, *Textual and Literary Criticism: The Sandars Lectures in Bibliography 1957–58* (New York: Cambridge University Press, 1966), 15.

106. Bowers, *Textual and Literary Criticism*, 15.

107. G. Thomas Tanselle, *A Rationale of Textual Criticism* (Philadelphia, PA: University of Pennsylvania Press, 1989), 38.

108. Bowers, *Textual and Literary Criticism*, 2.
109. Genette, *Paratexts*, 197.
110. Genette, *Paratexts*, 2.
111. Genette, *Paratexts*, 224.
112. Genette, *Paratexts*, 251.
113. Genette, *Paratexts*, 253.
114. Genette, *Paratexts*, 1.
115. Bibliographer Joan Crane labels the 1926 printing as a second edition based on "its existence as a different book in a different format, containing authorial revisions of the text," though she confesses that the book is not a true second edition "in the strict bibliographic sense." See Crane, *Willa Cather: A Bibliography* (Lincoln, NE: University of Nebraska Press, 1982), 66. Houghton Mifflin would eventually order fourteen printings of this revised printing. While the book was printed from the original Houghton Mifflin plates, Cather significantly revised only her introduction and asked for three minor corrections over the next six printings.
116. Genette, *Paratexts*, 221.
117. Genette, *Paratexts*, 221.
118. Genette, *Paratexts*, 253.
119. Toni Morrison, *The Bluest Eye*, 1970 (New York: Alfred A. Knopf, 1993), 215.
120. Morrison, *The Bluest Eye*, 1993, 216.
121. Genette, *Paratexts*, 253.

BIBLIOGRAPHY

Anesko, Michael. *'Friction with the Market': Henry James and the Profession of Authorship*. New York: Oxford University Press, 1986.

Barnes, James J. *Authors, Publishers, and Politicians: The Quest for an Anglo-American Copyright Agreement, 1815–1854*. Columbus, OH: Ohio State University Press, 1974.

Bloom, Harold. "Introduction." In *William Faulkner's* The Sound and the Fury, edited by Harold Bloom, 1–2. New York: Infobase Publishing, 2008.

Bourdieu, Pierre. "The Field of Cultural Production, or: The Economic World Reversed." 1993. In *The Broadview Reader in Book History*, edited by Michelle Levy and Tom Mole, 335–352. Toronto, ON: Broadview Press, 2015.

Bowers, Fredson. *Textual and Literary Criticism: The Sandars Lectures in Bibliography 1957–58*. New York: Cambridge University Press, 1966.

Bruccoli, Matthew J. *Some Sort of Epic Grandeur: The Life of F. Scott Fitzgerald*. 1981. 2nd Revised Edition. Columbia, SC: University of South Carolina Press, 2002.

Bruccoli, Matthew J., ed. *F. Scott Fitzgerald: A Life in Letters*. New York: Simon and Schuster, 1994.

Bruccoli, Matthew J., ed., with the assistance of Robert W. Trogdon, *The Only Thing That Counts: The Ernest Hemingway-Maxwell Perkins Correspondence*. Columbia, SC: University of South Carolina Press, 1996.

Bruccoli, Matthew J., and Margaret M. Duggan, eds., with the assistance of Susan Walker. *Correspondence of F. Scott Fitzgerald*. New York: Random House, 1980.

Charvat, William. *The Profession of Authorship in America, 1800–1870*. 1968, edited by Matthew J. Bruccoli. New York: Columbia University Press, 1992.

Cohen, Philip. "Faulkner by the Light of a Pale Fire: Postmodern Textual Scholarship and Faulkner Studies at the End of the Twentieth Century." In *Faulkner and Postmodernism*, edited by John N. Duvall and Ann J. Abadie, 167–191. Jackson, MS: University Press of Mississippi, 2002.

Conrad, Joseph. *The Nigger of the 'Narcissus'*. 1897. Garden City, NY: Doubleday, Page & Co., 1927.

Crane, Joan. *Willa Cather: A Bibliography*. Lincoln, NE: University of Nebraska Press, 1982.

Darnton, Robert. "What is the History of Books?" 1990. In *The Broadview Reader in Book History*, edited by Michelle Levy and Tom Mole, 231–250. Toronto, ON: Broadview Press, 2015.

Davies, Laurence, Frederick R. Karl, and Owen Knowles, eds. *The Collected Letters of Joseph Conrad*. Volume 6: 1917–1919. New York: Cambridge University Press, 2002.

Davis, Kenneth C. *Two-Bit Culture: The Paperbacking of America*. Boston, MA: Houghton Mifflin Co., 1984.

Fargnoli, A. Nicholas, and Michael Patrick Gillespie, *Critical Companion to James Joyce: A Literary Reference to His Life and Work*. New York: Facts On File, Inc., 2006.

Faulkner, William. "1699–1945 The Compsons." *The Portable Faulkner*. Malcolm Cowley, ed., 325–343. New York: Viking, 1946.

Fitzgerald, F. Scott. *The Great Gatsby*. 1925. Matthew J. Bruccoli, ed. New York: Cambridge University Press, 1991.

———. *Taps at Reveille*. 1935. James L. W. West III, ed. New York: Cambridge University Press, 2014.

Foucault, Michel. "What is an Author?" *Aesthetics, Method, and Epistemology*, James D. Faubion, ed., 205–222. New York: The New Press, 1998.

Genette, Gerard. *Paratexts: Thresholds of Interpretation*. 1987. Jane E. Lewin, trans. New York: Cambridge University Press, 1997.

Hemingway, Ernest. "Conrad, Optimist and Moralist." 1924. *By-Line: Ernest Hemingway*. William White, ed. 132–133. New York: Charles Scribner's Sons, 1967.

———. *Green Hills of Africa*. New York: Charles Scribner's Sons, 1935.

————. Letter to Bennett Cerf, 14 November 1952, Ernest Hemingway Collection, John F. Kennedy Library, Boston, MA.

Jaillant, Lise. "Canonical in the 1930s: Willa Cather's *Death Comes for the Archbishop* in the Modern Library Series," *Studies in the Novel* 45, no. 3 (2013): 476–499.

James, Henry. "*The American.*" 1907. *Literary Criticism: French Writers, Other European Writers, The Prefaces to the New York Edition*, Leon Edel, ed. 1053–1069. New York: Library of America, 1984.

————. "*The Portrait of a Lady.*" 1908. *Literary Criticism: French Writers, Other European Writers, The Prefaces to the New York Edition*, 1070–1085.

————. "*The Tragic Muse.*" 1908. *Literary Criticism: French Writers, Other European Writers, The Prefaces to the New York Edition*, 1103–1119.

————. "Volume XV." 1908. *Literary Criticism: French Writers, Other European Writers, The Prefaces to the New York Edition*, 1225–1237.

Joyce, James. "Appendix A: The Gilbert and Linati Schemata," *Ulysses: The 1922 Text*. Jeri Johnson, ed., 734–739. Oxford, UK: Oxford University Press, 2008.

Karl, Frederick R., and Laurence Davies, eds. *The Collected Letters of Joseph Conrad*. Volume 1: 1861–1897 (New York: Cambridge University Press, 1983.

————. *The Collected Letters of Joseph Conrad*. Volume 4: 1908–1911. New York: Cambridge University Press, 1990.

————. *The Collected Letters of Joseph Conrad*. Volume 5: 1912–1916. New York: Cambridge University Press, 1996.

Kuehl, John, and Jackson R. Bryer, eds. *Dear Scott/Dear Max: The Fitzgerald-Perkins Correspondence*. New York: Charles Scribner's Sons, 1971.

Madison, Charles A. *Book Publishing in America*. New York: McGraw Hill, 1966.

McGill, Meredith L. *American Literature and the Culture of Reprinting, 1834–1853*. Philadelphia, PA: University of Pennsylvania Press, 2002.

Melville, Herman. "The Piazza." *The Piazza Tales: and Other Prose Pieces, 1839–1860*. Harrison Hayford, Alma A. MacDougall, and G. Thomas Tanselle, eds., 1–12. Evanston, IL: Northwestern University Press, 1987.

Moretti, Franco. "Style, Inc. Reflections on Seven Thousand Titles (British Novels, 1740–1850)." *Critical Inquiry* 36, no. 1 (2009): 134–158.

Morrison, Toni. *Beloved*. 1987. New York: Vintage International, 2004.

————. *The Bluest Eye*. 1970. New York: Alfred A. Knopf, 1993.

Myers, Andrew. "'I Am Used to Being Dunned': F. Scott Fitzgerald and the Modern Library," *Columbia Library Columns* 25 (February 1976): 28–39.

Pearson, John H. *The Prefaces of Henry James: Framing the Modern Reader*. University Park, PA: Pennsylvania State University Press, 1997.

Radway, Janice A. *A Feeling for Books: The Book-of-the-Month Club, Literary Taste and Middle-Class Desire*. Chapel Hill, NC: University of North Carolina Press, 1997.

Ratner, Joshua Kopperman. *American Paratexts: Experimentation and Anxiety in the Early United States.* Dissertations available from *ProQuest.* 2011. AAI3500774. https://repository.upenn.edu/dissertations/AAI3500774

Rundle, Vivienne. "Defining Frames: The Prefaces of Henry James and Joseph Conrad," *The Henry James Review* 16, no. 1 (1995): 66–92.

Satterfield, Jay. *The World's Best Books: Taste, Culture and the Modern Library.* Amherst, MA: University of Massachusetts Press, 2002.

Tanselle, G. Thomas. *A Rationale of Textual Criticism.* Philadelphia, PA: University of Pennsylvania Press, 1989.

Trogdon, Robert W. *The Lousy Racket: Hemingway, Scribners, and the Business of Literature.* Kent, OH: Kent State University Press, 2007.

———. "Money and Marriage: Hemingway's Self-Censorship in *For Whom the Bell Tolls,*" *Hemingway Review* 22, no. 2 (2003): 6–18.

Turner, Catherine. *Marketing Modernism between the Two World Wars.* Amherst, MA: University of Massachusetts Press, 2003.

West, James L. W., III. *American Authors and the Literary Marketplace since 1900.* Philadelphia, PA: University of Pennsylvania Press, 1988.

The Willa Cather Archive team, eds. *The Complete Letters of Willa Cather.* The Willa Cather Archive, 2018. Accessed April 6, 2021. https://cather.unl.edu/writings/letters.

CHAPTER 2

A Proper Reading: Willa Cather's Introductions to *My Ántonia*

> *You either have to be utterly commonplace or else do the things people* <u>*don't*</u>
> *want, because it has not yet been invented. No really new and original thing
> is* <u>*wanted*</u>*: people have to learn to like new things.*
> —Willa Cather[1]

By 1934, Willa Cather had written the books central to her legacy: *O Pioneers!* (1913), *The Song of the Lark* (1915), *My Ántonia* (1918), *A Lost Lady* (1923), *The Professor's House* (1925), *Death Comes for the Archbishop* (1927), and, to a lesser degree, *One of Ours* (1922). In January she wrote friend Carrie Miner Sherwood, "as for ANTONIA she is really just a figure upon which other things hang. ... I was destined to write ANTONIA if I ever wrote anything at all."[2] Cather had recently been awarded a silver medal by the International Mark Twain Society, who had held a contest to determine "the most memorable and representative American novel in the last thirty-five years," and her letter to Sherwood expresses only mild appreciation, though she praises a citation by one judge for being well-written.[3] Instead she focuses on explaining her craft, something she felt reviewers and critics had, at times, recognized but mischaracterized. "You never can get it through peoples heads that a story is made out of an emotion or an excitement, and is <u>not</u> made out of the legs and arms and faces of one's friends or acquaintances," she declares. Her stories are pictures, but rather than pictures of actual people they are pictures of memories of those people. "If I had exaggerated my real feeling or stretched it one

© The Author(s), under exclusive license to Springer Nature
Switzerland AG 2021
R. K. Tangedal, *The Preface*, New Directions in Book History,
https://doi.org/10.1007/978-3-030-85151-4_2

inch," she argues, "the whole book would have fallen as flat as a pancake, and would have been a little ridiculous. There is just one thing you cannot fake or counterfeit in this world, my dear Carrie, and that is real feeling, feeling in people who try to govern their hearts with their heads."[4] Cather's strength in charting the life of her novel after publication merits special attention. Not only was she concerned with critics and readers seeing emotion and excitement in her creation, but she was also worried about the book as an object, where it would go and why, and how it would look.

Cather often referred to *Ántonia* as "she" and "her" in correspondence with editors and friends. For example, in a response to another of Houghton Mifflin editor Ferris Greenslet's suggestions to reissue the novel with new illustrations—this time in 1937—she pleads, "Why can't we let Antonia alone? She has gone her own way quietly and with some dignity, and neither you nor I have reason to complain of her behavior. She wasn't played up in the first place, and surely a coming-out party after twenty years, would be a little funny." She thinks it "wrong to dress her up and push her," since "we have saved her from text books, from dismemberment, from omnibuses." Colored illustrations or no, "I like her just as she is," the figure upon which other things hang.[5] She was dissatisfied with Houghton Mifflin's original advertising and marketing of the novel ("she wasn't played up in the first place"). Nearly twenty years earlier she had expressed her consternation over the handling of *Ántonia* to Greenslet. Houghton's publishers "don't believe they can make much on me, but they will be very careful not to lose much," and she "can work better for a firm that can give me some of its ingenuity and enthusiasm."[6] She moved to Alfred A. Knopf just three years later, and though she had an amiable working relationship, and lively correspondence, with Greenslet for the remainder of her life, Cather's insistence on keeping *Ántonia* "just as she is" provides a fitting way to frame the revisions she made to "her" between 1918 and 1926. The first edition of *My Ántonia* (1918) featured an original preface (titled an introduction by Cather), and eight years later, Cather reworked her introduction for a revised printing of *My Ántonia* (1926).[7] In the interim, a World War had raged, modernism had taken hold of the literary consciousness, and Cather had signed with a new publisher. The introductions are markedly different, with Cather's treatment of narrator Jim Burden the primary revision. But unlike many prefaces, Cather's introduction to *My Ántonia* has been the subject of scholarly focus. In what follows I examine Cather as editor in control of her novel and the impact of the 1926 revisions to the introduction, as well as the ways in which critics and scholars have accounted for the revisions she made to the introduction. Though prefaces, as I mentioned in Chap. 1, are rarely the focus of scholarly interest, the two versions of the introduction to *My Ántonia* and the attention they have received proves, partially, the value of engaging with prefaces as zones of control.

A Proper Reading: Cather as Editor in Control

Gerard Genette argues that "the way to guide the reading, to try to get a proper reading, is not only to issue direct orders. The way to get a proper reading is also—and perhaps initially—to put the (definitely assumed) reader in possession of information the author considers necessary for this proper reading."[8] Cather's introduction puts the reader in possession of the crucial editorial frame central to the novel. In it, Jim Burden delivers a manuscript to an unnamed narrator, presumably Willa Cather, about their shared childhood friend Ántonia. The narrator concludes that the present book is Burden's narrative, "substantially as he brought it to me."[9] On the surface, the introduction is rather straightforward: Cather introduces readers to her primary protagonist through a well-worn device, the preface. But Cather does more with the introduction than present Jim Burden; she presents herself. In May 1919 she wrote Will Owen Jones, an editor at the *Nebraska State Journal,* explaining the purpose of her "introductory chapter": "such a device is very often employed by Russian and French authors, when they wish their narrative to be colored by a certain mood and certain personal feelings throughout. It is a device, and since it is, the more frankly it is presented as such, the better." Her chief character, Ántonia, needed to be filtered "through a man's memory, because the most interesting things I knew about theseveral [sic] women of whom she was made, were told me by men," she said. It needed to be in the first person, "since it was so entirely a story of feel feeling and not of action," and the introduction "had to state the facts that the narrator of the story is a man of worldly experience,—for only those who know the world can see the past parish as it is—, that he has no children to plan for and is not particularly fortunate in his domestic life. If he were, he would not dwell upon the years of his first youth either so minutely or so sympathetically."[10] Cather displays a clear understanding of the preface-writing tradition, her book one of "mood and certain personal feelings" rather than action. But "determining the sender of a preface is a tricky matter," argues Genette, "first, because there are numerous types of preface-writers (real or otherwise), and second, because some of the situations thus created are complex—indeed, ambiguous or indeterminate."[11] The ambiguity central to Cather's experiment—is she the editor of Jim Burden's original manuscript?—positions the introduction as one of three kinds of preface: (1) "the alleged author of a preface may be the author ... of the text: this very common situation we will call the *authorial*, or *autographic*, preface"; (2) "the alleged author of a preface may be one of the characters in the action, when there are characters and action: this is the *actorial* preface"; or (3) "the alleged author of a preface may be a wholly different (third) person: the *allographic* preface."[12] Cather amplified her role as Jim's editor in the 1918 introduction, and she exhibited a nuanced "editorial" control over the "simple and faithful presentation" of Jim's memories. We are meant to see Jim Burden as the writer of the text, but "Willa Cather," in her role as narrator of the introduction and editor of the manuscript, becomes the link between Jim and the public. In essence, "Willa Cather" becomes the author of the book based on Jim's manuscript.

Cather's 1918 introduction compels not only a specific reading of the novel but a reading of Cather. Seeing Cather as an editor in control of the text shifts the narrative from a memorial to the American West to an examination of time and memory, and one of textual authority. But most importantly, in the 1918 introduction we *see* "Willa Cather," the implied narrator of the piece and the author of the book. Again, such a tactic is not new, but it can lead to a more complicated experience with the text. Daryl W. Palmer believes that "we know Jim Burden is not Willa Cather, even as we recognize that he shadows some important elements of the author's life."[13] The autobiographical dilemma that follows most writers of realistic fiction followed Cather. Late in her career, she wrote her brother about a particular scene in her novel, *Sapphira and the Slave Girl* (1940). "For years I wanted to write that actual scene," she wrote, "but I could never see a way to use it except in a personal autobiography, and I hate autobiographies."[14] She had written S. S. McClure's *My Autobiography* (1914) near the beginning of her writing career, which was first published in *McClure's* from October 1913 to May 1914; she never denied her work on the book nor was she denied any credit by the book's "author," McClure. He had called her "the real author" in an inscription to her personal copy of the book, since Cather "had authored the entirety of the autobiography, ostensibly recording, after-the-fact, the story as McClure told it."[15] Janis P. Stout contends that working on the McClure autobiography gave Cather "an experience of simultaneous involvement and distance: her modern perspective on fiction."[16] "Involvement and distance" proves an ample metaphorical frame for Cather's introduction to *My Ántonia*. Cather presents herself as the author of the book (Willa Cather is named on the cover, after all), "Willa Cather" as the implied narrator of the introduction and editor of Jim Burden's manuscript, and Jim Burden as the storyteller—"his" Ántonia. Cather distances herself immediately from Jim Burden, since the bulging portfolio he brings to her includes his version of their shared story, yet she portrays herself as intimately involved in bringing his work to the reader. Her tactic presents readers with an autographic preface (by the author of the work) disguised as an allographic preface (by a third party), her editorial role all the more amplified by her infusion of elements resembling an actorial preface (by a character from the work) into the introduction. Willa Cather, in an ambitious and thoroughly modern stroke, wrote an autographic, allographic, and actorial preface all in one, and with the 1918 introduction that comes from that experimentation, Cather displays the complex strands of textual and commemorative autonomy surrounding stories and who gets to tell them.

Cather's desire for control can be traced to very early in her career, as she told an interviewer for *The Bookman* in 1921, "I took a salaried position [with *McClure's*] because I didn't want to write directly to sell. I didn't want to compromise."[17] The clear control she had over both the physical specifications of her books *and* the control she exhibited in pieces like the introduction to *My Ántonia* confirm her willingness to remain true to her original conceit. Cather presents two authorities in her introduction, herself and Jim Burden. Oppositional authority is not new for Cather, as Merrill Skaggs points to the author's "reliance on evocative juxtapositions, so that scenes, lines, or facts placed side by side change each other," and how in *My Ántonia* "polarities determine the story's structural units, both large and small."[18] Though Skaggs characterizes these moments as "organizing habits" meant to challenge readers, they also rely on "her reader's ability to register the quiet explosion in the brain that juxtaposed volatile elements can produce."[19] Stout revises Skaggs's initial theory of polarities and determines that Cather's polarities were "rooted in a deep ambivalence of response to a shifting, increasingly uncertain modern world. This pervasive dividedness of mind produces in Cather's work a fiction far more complex, subtle, and uncertain than its appearance either of simplicity or of *resolved* polarity would indicate."[20]

Uncertainty permeates more than the fiction; the introduction implies a doubling of authority, though Stout and Skaggs agree that Burden is cloaked in Cather's authority and knowledge; this is an obvious notion considering the author's name on the dust jacket. But textually, Cather creates an ambiguous zone of authority. Her choice to create Jim Burden for narrative purposes reads differently if the introduction is not present. The polarity that puts Cather and Burden at odds exposes the fiction to possible misreadings and misinterpretations.

Unlike many writers of her time, Cather had significant editorial experience, having worked for *McClure's* from 1906 to 1912 (and as a managing editor for part of that span). Though she left *McClure's* to concentrate on her own work, her experience editing the magazine informed the remainder of her writing career. Cather's ability to shape her projects from minor details to overall completion marks her as a significant editorial force in American fiction. Given her editorial history, the way in which Cather obfuscates authority in *My Ántonia* while simultaneously celebrating it comes into sharper focus. Stout likens this dichotomy to "the evacuations of identity associated with postmodernism" several years later and notes "the idea of the plurality of the self and the falsity of unitary conceptions of meaning" in the novel.[21] The novel displays a complex treatment of memory that both celebrates the past and broadens the conception of that past. David Stouck sees the introduction placing "the narrator's memories in a perspective that creates dramatic tension in the book,"[22] and though that dramatic tension drives the novel, it is Cather's introduction that allows for Burden to narrate in the first place. Cather's introduction shows the duality of expression, the editor and the writer, and the question of who controls the story emerges.

But in the early stages of composition, Cather's confidence in the novel was less than emphatic. She told her brother Roscoe that her new novel idea was "not very new, none of my ideas ever are," but the delivery of her novel featured a significant change: "the trouble about this story is that the central figure must be a man, and that is where all women writers fall down." In reference to her earlier work Cather continued,

> I get a great many bouquets about my men, but if they are good it is because I'm careful to have a woman for the central figure and to commit myself only through her. I give as much of the men as she sees and has to do with—and I can do that with the utmost authority. But I hate to try more than that. And yet, in this new-old idea, the chief figure must be a boy and man.[23]

She informs Roscoe of a "new-old idea," in reference to her process of creating male characters observed from a female perspective. As we find in *My Ántonia*, Cather instead creates Jim Burden, a middle-aged man recollecting a strong female character (Ántonia). By making the change, Cather is able to present a female as seen through the eyes of a man. This point has been the center of critical controversy, as Stout believes "countless readers as well as numerous critics have accepted Jim's heartfelt tribute at face value."[24] Many readers fail to recognize the double perspective at the heart of the novel: Cather as editor to Jim's "manuscript." Readers are exposed to a different type of novel where "the invented narrator is not a professional writer, the apparent artlessness of his memories seems perfectly logical, and the reader is willing to suspend his belief that he is in the presence of a perfectly controlled art," according to James Woodress.[25] Though Woodress articulates the invention clearly, Stout takes issue with Woodress simplifying Jim's memories as, "of course, [Cather's] memories."[26] Stout calls for a further examination of Cather's role in *My Ántonia*, for by simply conflating Burden and Cather critics miss out on the editorial perspective that Cather was able to create in the finished novel. We must consider the complex narrative perspective at the core of Cather's novel, which her introduction frames for the reader.

The frame also ruptures our received notions of authenticity. "Willa Cather" makes an agreement with Jim, after he had made her "see" Ántonia again, "feel her presence, revived all my old affection for her" on their train ride through Iowa. "I told him I had always felt that other people—he himself, for one—knew her much better than I. I was ready, however, to make an agreement with him; I would set down on paper all that I remembered of Antonia if he would do the same. We might, in this way, get a picture of her."[27] He agrees and, with "sudden clearness" in his eyes, tells her that "I should have to do it in a direct way, and say a great deal about myself. It's through myself that I knew and felt her, and I've had no practice in any other form of presentation."[28] Here we see Jim, with "his naturally romantic and ardent disposition," who "has helped young men out there to do remarkable things in mines and timber and oil." His impulsiveness drives his success, and "he never seems to me to grow older." His "quick-changing blue eyes are those of a young man," and his "sympathetic, solicitous interest in women is as youthful as it is Western and American."[29] He is ageless, and according to Marilee Lindemann, his romantic disposition is "written on a body that seems unmarked by time yet is carefully particularized in terms of gender, race, region, and nation."[30] For Lindemann and others, the transfer of text from Burden to "Willa Cather" complicates authority by actually doubling down on the aspect of control central to Cather's experiment.[31] "The transfer from 'Cather' to Jim, true or false," argues Lindemann, "is crucial to the text's interrogation of the sociopolitical technologies of vision and visibility, the conditions that determine access to cultural power and narrative authority."[32] Because he cannot "see clearly or neutrally"[33] due to his romantic disposition, Jim puts the burden of structuring and shaping his childlike memories on the shoulders of a more balanced adult: "Willa Cather." In the sweeping descriptors of Jim Burden we must also *see* the real Willa Cather, who feels that Jim's youthful vigor can neither help him pin down his past with Ántonia without her encouragement nor result in a structured narrative without her intervention. Further, Cather sympathizes with Jim indirectly, which only adds to the belief that Jim cannot grow up because of his marriage to Genevieve Whitney Burden, "a restless, headstrong girl" who came from means, lifting her husband out of struggle and obscurity by simply marrying him. Cather gives the impression that Jim's "quiet tastes" are no match for his wife's role as "the patroness to a group of young poets and painters of advanced ideas and mediocre ability."[34] Her fortune is hers, and she "lives her own life," whereas Jim lights out in new directions, raising capital for "new enterprises in Wyoming and Montana," even though he lives in New York City with his socialite wife. In Cather's sympathetic portrayal, Jim appears industrious and thoughtful, and his youthful exuberance and authentic passion are seen, for the most part, as personal strengths, even though such strengths can lead him to "lose himself in those big Western dreams."[35] Still, someone must give order to his memories. Someone must remain grounded while Jim loses himself in dreams.

Cather encourages readers, albeit subtly, to see Jim's strengths as authorial weaknesses, for when she encourages him to write down his memories of Ántonia, a "Bohemian girl whom we had known long ago, and whom both of us admired," Jim reacts with almost childlike frankness: "He rumpled his hair with a quick, excited gesture, which with him often announces a new determination, and I could see that my suggestion took hold of him. 'Maybe I will, maybe I will!' he declared. He stared out of the window for a few moments, and when he turned to me again his eyes had the sudden clearness that comes from something the mind itself sees."[36] Jim is the idea man, the man who can raise capital in order to make something happen, and the man who can dream. His youthful naiveté stands in opposition to the more adult "Willa Cather" of the introduction, who tells him that "how he knew her and felt her was exactly what I most wanted to know about Ántonia. He had had opportunities that I, as a little girl who watched her come and go, had not."[37] Jim's status as a boy and now a man provides him with a much different relationship to memory and mobility than his female friend. Cather the narrator's part of the agreement goes unfulfilled. Sometime after the train ride Jim arrives at her apartment, "with a bulging legal portfolio sheltered under his fur overcoat." After tapping his "thing about Ántonia" with pride he asks about Cather the narrator. "I had to confess that mine had not gone beyond a few straggling notes," she writes. After Jim titles his manuscript "My Ántonia," he instructs his friend to read it immediately, "'but don't let it influence your own story.'" The narrator's story goes unwritten, "but the following narrative is Jim's manuscript, substantially as he brought it to me."[38] In the 1918 introduction, Cather presents herself as a writer in her own right, though technically a failed one. Melissa J. Homestead argues that "the 1918 Introduction concludes with the failure of the narrator, a female professional author who spent her childhood in Nebraska but lives in New York, to produce an account of Ántonia." "Because she has failed," Homestead concludes, "she merely introduces the slightly edited manuscript of her amateur friend."[39] Burden is the man with the means to take time with his memories and write down what those memories mean to him. While Cather the narrator certainly shares in the advantages of mobility and independence, she still lacks the status of a vibrant, blue-eyed, sandy-haired man taken regularly by passionate reminiscences of their shared childhood. Jim's privilege cannot go unnoticed, nor can Cather's examination of authenticity and its impact on story.

Milton Orvell believes that Cather uses the introduction "to disarm our expectations of 'art,' offering instead a narrative that promises to be the real thing itself, an authentic narrative of Ántonia by someone who knew her and is, for reasons we may never fully understand, obsessed with her."[40] Conversely, Sharon O'Brien argues that the introduction "shows how aesthetically shaped and modernist *My Ántonia* is ... we are aware from the beginning that we are encountering someone's story about the past rather than 'the real' itself. Because we have the framing device, we see Jim Burden as a character with a particular slant on 'my' Ántonia and are ready to be readers who can see how his own story colors his portrait of her."[41] Stout goes on to explain the knowledge that Cather holds over Burden by alleging the work had been done by Jim, as if heightened art would spoil or detract from our understanding of, and Jim's memories regarding, Ántonia. But if authenticity is the goal, and Cather insists upon, according to Orvell, "making a virtue out of the naïveté of her narrator,"[42] then Stout's assertion that Cather "can see beyond his sentimentality—in part because as a woman she can see beyond the perspective of a man observing a woman's experience" complicates things even further.[43] Cather questions the ways readers receive stories and how that reception is manipulated by seemingly authentic guideposts. No one doubts that Cather wrote *My Ántonia*, created Jim Burden for narrative purposes, and presented his supposed memories as somehow removed from her own perspective, though edited together with her skill and attention to authenticity. Even further, the idea that Cather created a less artful novel for the sake of authenticity begs repeating the following question: for what purpose does her introduction exist? If we are dealing with authorial effacement—such as T. S. Eliot's notion of poetry being "not a turning loose of emotion, but an escape from emotion; it is not the expression of personality, but the escape from personality"[44]—can we assert confidently that Cather intended for her own narrative to be subdued in favor of another? The simple fact that Cather created Jim Burden and his narrative, critiqued the inception of that narrative in her introduction, and continued to defend the novel as her central work of fiction for the remainder of her life, buttresses the argument that editorial control and authenticity were primary concerns for Cather.

Even so, Cather's editorial concerns go beyond the complications she establishes in her introduction. When finalizing the W. T. Benda illustrations for the novel Cather wrote R. L. Scaife asking for "the exact size of the page" and "a sheet of the paper you will use" so she "may size the cuts" herself, rather than put it in the hands of copiers.[45] She informed Greenslet on 1 February 1918 that "the Introduction will be almost the last thing I write" before commencing with an editorial concern over her name: "My name on the cover is 'Willa S. Cather'; if it is not too much trouble I wish you could ask them to cut out the S and solder the plate, leaving it simply 'Willa Cather.' I think the S looks too business-like for the queer title above it."[46] Prior to *Ántonia*, all Cather books had featured either "S" or "Sibert" in her name, but with her new novel she wanted something different, akin to her eventual introduction. Upon reviewing the first proofs Cather told Greenslet on 2 July that "the proofs are going well, except that the Riverside copy reader changed the spelling of Mama to Mamma—too sophisticated a form for these country people—and I have to change it back in every case" before concluding that "most of the copy-reader's changes were good, by the way."[47] Her 11 July letter to Greenslet voices her editorial concerns: "You know I am particularly anxious that the cuts should be printed on the same paper as the text, and not on coated paper. I wrote asking for page proofs of the cuts, so that I can see how they are set on the page. (In the dummy the cuts were set too high in each case.)"[48] Her directness regarding not only the illustrations but also their position (to the inch) on the page shows how far Cather was willing to go in service to her vision. Cather was not in the business of letting others determine the look of her texts, a chief reason for her willingness to deal directly with the publication details. But her attention to these minute printing details grates against the more passive persona she develops for "Willa Cather" in the 1918 introduction. Yet in that persona, Cather still has Jim leave his bulging portfolio with her; she controls the future of Jim's narrative. Cather knew what the impact of her introduction would mean for the novel.

Given these editorial concerns, one can read *My Ántonia* and its introduction as the result of craft and precision, with nothing achieved accidentally. Immediately following the release of the novel Cather insisted to friend Irene Miner Weisz that "a stranger, if he has an eye trained for literary values, is apt to get the whole picture more <u>as a whole</u> than anyone who knew the people from whom the characters were sketched" and felt that "the further you stand away from a picture of this kind, the more you get the painter's intention."[49] Cather uses symbolism at several points in the novel to foreground editorial control and authorial ambiguity in the face of Jim's memories. After all, *My Ántonia* is a novel about memory and therefore a novel about perspective. Early on Jim regards his new home as "nothing but land: not a country at all, but the material out of which countries are made" and gives the feeling of being "erased, blotted out" by the vastness of the landscape.[50] He has yet to produce a shadow, a symbol of the novel imbued with narrative possibility, mostly due to his being a shadow of several people Cather knew. Because of the introduction we forget, albeit momentarily, that there is no Jim Burden and therefore no Burden manuscript. There is only Willa Cather and the novel in our hands. However, the introduction manipulates readers and essentializes the narrator and his relationship to the text. Cather's many veiled symbols are signposts of editorial authority playing through Jim's narrative to remind readers of her complete artistic control. One of the most famous lines in the novel describes happiness as becoming "a part of something entire, whether it is sun or air, or goodness and knowledge" and "to be dissolved into something complete and great."[51] Cather wants readers to read her narrative as Jim's, and by creating a dual authorial perspective she is able to present an essential American vision of memory. Her "new-old" idea rested on producing a male view with female control. Jim recalls, "it must have been the scarcity of detail in that tawny landscape that made detail so precious,"[52] and Cather illuminates her own authority in the process by recognizing the effect Jim's narrative role would have over the entire work.

Still, Stout reminds us that "however closely [Jim Burden] may represent Willa Cather, his knowledge is less than hers. The result is an undercurrent of resistance to Jim Burden's voice and to his vision and judgment of Ántonia."[53] Jim refers to the "jealousy and envy and unhappiness" of closed up homes in Black Hawk, noting that

> this guarded mode of existence was like living under a tyranny. People's speech, their voices, their very glances, became furtive and repressed. Every individual taste, every natural appetite, was bridled by caution. The people asleep in those houses, I thought, tried to live like the mice in their own kitchens; to make no noise, to leave no trace, to slip over the surface of things in the dark.[54]

In referring to these homes as spaces of alternate histories and practice, and "made up of evasions and negations,"[55] Cather reminds readers that Jim is less attached to stories other than his own. His perspective, though present, is far from the only one present in the novel. "Jim's focus on 'his' Ántonia," argues Stout, "is repeatedly exposed to correction."[56] Subtle hints such as this allow for Cather to situate Burden as simply "a" storyteller rather than "the" storyteller. But by doing so Cather calls careful attention to expectations and roles given to women like Ántonia and businessmen like Burden. Stout notes Jim's role in distorting the past as much as recounting it, and through the double authority of the novel—Cather and Jim Burden—we are presented with an exercise in perspective.[57]

Cather asserts her control further when Jim recalls the setting sun engulfing a black plough, as "the long fingers of the sun touched their foreheads." Jim focuses on its curiosity "magnified across the distance by the horizontal light, it stood out against the sun, was exactly contained within the circle of the disc; the handles, the tongue, the hare—black against the molten red. There it was, heroic in size, a picture writing on the sun." A variety of interpretations abound here: (1) the plough is Jim, someone who's portrayal of Ántonia and her legacy only gains clarity when emblazoned by the sun's (Cather's) rays. As it focuses every so often (much like memory), the beauty of its composition becomes apparent, presenting a clear image of the past; (2) the sun may be memory itself, as the plough is "a picture writing on the sun."[58] Cather recognizes the futility of memory alone and how important the linking of several memories together is in forming a coherent narrative. Cather's editorial concerns are in clear view: the plough "had sunk back to its own littleness somewhere on the prairie,"[59] and by failing to feel Cather's guiding hand readers would misinterpret what makes the novel possible. "The objects are symbols, and the symbols send an elegiac message," argues Brian Gingrich. "There was a time when we could live naively in simple nature, and even a moment when we could act on nature with simple implements; those times have passed."[60]

Similarly, Jim describes a windmill against the night sky once he returns to his childhood home, now occupied by Widow Steavens: "I lay awake and watched the moonlight shining over the barn and the stacks and the pond, and the windmill making its old dark shadow against the blue sky."[61] The image of a static object engulfed in the light of a natural body, producing a shadow and issuing a secondary form, plays to the specific double consciousness Cather seeks to enact from the beginning. Jim's narrative comprises only one part of the picture, one source of insight. By denying the existence of other sources readers fail to understand Cather's textual experimentation. Because of the introduction, the novel encourages readers to question narrative authority and control. Gingrich realizes that Jim's visions "refer back to singular natural objects in the story," since for Jim, they are concrete objects in his memory. But those same objects evolve into "the form of abstract metaphors the moment the discourse seeks to inhabit them," leaving readers to consider a plough, a windmill, or a barn as symbols of something more.[62] Michael Martone sees the Midwest as an abstract landscape, where "our response to the geology of the region might be similar to our response to the contemporary wall of paint in the museums." In what he calls the flatness, "everywhere is surface. This landscape can never take us emotionally in the way smoky crags or crawling oceans can. We stare back at it. Beneath our skins, we begin to disassemble the mechanisms of how we feel. We begin to feel."[63] The landscape burrows into Martone, deep beneath his surfaces, making as much of an impression on him over time as the immediate sensations of mountains and oceans do in moments. Ántonia "seemed to mean to us the country, the conditions, the whole adventure of our childhood," notes the narrator of the 1918 introduction. "To speak her name was to call up pictures of people and places, to set a quiet drama going in one's brain."[64] Ántonia is the past, motherhood, the land, stoicism, resilience, the feeling. Where the person ends and the symbol begins is as complicated and drawn out as Martone's Midwestern flatness. We feel her as we feel the plough sinking into its littleness and the windmill making its shadow. We feel Cather guiding Jim, and the original introduction helps us discover that for ourselves.

Once Jim concludes that he and Ántonia share "the precious, the incommunicable past,"[65] his entire narrative comes into question. If the past remains incommunicable, how then did he create his manuscript, and how was he able to transcribe something so precious he feels it immaterial outside of his own real, lived experience with Ántonia? The introduction sheds light on this issue. Jim's feelings in the 1918 introduction feed on his energy, as he "impetuously" asks the narrator why she has not written anything about Ántonia, as if she too required the exercise of memory to make whole her existence.[66] By describing the narrative crux of her invention (a female writing from a male perspective), Cather parlays a role as co-writer into her role as editor, where she casts herself as the controlling agent of Burden's recollections. Jim needed to write his narrative to feel complete, whereas Cather the narrator did not require the same textual therapy. But Jim's romanticism, his idealism painted against the backdrop of adult mundanity in the form of Cather as narrator, makes him more than ordinary or plain. He and Cather share the "freemasonry" of growing up in a little prairie town "buried in wheat and corn," and they share the distance that separates each of them from the past that Ántonia represents.[67] Without Jim's enthusiasm and vigor, and without Cather's caretaking, both presented in the 1918 introduction, Jim's "My Ántonia" would never have become Cather's *My Ántonia*.

THE IMPACT OF THE 1926 REVISIONS

Some early reviews of *My Ántonia* noted the introduction. One praised Cather's choice to tell the story from Jim's perspective and allude to it in an introduction: "By deliberately and at the outset surrendering the story teller's most valuable prerogatives Miss Cather has won a complete victory over the reader, shattering his easeful assumptions of the unreality of it all, routing his ready-made demand for the regulation thrills and taking prisoner his sense of what is his rightful due."[68] N. P. Dawson believed Cather "cleverly and with art explains the male medium of story-telling" in the introduction, then quoted the second half of the first paragraph, where the narrator and Jim agree that growing up in a small prairie town gives them a "kind of freemasonry."[69] The introduction had the impact Cather intended, which makes her choice to revise it eight years later all the more interesting. Of all her books Cather was the most protective of *My Ántonia*, with Sharon O'Brien charting the decades-long battle Cather waged to keep her novel safe from mass marketing, paperback editions, and other forms of popular repurposing.[70] In February 1924, Cather wrote her now former editor from Houghton Mifflin, Ferris Greenslet, insisting that she edit and provide a preface for a new edition of her one-time mentor Sarah Orne Jewett's collected stories: "I think the stories ought to have a fresh envelope and be issued in standard-sized volumes with good clear type,— (I would suggest type like that you used in 'Antonia')—some type that does not look like textbook type. I don't mean that I think the books ought to look loud, naturally, but modern."[71] Her use of "modern" is crucial here given the structure and purpose of her introduction to *My Ántonia*. Perhaps most effective is her evocative definitions of beauty in her finished preface for the Jewett volume, one concerning ornamentation and the other concerning modern non-ornamentation. Comparing the latter to a modern yacht, she claims "our whole sensation of pleasure in watching a yacht under sail comes from the fact that every line of the craft is designed for one purpose, that everything about it furthers that purpose, so that it has an organic, living simplicity and directness."[72] The same can be said for Cather's 1926 introduction, where she emphasizes simplicity and directness rather than the more fully realized impression she had left in 1918. The purpose of the 1926 introduction to *My Ántonia* is not the same as the purpose of the 1918 introduction, so where did Cather feel her design lacking? Which part of the craft was not furthering her purpose? Was her original introduction neither simple nor direct enough to aid in the success of the novel?

Gerard Genette points out that secondary prefaces result from a reaction to the first edition's response, both critically and publicly,[73] and in most cases a negative response prompts a new authorial response in which the author resituates the work for a new readership. The oddity of the *Ántonia* introduction is that initial reviews of the novel were strong,[74] with many declaring the novel one of the year's best. Sales were moderate due to the United States' involvement in World War I, but Cather's novel never fell out of critical favor. Why then revise the introduction? First and foremost, Greenslet wanted to get out a new edition due to Cather's continued success with Alfred A. Knopf, the publisher she had left Houghton Mifflin for after *My Ántonia* was released. She had won a Pulitzer Prize in 1923 for her Great War novel *One of Ours*, and her subsequent titles with Knopf had been critically acclaimed and steady sellers. Greenslet did not want to let the opportunity pass, asking Cather to consider a new edition. Cather wrote Greenslet that the introduction was "not very good" and that it was "the only thing about the story that was laborious," though she insisted that it was necessary in order to get a picture of Jim's "unsuccessful personal life," meaning that his reminiscences were not objective or omniscient but rather colored by his own personal disappointment.[75] Cather understood the function of her introduction, and Greenslet, who preferred to remove it altogether by 1926, acquiesced to her revisions.[76] Jim is calmer and more collected, and he expresses a more restrained romanticism, one of recollection, as he hopes to organize his memory for better or worse. Most importantly, the 1926 introduction carries the essence of Cather's technique, whereas the earlier introduction plots it out explicitly. The 1918 introduction makes Jim an energetic lightning rod of memory, while the 1926 version presents him more practically, a man whose faith and knowledge (and perceived ordinariness) produce greater insight than a boy losing himself in dreams.[77] Homestead reports that Greenslet's desire to re-release the novel paid off, as sales grew and remained steady for the firm and Cather.[78] But the introduction, both the original and revised versions, remained an afterthought for decades, and many reprintings of Cather's novel included the 1926 introduction well into the 1990s.

Given the market opportunity, one can see Greenslet's perspective, though Cather's is still somewhat muddied. The following revisions were made to the introduction: (1) Cather removes most of the paragraph about Jim Burden's wife, whom she does not name in the revised introduction;[79] (2) Cather reduces Jim's biography, emending a full-page paragraph to eight lines;[80] (3) the narrator does not make an agreement with Jim regarding writing down his memories about Ántonia, instead Jim has been writing about her "from time to time" on his "long trips across the country"[81] for amusement; (4) Cather removes any notion of the narrator being a writer or engaging in the writing process with Jim, reducing the narrator's "few straggling notes"[82] in 1918 to nothing by 1926;[83] (5) in the 1918 introduction, the narrator reinforces that the following narrative is "Jim's manuscript, substantially as he brought it to me."[84] In the 1926 introduction, the narrator does not reference any editorial activity after Jim turns over the manuscript. It simply ends with Jim's satisfaction from naming the manuscript "My Ántonia."[85] Essentially, Cather removes any trace of herself, either as character or as author, from the introduction, which now focuses solely on Jim Burden. The introduction shifts from an autographic–allographic–actorial preface to something else. There are few if any autographic or allographic elements, since we cannot say with confidence that the narrator is Willa Cather, either the author or the third-party editor. The best we can surmise is that the narrator is a character (actorial) who edits and brings Jim's manuscript out. With Jim reduced to a more mundane and composed character, the narrator lessened to a far less engaged individual force, and Willa Cather or "Willa Cather" removed altogether, the revised introduction all but negates the ambitious qualities of the original. There is no ideal way to understand Cather's intentions here, though scholars have tried to comprehend the sharp departure she took between 1918 and 1926. The impact of Cather's revisions to her introduction signals one of the few times that prefatory material has been scrutinized and investigated as a critical piece of a narrative text.

The two versions of the introduction offer a competing vision of textual control, relying on readers to discern who controls narrative and to what end. In the 1926 introduction Burden proclaims: "I didn't take time to arrange it; I simply wrote down pretty much all that her name recalls to me."[86] Burden's spontaneous, chaotic, and energetic display from the 1918 introduction, with his bulging portfolio and fur overcoat, is gone. The second introduction finds Burden reticent, composed, and even somber when presenting Cather with his manuscript. He claims time kept him from arranging the text, though the original introduction makes no such claim. Such a suggestion makes Burden less the romantic and more the practical memorializer. Pride and youth have been replaced with practicality and experience, as Jim sits and warms his hands.[87] The energy is lacking, the charisma removed and replaced with quiet satisfaction rather than gusto. Keith Wilhite argues, convincingly, that "if the introduction functions at all as a guide for readers, it serves as a warning against the trap of privileging storytelling over narrative or trying to disentangle acts of feminine and masculine artistry in the novel," with the 1926 revision strengthening and supporting that reading.[88] Wilhite wants us to "resist reading one voice or artistic practice as 'authorially endorsed'" so that "we can read the introduction as a text that anticipates the more pervasive instability that both Ántonia's stories and Jim's narrative articulate."[89] Emmy Stark Zitter makes a similar argument, suggesting that the revised introduction moves Cather "toward rejecting the male/female, artist/nonartist dichotomy" set up in the original, and "by abandoning the pose of the woman as failed author, she can speak more confidently about Jim Burden, her own artistic creation."[90] Stout feels that Cather "hit on a narrating character whose yearning and devotion toward the central figure are evident, and who tells the 'burden' of the story, while at the same time the story itself shows us far more than his own fixation encompasses."[91] With Jim's muted personality in the 1926 introduction, Wilhite's reading amplifies the indeterminacy of the framework. Had the 1918 introduction remained a consistent part of the novel, we would be better equipped for Jim's fixation and his vibrant, romantic disposition. Instead, readers are actually better prepared for narrative ambiguity thanks to Cather's choice to revise Jim and the narrator. Less, for lack of a better phrase, is more.

Early scholarship grappled with the significance of the introduction. David Daiches labeled the original "relatively unimportant,"[92] while E. K. Brown believed the 1926 revision improved the introduction. "The earlier text left one wondering whether Jim was not ignominiously weak in continuing to lend himself to the purposes of such a creature," he noted. "Unless Jim can satisfy the reader that his impressions and judgments about women are sound, his value as an appreciative recorder of Ántonia is threatened."[93] Of course, as Wilhite and others have since pointed out, it is crucial that we question Jim and his narrative, and both versions of the introduction actually encourage our skepticism. Lindemann sees the treatment of "Cather" the narrator "as a sign of Cather's deep skepticism about women's ability to compete in the contest to figure themselves in a culturally powerful way."[94] Homestead extends, to a degree, Lindemann's key point by offering another compelling and convincing analysis of the revisions, arguing that Cather removed herself from the 1926 introduction "to make her novel stand as an autonomous work of art produced by a modern author unconstrained by gender rather than as a regionalist novel contained within a women's literary tradition."[95] Cather needed to shed her association with Houghton, which showcased her performance as a "regionalist woman author" next to Jim's unalloyed masculine charm. Her reputation as a modern author with Knopf required a striking erasure, a removal, a distancing from Houghton. For Homestead, there was no better way for Cather to achieve her severance than blotting

herself out of the introduction. Zitter concludes that in the revised introduction, "Cather places greater distance between herself, the woman who
has succeeded as a writer, and the male narrative voice she had found it
necessary to use earlier in her career." "Autobiography and fiction," she
notes, "are growing farther apart, if not divorcing altogether."[96] And
Robert Thacker, in drawing additional parallels between McClure's autobiography and *My Ántonia*, sees Cather "defining a relation between storyteller and single listener, an audience of one motivated most explicitly be
her own sympathies. This motive, and this relation, lay at the core of *My
Ántonia.*"[97]

Some critics relate the 1926 revisions to ruptures in Cather's personal
life and liken her revised introduction to her 1925 novel *The Professor's
House*, which features a rural southwestern section placed between two
domestic, urban episodes. Richard C. Harris concludes that Cather, like
her professor Godfrey St. Peter, "found herself unable to accept or cope
with the world around her."[98] In her essay detailing the editorial role of
Cather regarding W. T. Benda's illustrations to *My Ántonia*, Jean Schwind
argues that "by dropping the fiction of a co-authored *Ántonia*, Cather
strengthens the fiction of her editorial authority over Jim's work," for she
acts exclusively as Jim's editor by 1926.[99] Schwind concludes that by revising her introduction, Cather lessens the impact of Benda's illustrations,
though her editorial role is elevated. Such dialectical positioning finds the
novel in a constant state of flux. Harris also contends that the second
introduction reflects Cather's postwar mindset, of a time Cather famously
wrote "the world broke in two in 1922, or thereabouts."[100] Steven Trout,
in analyzing Cather's understudied relationship to the Great War, argues
that her other achievements "overshadowed her compulsive examination
of the international cataclysm that coincided with the arrival of her artistic
maturity."[101] Her novels *One of Ours* (1922) and *The Professor's House*
(1925) were released in this period, and prior to her revised introduction
to *My Ántonia*. But if Cather sought to engage in authorial self-effacement
by revising her second introduction, she takes away her own control and
grants Burden more control over the material. As O'Brien articulates, "In
both editions, then, we see that the power of a writer is circumscribed
because she alone cannot bring the text to the reader: for that act of connection, a publisher is needed."[102] The introduction exposes the process of
publication as more than a few straggling notes pasted together by an editor. The book in our hands is more than that, and the 1926 introduction
does more than complicate the novel it prefaces. It reinforces Cather's

desire to be seen as she wished, and her will to break with an original introduction that, regardless of her letters to the contrary, she always wanted in her book. By erasing herself from the introduction, Cather ensures that we actually *see* her more clearly in the way she intended to be seen.

SOMETHING COMPLETE AND GREAT

Merrill Skaggs credits Mildred Bennett's work with proposing that for Cather "the imagination importantly expresses itself through arrangement, as well as invention."[103] With two available versions of the introduction in various editions of the book, we are apt to follow the version closest to the first edition, aligning with the Cather Scholarly Edition's principles.[104] However, since Cather revised her introduction substantially following both her alleged dissatisfaction with the original and Ferris Greenslet's insistence, the 1926 introduction could be seen as Cather's preferred entry. The scholarly edition reprints Cather's 1918 introduction as written, with the 1926 introduction available only in fragments as rejected substantives.[105] In doing so, the editors determine that Cather's edits, though substantive, do not reflect Cather's ideal text. While evidence of Cather's disappointment with the original introduction exists in letters to Greenslet, and the editors recognize that "the alterations Cather made in the introduction were beyond minor stylistics, and were closely related to a reassessment of Jim's role as a narrator, and thus basic to a revised point of view in the novel,"[106] they do not reproduce the 1926 introduction in an appendix, or as an auxiliary document. If the 1926 introduction "suggests a reassessment of the function of the introduction" for Cather, then it should be included in the edition in full, rather than as rejected substantives.[107] However, the editors treat both versions of the introduction as crucial, rather than castaway, elements of Cather's book. Their determination, that the 1918 introduction should preface a scholarly edition, and that the 1926 printing should be characterized as a new edition due to the heavy revisions to the introduction, proves again that the introduction moves beyond the standard trappings of the authorial preface. As a piece with nearly forty years of criticism behind it, Willa Cather's introduction to *My Ántonia* turns the novel into something complete and, depending on which version one reads, great.

NOTES

1. Willa Cather, "#2083: Willa Cather to Roscoe Cather, [November 28, 1918]," in *The Complete Letters of Willa Cather*, eds. the Willa Cather Archive team. The Willa Cather Archive, 2018. Accessed April 14, 2021, https://cather.unl.edu/writings/letters/let2083.
2. Willa Cather, "#1214: Willa Cather to Carrie Miner Sherwood, January 27, 1934," in *The Complete Letters of Willa Cather*, eds. the Willa Cather Archive team. The Willa Cather Archive, 2018. Accessed April 14, 2021, https://cather.unl.edu/writings/letters/let1214.
3. Cather wanted Sherwood to have a copy of the citation "because it particularly takes notice of the fact that, though there have been many imitations of ANTONIA and some of them good, I really was the one who first broke the ground." See Cather, "#1214: Willa Cather to Carrie Miner Sherwood, January 27, 1934."
4. Cather, "#1214: Willa Cather to Carrie Miner Sherwood, January 27, 1934."
5. Willa Cather, "#1385: Willa Cather to Ferris Greenslet, [December 29, 1937]," in *The Complete Letters of Willa Cather*, eds. the Willa Cather Archive team. The Willa Cather Archive, 2018. Accessed April 14, 2021, https://cather.unl.edu/writings/letters/let1385.
6. Willa Cather, "#0461: Willa Cather to Ferris Greenslet, May 19 [1919]," in *The Complete Letters of Willa Cather*, eds. the Willa Cather Archive team. The Willa Cather Archive, 2018. Accessed April 14, 2021, https://cather.unl.edu/writings/letters/let0461.
7. Bibliographer Joan Crane labels the 1926 printing as a second edition based on "its existence as a different book in a different format, containing authorial revisions of the text," though she confesses that the book is not a true second edition "in the strict bibliographic sense." See Crane, *Willa Cather: a Bibliography* (Lincoln, NE: University of Nebraska Press, 1982), 66. Houghton Mifflin would eventually order fourteen printings of this revised printing. While the book was printed from the original Houghton Mifflin plates, Cather significantly revised only her introduction and asked for three minor corrections over the next six printings. Though the editors of the 1994 scholarly edition of *My Ántonia* agree with Crane, and they cite Fredson Bowers's *Principles of Bibliographical Description* as evidence, I prefer to label the book the 1926 revised printing since the 1918 plates were reused in preparing the 1926 printing, save for the reset introduction. However, the choice of Crane and the scholarly edition editors to treat the 1926 printing as an edition in its own right provides further evidence that the introduction was more than an auxiliary device to Cather. See my analysis later on.

8. Gerard Genette, *Paratexts: Thresholds of Interpretation*. 1987. Trans. Jane E. Lewin (New York: Cambridge University Press, 1997), 209.

9. Willa Cather, *My Ántonia*, 1918 (Lincoln, NE: University of Nebraska Press, 1994), xiii.

10. Willa Cather, "#0462: Willa Cather to Will Owen Jones, [May 19, 1919]," in *The Complete Letters of Willa Cather*, eds. the Willa Cather Archive team. The Willa Cather Archive, 2018. Accessed April 26, 2021, https://cather.unl.edu/writings/letters/let0462.

11. Genette, *Paratexts*, 178.

12. Genette, *Paratexts*, 178–179.

13. Daryl W. Palmer, *Becoming Willa Cather: Creation and Career* (Reno, NV: University of Nevada Press, 2019), 221.

14. Willa Cather, "#2172: Willa Cather to Roscoe Cather, October 5, 1940," in *The Complete Letters of Willa Cather*, eds. the Willa Cather Archive team. The Willa Cather Archive, 2018. Accessed April 26, 2021, https://cather.unl.edu/writings/letters/let2172.

15. Opening commentary to S. S. McClure, *My Autobiography*. See Andrew Jewell, ed. Willa Cather Archive, University of Nebraska–Lincoln. https://cather.unl.edu/writings/books/index.mcclure (accessed April 26, 2021).

16. Janis P. Stout, *Cather Among the Moderns* (Tuscaloosa, AL: University of Alabama Press, 2019), 72. Stout references Robert Thacker's work in developing the connections between *My Autobiography* and *My Ántonia*. See Stout, *Cather Among the Moderns*, 71–72.

17. Latrobe Carroll, "Willa Sibert Cather," *Bookman*, May 3, 1921, in *Willa Cather in Person: Interviews, Speeches, and Letters*, ed. L. Brent Bohlke (Lincoln, NE: University of Nebraska Press, 1986), 21.

18. Merrill Skaggs, *After the World Broke in Two: The Later Novels of Willa Cather* (Charlottesville, VA: University of Virginia Press, 1990), 15.

19. Skaggs, *After the World Broke in Two*, 15.

20. Janis P. Stout, *Willa Cather: The Writer and Her World* (Charlottesville, VA: University of Virginia Press, 2000), 145.

21. Stout, *The Writer and Her World*, 150.

22. David Stouck, "Perspective as Structure and Theme in *My Ántonia*," *Texas Studies in Literature and Language* 12, no. 2 (1970): 287.

23. Willa Cather, "#2073: Willa Cather to Roscoe Cather, July 8 [1916]," in *The Complete Letters of Willa Cather*, eds. the Willa Cather Archive team. The Willa Cather Archive, 2018. Accessed April 14, 2021, https://cather.unl.edu/writings/letters/let2073.

24. Stout, *The Writer and Her World*, 145.

25. James Woodress, *Willa Cather: A Literary Life* (Lincoln, NE: University of Nebraska Press, 1987), 290.

26. Woodress, *A Literary Life*, 290.
27. Cather, *My Ántonia*, 1994, xii.
28. Cather, *My Ántonia*, 1994, xii.
29. Cather, *My Ántonia*, 1994, xi.
30. Lindemann, Marilee. *Willa Cather: Queering America* (New York: Columbia University Press, 1999), 62.
31. Lindemann references the work of Judith Butler and Teresa de Lauretis, among others, concluding that the novel is "profoundly pessimistic about the possibility of what de Lauretis calls 'the standard of vision, ... of *what can be seen*.'" See Lindemann, *Willa Cather: Queering America*, 62.
32. Lindemann, *Willa Cather: Queering America*, 63.
33. Lindemann, *Willa Cather: Queering America*, 62.
34. Cather, *My Ántonia*, 1994, x.
35. Cather, *My Ántonia*, 1994, xi.
36. Cather, *My Ántonia*, 1994, xii.
37. Cather, *My Ántonia*, 1994, xii–xiii.
38. Cather, *My Ántonia*, 1994, xiii.
39. Melissa J. Homestead, "'Live Property': Cather's 1926 Revisions to the Introduction of *My Ántonia* and the Specter of Nineteenth-Century Women's Regionalism," in *"Something Complete and Great": The Centennial Study of* My Ántonia, ed. Holly Blackford (Madison, NJ: Fairleigh Dickinson University Press, 2017), 90.
40. Milton Orvell, "Time, Change, and the Burden of Revision in *My Ántonia*," in *New Essays on* My Ántonia, ed. Sharon O'Brien (New York: Cambridge University Press, 1999), 33–34.
41. Sharon O'Brien, "Possession and Publication: Willa Cather's Struggle to Save *My Ántonia*," *Studies in the Novel* 45, no. 3 (2013): 471.
42. Orvell, "The Burden of Revision," 35.
43. Stout, *The Writer and Her World*, 146.
44. T. S. Eliot, "Tradition and the Individual Talent," *Perspecta* 19 (1982): 42.
45. Willa Cather, "#0400: Willa Cather to Roger L. Scaife, December 1 [1917]," in *The Complete Letters of Willa Cather*, eds. the Willa Cather Archive team. The Willa Cather Archive, 2018. Accessed April 14, 2021, https://cather.unl.edu/writings/letters/let0400.
46. Willa Cather, "#0407: Willa Cather to Ferris Greenslet, [January 1918]," in *The Complete Letters of Willa Cather*, eds. the Willa Cather Archive team. The Willa Cather Archive, 2018. Accessed April 14, 2021, https://cather.unl.edu/writings/letters/let0407.
47. Willa Cather, "#0421: Willa Cather to Ferris Greenslet, July 2 [1918]," in *The Complete Letters of Willa Cather*, eds. the Willa Cather Archive team. The Willa Cather Archive, 2018. Accessed April 14, 2021, https://cather.unl.edu/writings/letters/let0421.

48. Willa Cather, "#0423: Willa Cather to Ferris Greenslet, July 11 [1918]," in *The Complete Letters of Willa Cather*, eds. the Willa Cather Archive team. The Willa Cather Archive, 2018. Accessed April 14, 2021, https://cather.unl.edu/writings/letters/let0423.
49. Andrew Jewel and Janis Stout, eds., *The Selected Letters of Willa Cather* (New York: Alfred A. Knopf, 2013), 260.
50. Cather, *My Ántonia*, 1994, 7.
51. Cather, *My Ántonia*, 1994, 18.
52. Cather, *My Ántonia*, 1994, 28.
53. Stout, *The Writer and Her World*, 146.
54. Cather, *My Ántonia*, 1994, 212.
55. Cather, *My Ántonia*, 1994, 212.
56. Stout, *Cather Among the Moderns*, 70. She continues: "Cather lets her readers see, for example, that he fails to notice how Ántonia has led her children to think of Frances Harling as a potential model, and thus he misses the implication that she sees her life of hard domestic work and childbearing as less than fully desirable."
57. Stout, *The Writer and Her World*, 151.
58. Cather, *My Ántonia*, 1994, 237.
59. Cather, *My Ántonia*, 1994, 238.
60. Brian Gingrich, "Willa Cather's Naivete." *Twentieth Century Literature* 66, no. 1 (2020): 314.
61. Cather, *My Ántonia*, 1994, 310.
62. Gingrich, "Willa Cather's Naivete," 319.
63. Michael Martone, "The Flatness," in *The Flatness and Other Landscapes* (Athens, GA: University of Georgia Press, 2000), 5.
64. Cather, *My Ántonia*, 1994, xii.
65. Cather, *My Ántonia*, 1994, 360.
66. Cather, *My Ántonia*, 1994, xii.
67. According to Mark A .R. Facknitz, "Remarkably, this narrative travels in two directions; first, west through nostalgia and compromise into the past, from the prairie town that Burden long ago escaped to a place in the here and now, Ántonia's garden. Second, once the story is vivid and coherent, it moves east and penetrates through the geographical, social, and class distances that separated Burden from Ántonia." His analysis of distances, trains, and the way the narrative travels is more meaningful when applied to the 1918 introduction, rather than the revision. See Facknitz, "Changing Trains: Metaphors of Transfer in Willa Cather," *Cather Studies* 9 (2011): para. 14. Willa Cather Archive. https://cather.unl.edu/scholarship/catherstudies/9/cs009.facknitz (accessed April 22, 2021).

68. "My Nebraska Antonia," *Sun* (New York), October 6, 1918. Reprinted in *Willa Cather: The Contemporary Reviews*, ed. Margaret Anne O'Connor (New York: Cambridge University Press, 2001), 81.

69. N. P. Dawson, "Miss Cather's *My Ántonia*, "*Globe and Commercial Advertiser* (New York), January 11, 1919. Reprinted in *Willa Cather: The Contemporary Reviews*, ed. Margaret Anne O'Connor (New York: Cambridge University Press, 2001), 86.

70. See O'Brien, "Possession and Publication," 460–475.

71. Willa Cather, "#0718: Willa Cather to Ferris Greenslet, February 17 [1924]," in *The Complete Letters of Willa Cather*, eds. the Willa Cather Archive team. The Willa Cather Archive, 2018. Accessed April 14, 2021, https://cather.unl.edu/writings/letters/let0718.

72. Willa Cather, "Preface," in Sarah Orne Jewett, *The Best Stories of Sarah Orne Jewett*, ed. Willa Cather (Boston, MA: Houghton Mifflin, 1925), xix.

73. Genette, *Paratexts*, 240.

74. Of the fourteen contemporary (1918–1921) reviews collected in *Willa Cather: The Contemporary Reviews*, none are negative, with each endorsing the novel for a variety of reasons. *The New York Times Book Review* recognized Cather's book as a "carefully detailed picture rather than a story"; *The Sun* felt that "a young writer who wants to deal with a variety of difficult things can learn big lessons from reading this book"; *New York Call Magazine* called the book a "fresh and sincere piece of work," and H. W. Boynton, writing for *Bookman*, concluded that "we may be hardly conscious how much of the total effect of the portrait is owing to the quiet beauty and purity of the artist's style"; 'It is a story of great truth and great beauty," wrote N. P. Dawson for the *Globe and Commercial Advertiser*, and H. L. Mencken, a frequent champion of Cather's novels, referred to the book as "one of the best that any American has ever done, East or West, early or late. It is simple; it is intelligent; it is moving." See Margaret Anne O'Connor, ed. *Willa Cather: The Contemporary Reviews* (New York: Cambridge University Press, 2001), 79–94.

75. Willa Cather, "#0824: Willa Cather to Ferris Greenslet, February 15, 1926," in *The Complete Letters of Willa Cather*, eds. the Willa Cather Archive team. The Willa Cather Archive, 2018. Accessed April 14, 2021, https://cather.unl.edu/writings/letters/let0824.

76. For an excellent analysis of the correspondence between Greenslet and Cather concerning the 1926 introduction, see Homestead, "'Live Property,'" 88–90.

77. Cather, *My Ántonia*, 1994, xi.

78. Homestead, "'Live Property,'" 96.

79. Willa Cather, *My Ántonia*, 1918 (Boston, MA: Houghton Mifflin & Co., 1926), viii.

80. Cather, *My Ántonia*, 1926, viii.
81. Cather, *My Ántonia*, 1926, ix.
82. Cather, *My Ántonia*, 1994, xiii.
83. Cather, *My Ántonia*, 1926, ix.
84. Cather, *My Ántonia*, 1994, xiii.
85. Cather, *My Ántonia*, 1926, ix.
86. Cather, *My Ántonia*, 1926, xi.
87. Cather. *My Ántonia*, 1926, xi.
88. Keith Wilhite, "Unsettled Worlds: Aesthetic Emplacement in Willa Cather's *My Ántonia*," *Studies in the Novel* 42, no. 3 (2010): 273.
89. Wilhite, "Unsettled Worlds," 274.
90. Emmy Stark Zitter, "Making Herself Born: Ghost Writing and Willa Cather's Developing Autobiography," *Biography* 19, no. 3 (1996): 295.
91. Stout, *Cather Among the Moderns*, 70.
92. David Daiches, *Willa Cather: A Critical Introduction* (Ithaca, NY: Cornell University Press, 1951).
93. E. K. Brown, *Willa Cather: A Critical Biography* (New York: Alfred A. Knopf, 1953), 200–201.
94. Lindemann, *Willa Cather: Queering America*, 64.
95. Homestead, "'Live Property,'" 94.
96. Zitter, "Making Herself Born," 294.
97. Robert Thacker, "'It's Through Myself that I Knew and Felt Her': S. S. McClure's *My Autobiography* and the Development of Willa Cather's Autobiographical Realism," *American Literary Realism* 33, no. 2 (2001): 132.
98. Richard C. Harris, "Jim Burden, Willa Cather and the Introductions to *My Ántonia*," *Willa Cather Pioneer Memorial Newsletter* 30, no. 3 (1986): 33.
99. Jean Schwind, "The Benda Illustrations to *My Ántonia*: Cather's 'Silent' Supplement to Jim Burden's Narrative," *PMLA* 100, no. 1 (1985): 54.
100. Willa Cather, *Not Under Forty* (New York: Alfred A. Knopf, 1936), v.
101. Steven Trout, *Memorial Fictions: Willa Cather and the First World War* (Lincoln, NE: University of Nebraska Press, 2002), 191.
102. O'Brien, "Possession and Publication," 462.
103. Skaggs, *After the World Broke in Two*, x. Bennett published one of the first scholarly works on Cather, *The World of Willa Cather* (1951).
104. "The policy of the Cather Edition is to present the work as Cather intended it at first publication in book form, emended only to admit corrections authorized by Cather herself or deemed necessary by the present editors. Such a policy necessarily precludes incorporation of those later revisions made by Cather that alter the substance of the work or its aesthetic intention." See Cather, *My Ántonia*, 1994, 505.

105. See "Rejected Substantives" in *My Ántonia*, 1994, 529–532.
106. Cather, *My Ántonia*, 1994, 513.
107. Cather, *My Ántonia*, 1994, 520.

BIBLIOGRAPHY

Brown, E. K., *Willa Cather: A Critical Biography*. New York: Alfred A. Knopf, 1953.
Carroll, Latrobe. "Willa Sibert Cather," *Bookman*, May 3, 1921. In *Willa Cather in Person: Interviews, Speeches, and Letters*, edited by L. Brent Bohlke, 19–24. Lincoln, NE: University of Nebraska Press, 1986.
Cather, Willa. *My Ántonia*. 1918. Boston, MA: Houghton Mifflin & Co., 1926.
———. *My Ántonia*. 1918. The Willa Cather Scholarly Edition. Eds. Charles Mignon and Kari Ronning. Lincoln, NE: University of Nebraska Press, 1994.
———. *Not Under Forty*. New York: Alfred A. Knopf, 1936.
Crane, Joan. *Willa Cather: A Bibliography*. Lincoln, NE: University of Nebraska Press, 1982.
Daiches, David. *Willa Cather: A Critical Introduction*. Ithaca, NY: Cornell University Press, 1951.
Dawson, N. P. "Miss Cather's *My Ántonia*." *Globe and Commercial Advertiser* (New York), January 11, 1919. Reprinted in *Willa Cather: The Contemporary Reviews*, edited by Margaret Anne O'Connor, 85–86. New York: Cambridge University Press, 2001.
Eliot, T. S. "Tradition and the Individual Talent." *Perspecta* 19 (1982): 36–42.
Facknitz, Mark A. R. "Changing Trains: Metaphors of Transfer in Willa Cather." *Cather Studies* 9 (2011). Willa Cather Archive. https://cather.unl.edu/scholarship/catherstudies/9/cs009.facknitz (accessed April 22, 2021).
Genette, Gerard. *Paratexts: Thresholds of Interpretation*. 1987. Jane E. Lewin, trans. New York: Cambridge University Press, 1997.
Gingrich, Brian. "Willa Cather's Naivete." *Twentieth Century Literature* 66, no. 1 (2020): 305–332.
Harris, Richard C. "Jim Burden, Willa Cather and the Introductions to *My Ántonia*." *Willa Cather Pioneer Memorial Newsletter* 30.3 (1986): 33–34.
Homestead, Melissa J. "'Live Property': Cather's 1926 Revisions to the Introduction of *My Ántonia* and the Specter of Nineteenth-Century Women's Regionalism." In *"Something Complete and Great": The Centennial Study of* My Ántonia, edited by Holly Blackford, 81–101. Madison, NJ: Fairleigh Dickinson University Press, 2017.
Jewell, Andrew and Janis Stout, eds. *The Selected Letters of Willa Cather*. New York: Alfred A. Knopf, 2013.
Jewett, Sarah Orne. *The Best Stories of Sarah Orne Jewett*. Willa Cather, ed. Boston, MA: Houghton Mifflin, 1925.

Lindemann, Marilee. *Willa Cather: Queering America*. New York: Columbia University Press, 1999.

Martone, Michael. "The Flatness." *The Flatness and Other Landscapes*. 1–5, Athens, GA: University of Georgia Press, 2000

"My Nebraska Antonia," *Sun* (New York), October 6, 1918. Reprinted in *Willa Cather: The Contemporary Reviews*, edited by Margaret Anne O'Connor, 79–81. New York: Cambridge University Press, 2001.

O'Brien, Sharon. "Possession and Publication: Willa Cather's Struggle to Save *My Ántonia*." *Studies in the Novel* 45, no. 3 (2013): 460–475.

O'Connor, Margaret Anne, ed. *Willa Cather: The Contemporary Reviews*. New York: Cambridge University Press, 2001.

Orvell, Milton. "Time, Change, and the Burden of Revision in *My Ántonia*." In *New Essays on* My Ántonia, edited by Sharon O'Brien, 31–56. New York: Cambridge University Press, 1999.

Palmer, Daryl W. *Becoming Willa Cather: Creation and Career*. Reno, NV: University of Nevada Press, 2019.

Schwind, Jean. "The Benda Illustrations to *My Ántonia*: Cather's 'Silent' Supplement to Jim Burden's Narrative." *PMLA* 100, no. 1 (1985): 51–67.

Skaggs, Merrill. *After the World Broke in Two: The Later Novels of Willa Cather*. Charlottesville, VA: University of Virginia Press, 1990.

Stouck, David. "Perspective as Structure and Theme in *My Ántonia*." *Texas Studies in Literature and Language* 12.2 (1970): 285–294.

Stout, Janis P. *Cather Among the Moderns*. Tuscaloosa, AL: University of Alabama Press, 2019.

———. *Willa Cather: The Writer and Her World*. Charlottesville, VA: University Press of Virginia, 2000.

Thacker, Robert. "'It's Through Myself that I Knew and Felt Her': S. S. McClure's *My Autobiography* and the Development of Willa Cather's Autobiographical Realism." *American Literary Realism* 33, no. 2 (2001): 123–142.

Trout, Steven. *Memorial Fictions: Willa Cather and the First World War*. Lincoln, NE: University of Nebraska Press, 2002.

Wilhite, Keith. "Unsettled Worlds: Aesthetic Emplacement in Willa Cather's *My Ántonia*." *Studies in the Novel* 42, no. 3 (2010): 269–286.

The Willa Cather Archive team, eds. *The Complete Letters of Willa Cather*. The Willa Cather Archive, 2018. Accessed April 6, 2021. https://cather.unl.edu/writings/letters.

Woodress, James. *Willa Cather: A Literary Life*. Lincoln, NE: University of Nebraska Press, 1987.

Zitter, Emmy Stark. "Making Herself Born: Ghost Writing and Willa Cather's Developing Autobiography." *Biography* 19, no. 3 (1996): 283–301.

CHAPTER 3

Stepping In or Turning Back: Ring Lardner and Authorial Resistance

A long solemn-faced man. The face was wonderful. It was a mask. All the time when you were with him, you kept wondering. ... 'What is going on back there?'
—Sherwood Anderson[1]

Lardner actually knows more about the management of the short story than nine-tenths of its most imminent practitioners. His stories are always built very carefully, and yet they always seem to be wholly spontaneous, and even formless.
—H. L. Mencken[2]

Ring Lardner had wanted to call his final story collection of the 1920s "Ensemble," after considering "Our Kind," "Some of Ours," "Such as We," and "Sorts and Conditions," but Maxwell Perkins, his editor at Charles Scribner's Sons, settled on *Round Up*.[3] Lardner didn't like the title, thinking it too Western. Published in 1929, the collection featured stories that had already been published in newspapers and magazines, with Lardner revising none of his previous work. The book sold 80,000 copies

---

Parts of this chapter appeared as "Refusing the Serious: Authorial Resistance in Ring Lardner's Prefaces for Scribner's." *Authorship*, 5, no. 2 (2016): 1–11. I wish to thank Ghent University, as well as editors Gert Buelens and Koenraad Claes, for permission to reprint portions of that essay in this book.

R. K. Tangedal, *The Preface*, New Directions in Book History, https://doi.org/10.1007/978-3-030-85151-4_3

65

by the end of 1929, netting Lardner nearly $12,000 in royalties (US $190,000 in 2021).[4] These numbers are on par with Ernest Hemingway's *A Farewell to Arms* (1929), which had sold nearly 70,000 copies by the end of the year,[5] though they were a far cry from 1920s literary titan Sinclair Lewis, whose *Dodsworth* (1929) furthered his streak of selling in the hundreds of thousands.[6] Lardner's relatively short book career (roughly 20 years) never included a novel, the form that Perkins encouraged all of his writers to pursue in order to further their art and, more importantly, their profits. Lardner was content to republish old stories, and he had successfully resisted the temptations (and pressures) to write a novel by the time he died in 1933 at age 48.

But all the more remarkable is that Lardner, for most of his adult life, was best described as a baseball writer who produced some of the most popular magazine work of the time during his editorship of "In the Wake of the News" (1913–1919), and his "Weekly Letter" for the Bell Syndicate reached a circulation of eight million by the mid-1920s.[7] Many of his short stories appeared in *The Saturday Evening Post* and *Cosmopolitan*, and his popular "Busher" baseball stories (eventually collected and published as *You Know Me Al* in 1916) set a new precedent for the use of realistic American vernacular in fiction, not unlike his predecessor Mark Twain, to whom he was frequently compared. Lardner became one of the most recognizable and popular men in America from coast to coast due to his wide syndication. A young Hemingway wrote stories under the pseudonym "Ring Lardner, Jr." for his high school newspaper, and his work was championed by H. L. Mencken, Sherwood Anderson, and F. Scott Fitzgerald. English novelist Virginia Woolf famously compared Lardner to Sinclair Lewis, Anderson, and Willa Cather in a review of *You Know Me Al*,[8] and Dorothy Parker, in her review of *Round Up* for *The New Yorker*, argued that "It is difficult to review these spare and beautiful stories; it would be difficult to review the Gettysburg address. What more are you going to say of a great thing than it is great?" She praises his "unparalleled ear and eye, his strange, bitter pity, his utter sureness of characterization, his unceasing investigation, his beautiful economy" before concluding that "Lardner's qualities are not to be listed, but to be felt, as you read his work."[9] His unique style, which oftentimes eschewed third-person omniscience in favor of a first-person account—usually in the guise of the "wise boob" character he created and popularized—allowed Lardner to present the mores of social class and wealth from a humorous yet realistic perspective. Lardner put his finger on the pulse of the American reader, namely through separating his real voice from the voice of his characters and allowing each to describe themselves rather than be described.[10] Though much has been done to resurrect Lardner's best work (two full-length biographies, multiple letters collections, dozens of articles, etc.), the reputation of his writing still lags behind contemporaries Hemingway, Fitzgerald, and Cather.

However, in early 1924 Lardner partnered with major publishing house Charles Scribner's Sons, where editor Max Perkins wished to transform him into a serious writer. By "serious" the firm meant more literary, an author concerned with the literary and cultural influence his work has (and may have) on present and future readers/writers. Perkins's initial intention was to lure Lardner to the firm and convince him to produce a novel, the form the editor consistently pushed his writers to produce. Perkins knew that a "big" book would produce positive financial and critical results, more so than other genres. One need only look to his correspondence with F. Scott Fitzgerald and Ernest Hemingway to establish the editor's preferred publication genre. Concerning the follow-up to Fitzgerald's *The Great Gatsby* (1925), Perkins wrote Fitzgerald on 3 January 1928 that "we feel no anxiety whatever about the novel," though he immediately reminded his author, "I have worried a little about the length of time elapsing between [a new novel] and 'The Great Gatsby.'"[11] He similarly wrote Hemingway on 30 August 1935: "When you're ready to do a novel. That's what they all must want. That's what they all tell me they want + want me to tell you. I don't think I can tell you anything."[12] Perkins showed similar persistence with Lardner, who responded favorably to Perkins's luring but never wholly acquiesced to the editor's policies. At no point did Perkins or the firm wish to curtail Lardner's humor or satire. Lardner's early correspondence with Perkins shows his relative indifference to the firm's willingness to recast him as more than the writer he was. For instance, he wrote Perkins on 21 July 1924 that he would "come to one of those literary luncheons if you think it advisable, but it is my secret ambition not to."[13] He further distanced himself from novel writing later that year, when he wrote Perkins: "Don Stewart's 'Mr. and Mrs. Haddock Abroad' was a blow to me. That is the kind of 'novel' I had intended to write, but if I do it now, the boys will yell stop thief."[14] In 1926, Perkins assured Lardner that "a continuous book always has an advantage,"[15] and in 1928 he told Lardner that "I do not know of any publishing news that would be more interesting than that such a book by you was to come out."[16] The editor knew that with Lardner he had a saleable commodity with over a decade of considerable success and readership, but he never could convince Lardner to produce a long work. Nevertheless, the firm benefitted greatly from the association. Lardner's books sold steadily and well, with the aforementioned *Round Up* selling upwards of 100,000 copies in its first two years.

Along with Perkins, Lardner's close friend and fellow Scribner's author F. Scott Fitzgerald stumped for the sportswriter whenever he could. He wrote to Perkins regularly (also Fitzgerald's editor) about the prospect of a Lardner novel. By May 1926, Fitzgerald had become generally frustrated by his friend's insistence on story writing. He wrote Perkins, "God, I wish he'd write a more or less personal novel. Couldn't you persuade him? The real history of an American manager, say a Ziegfeld or a theatrical girl."[17] The sentiment was repeated three years later: "*Why* won't he write about Great Neck, a sort of Oddysee of man starting in theatre business."[18] Perkins responded in more pragmatic terms: "I am sure if Ring made a lot of money [writing plays], he would do even less writing of the kind we can use, than even now.—And he is writing another play too, and once a man gets going at that, it is a question if he will ever do anything else, except by necessity" (157). The kind of writing Scribner's could "use" was a novel, and since Lardner began his writing career in the short-form market, he had never needed to write another way. It is hard to ignore Perkins's disinclination toward playwriting in his letter to Fitzgerald; the editor had watched Fitzgerald fail at writing theater with his play *The Vegetable* just four years earlier, resulting in the need to write more stories to make up for lost profits. Fitzgerald always saw his stories as necessities rather than art, even if some featured shades of the talent that built his career. Lardner never ventured into any other form of writing besides nonfiction and short stories, save for a handful of plays co-written with other established playwrights. But his decision to sign with Scribner's when he did signaled, to some, a desire to mature, to grow, to write seriously.

By the mid-1920s, the most scathing critique of Lardner's refusal to enter into a serious writing career came from prominent critic Edmund Wilson. In a July 1924 review of Lardner's *How to Write Short Stories (with Samples)* for the *Dial*, Wilson wrote:

> Will Ring Lardner, then, go on to his *Huckleberry Finn* or has he already told all he knows? … But you never know: here is a man who has had the freedom of the modern West no less than Mark Twain did of the old one, who approaches it, as Mark Twain did, with a perceptive interest in human beings instead of the naturalist's formula—a man who lives at a time when if

one be not sold irredeemably into bondage to the *Saturday Evening Post*, it is far easier for a serious writer to get published and find a hearing than it was in Mark Twain's day. If Ring Lardner has anything more to give us, the time has now come to deliver it.[19]

For Perkins, Fitzgerald, and Wilson, to write short stories was to postpone talent that should be spent on writing novels. Short stories were the means to an end, namely precursors to the great event: the novel. Wilson concluded: "When [Sinclair] Lewis himself, in his earlier phase a humorist for the *Saturday Evening Post*, took a chance and composed in *Main Street* his satire upon its readers, he received unexpected support. It turned out that there were thousands of people who were ready to hear what he wanted to say."[20] It appears that Wilson willfully ignored the fact that Lardner's columns and stories reached millions of readers each day, as he casually dismissed Lardner's writing in the "popular vein" as thoroughly "worked out" by 1924.[21] Regardless of Lardner's established reach, he was "too much of an artist to make the biggest kind of success as a clown," leading Wilson to conclude, "What bell might not Lardner ring if he set out to give us the works?"[22] Given the pressure to prepare a long work, Lardner's foray into a "serious" literary career with Scribner's is best characterized as an act of public authorial resistance, for he chose to lampoon himself, authorship, publishing, and serious writers rather than enter completely into their fraternity.

Once signed by Scribner's, Lardner used his considerable market position to maintain rather than evolve his public authority, and he resisted overtures to rebrand himself by playing to his strengths: satire, comedy, and manipulation. His prefaces to *How to Write Short Stories (with Samples)* (1924) and *The Love Nest and Other Stories* (1926) are pieces as textually nonsensical and arbitrary as many of his writings on the surface, yet they are carefully constructed to expose the underside of socio-cultural mores and the publishing industry. With these prefaces, Lardner displayed his resistance to a more serious authorial persona that he never intended to inhabit, offering instead another level of satire to his penchant for textual comedy. He was keenly aware of the functions of prefaces as they pertained to his fiction. Charles Holmes concludes that Lardner "was not a frustrated genius who turned out journalistic pieces with cynical indifference, but a scrupulous craftsman, a writer who was a master of his medium and who treated it with respect."[23] Lardner respected satire, abhorred fakery, skewered hypocrisy, and stuck to his writing persona. His prefaces are satires of prefaces, he the satirist of preface-writers. All along, Lardner certainly knew what the space was supposed to include, thanks in large part to Perkins. Consequently, he knew how best to lampoon that space as the writer who resisted the pressures of serious authorship.

More than anything, Lardner's work for Scribner's promotes the persona he wanted to maintain, leaving his editor if not frustrated then certainly disappointed. Had Perkins convinced Lardner to write the big book, who knows how many copies it would have sold, and how much more successful Lardner would have become. Douglas Robinson contends that Lardner "wrote for two audiences" and that "in a culture dedicated to ideals of egalitarianism and excellence, democracy and genius, pleasing both the masses and the elite spells success—a success only a few of our writers have attained" (265). Suggesting that Lardner intended for his work to satisfy both the popular and critical communities is uneven territory. Lardner did not need to produce new fiction for Scribner's nor cast himself as a "serious author" worthy of critical acclaim; he made more than enough money in various print markets. While some have argued for Lardner's possible desire—albeit miniscule—to become more than a humorist, the prefaces under examination show Lardner at his popular best, as he angles into a critical community on his own terms. Indeed, the vast majority of his Scribner's titles feature reworked magazine pieces previously published in a variety of venues, with very little new material written exclusively for Scribner's.[24] Unlike Fitzgerald, Hemingway, or Thomas Wolfe, Lardner's primary goals were always firmly established in the magazine market. He knew how to write to make money, and he did it with a knack for understanding readers. Lardner cared little for literary pretension, evidenced by his satiric prefaces, which complicate the intended function of the preface—the most important of which, per narratologist Gerard Genette, "is to provide the author's interpretation of the text or, if you prefer, his statement of intent"—by indirectly commenting on the business of literature through comedic misdirection.[25] Perkins may well have intended for the prefaces and reprints to reposition Lardner in hopes of attracting new readers. However, it is clear that Lardner sought to reinforce an already established authorial persona to an already established set of consumers. He refused to fix what wasn't broken. Though difficult to position because of his relative indifference to the literati, Lardner and his work for Maxwell Perkins at Charles Scribner's Sons provides a sterling example of authorial resistance in the face of expected evolution. Ring

Lardner altered the preface from a place of serious textual positioning into a space of textual resistance, resulting in biting commentaries on the "literary game" from the only perspective he knew: his own.

AUTHORIAL RESISTANCE

In the examination that follows, we see Ring Lardner resisting the urge to become an author of serious fiction, and his prefaces for Scribner's were windows into a resistance few understood. What can we make of a writer taking part in the responsibilities of authorship, putting himself through the paces to keep an amicable relationship with his editor, only to deprecate his role so fully that to call the pieces satire would be generous? The private function of writing (the writer) clashes inherently with the public function of writing (the author), as one represents creation and the other represents consumption. Lardner's indifference to revising his work for the Scribner's collections suggests a nonchalant creative self and neutral peddler of past works. And maybe, as readers in the twenty-first century, we should be willing to part with our myths of writers caring about everything they wrote, every book they produced, and every reading they gave. Needless to say, Lardner cared deeply for his craft, knowing how best to make a profit on the creation of unique and relatable characters like Jack Keefe in *You Know Me Al*, Tom Finch in *The Big Town*, and Whitey the barber in "Haircut." One cannot make a living with words if one does not care for and understand one's characters. But herein lies the core contradiction at the center of Ring Lardner and his fiction: he was talented enough and smart enough to carve out a lucrative magazine career that never put him in the poor house during his adult life; but that talent and intelligence, as popular as it made him, should have taken him farther than he let it. Critics, his editor, friends, and scholars note their surprise that Lardner never took the baton from Mark Twain as the preeminent long-form (and short-form) humorist in America. Expectations fueled many a writer to evolve beyond their early preconceptions of self, and for the most part, writers that last in the market develop and progress as times and readers change. Lardner was fully formed by the late 1910s, with the Black Sox Scandal catalyzing his commitment to reach readers with satire in their own language, wit in their own tongue, and truth packaged as farce.

Personally, I would like to think that Lardner knew how good he was. In the knowing, he may have purposefully steered clear of the damage he'd seen "serious" writers do to themselves. Never satisfied with short stories for magazines, F. Scott Fitzgerald always saw himself as a novelist, a serious writer making a substantial mark on the culture. Lardner, who was friends with Fitzgerald for over a decade, listened to his friend decry the business of literature, the vitriol of critics, the indifference of readers. And Fitzgerald knew how popular Lardner was, how talented he had proven to be in the early years of the twentieth century. Ironically, though Fitzgerald pushed Perkins to persuade Lardner to write a great comic novel, thereby moving Lardner away from stories and the new plays he was working on, Ernest Hemingway had admonished Fitzgerald in the late 1920s for selling out his talent to the *Post* and other slicks. "You damned fool," he wrote, "Go on and write the novel."[26] In the intervening years between the success of *This Side of Paradise* (1920), the mixed reaction to *The Great Gatsby* (1925), and the slow development of *Tender Is the Night* (1934), Fitzgerald had gone from quasi-agent to Lardner and Hemingway (having been involved in bringing them both to Perkins and Scribner's) to the least popular of the three. Lardner even penned a popular musical play with George S. Kaufman (*June Moon*, 1929), while Fitzgerald's only play, *The Vegetable* (1922), bombed upon release. On the surface, Lardner had many aspects of the literary career that Fitzgerald wanted, save for the serious novelist moniker he craved. Almost everything Lardner touched turned a profit: essays, sports columns, syndicated columns, short stories, and so on. We have no way of knowing if Lardner took his friend's experiences in the marketplace as a cautionary tale. Lardner too shared a fondness for alcohol, and he was known to battle bouts of depression. But no matter the wooing, Lardner maintained a comfortable lifestyle as a result of his literary choices.

Douglas Noverr argues that Lardner's early commitment to sports writing steeled his resolve against the hierarchy of professional writing, a resolve that someone like his friend Fitzgerald struggled to cultivate. "He had to learn how to develop a thick skin and to use his ironic and sarcastic wit to succeed and survive," writes Noverr. "He had to keep up with the fast and often bewildering pace of his career in order to earn the big money."[27] With success and survival as goals, Lardner wrote about regular people in the language that they spoke. He spent time with ball players, managers, umpires, fans, club owners, sportscasters, fellow writers, and the guys that cleaned the stadiums. He succeeded in recreating an authentic dialect found among ballplayers at first, and then whom he called "wise boobs" later on. He survived by knowing what to do with his writing: sell it. Lardner married opportunity with ability when he exposed the American vernacular as an outgrowth of social class, especially after the Great War had ravaged much of Europe and sent writers into new and terrifying territory. "I knowed they would like my stuff when they seen it,"[28] writes busher Jack Keefe, Lardner's most famous early character. Called up from the second team to the first team in the Chicago White Sox minor league system, Keefe ultimately pitches for the White Sox, proclaiming to his friend, Al, that "You will see by the papers what I done to them before we get threw."[29] Prominent American critic and editor H. L. Mencken, noted champion of the naturalist fiction of the early twentieth century, called Lardner's investigations into ordinary people "alert, ingenious and brilliant." "The character he finally sets before us," he concludes, "is so astoundingly realistic as to hide that the effect is indistinguishable from that of life itself."[30] English novelist Virginia Woolf, in her essay "American Fiction," remarked upon Lardner's "extraordinary ease and aptitude" with character: "[Lardner] is not merely himself intent on his own game, but his characters are equally intent on theirs. ... Mr. Lardner's interest in games has solved one of the most difficult problems of the American writers; it has given him a clue, a centre, a meeting place for the diverse activities of people whom a vast continent isolates, whom no tradition controls." Lardner's work is "unique in its kind, something indigenous to the soil," rather than a retread of earlier traditions.[31] Given Woolf's praise, one begins to see the ingenuity in the language Lardner created, and the heart it took to recognize and respect the characters he made for readers.

But equally fascinating, then, is Lardner's penchant for resisting legacy building. "I suppose I ought to keep copies of my stuff, but I never have,"[32] he wrote Hewitt Howland, his editor at Bobbs-Merrill, where most of his work was published in book form prior to his association with Scribner's and Max Perkins. He apologized to Perkins for not being better at keeping his material, leaving to his new editor the trouble of "gathering the stuff"[33] that would become *How to Write Short Stories (with Samples)*. The practice no doubt came from his sports writing days, deadlines driving the work rather than artistic temperament. Casting off pages for quick print and quicker cash took precedence over careful historiography. Unlike Fitzgerald, who kept nearly everything he ever wrote, Lardner lived his writing life from piece to piece, story to story. There was a freedom to Lardner's conception of authorship, as his reading public grew largely from his ability to be prolific and precise. He had novels in him, but to write those novels would have meant stalling his desire to succeed and his need to survive. Mencken wondered, upon the publication of *How to Write Short Stores (with Samples)*, "can it be that the Scribners are trying to make good Ring respectable? If so the effort will fail. ... He is doomed to stay outside where the gang is."[34] Like Mencken expected, and Wilson denounced, Lardner embraced his persona, spending much time with friends and well-wishers, especially into the 1920s, when his profile reached its zenith. But even in his heyday, Lardner rarely changed his demeanor regarding the magazine and publishing industries that he had mastered. While he was a professional in a difficult game, he maintained the freedom and manufactured aloofness of his best characters. Like Jack Keefe, he knew how good his stuff was, but he saw himself as a saleable property more than a singular talent. He knew the game he was playing, never thinking beyond the present, since he would be forgotten were he to stop producing, just like a journeyman ballplayer.

"What we all felt for him was warm affection," wrote Sherwood Anderson after meeting Lardner for the first time. "I had never known anyone just like him writing in America. He awoke a certain feeling. You wanted him not to be hurt, perhaps to have some freedom he did not have."[35] He mentions Lardner being behind a mask for guests at the party, the confident storyteller and literary celebrity entertaining everyone. Anderson later recalls picking Lardner up from a party in New Orleans, the two of them stealing booze to drink on their own far away from partygoers and hangers-on. Anderson notices that Lardner, his mask removed, may have wanted to ask their driver to join them, but that he had refrained out of respect for Anderson. "This was a different Ring Lardner from the one I had seen in the room with all those people," he wrote. "This one was a shy man ... he was a man whose habit it was to wear a mask, and it had slipped off, and at the moment I was like a man standing in the dressing-room of a theater and watching an actor at work on his make-up. I saw him put the mask back on his face and he wore it for the rest of the evening."[36] Anderson uncovers a complex man, sharing in the "common tragedy, the tragedy of every creative man, big or little, in our day. No one of us escapes it. How can he?"[37] Friends like Anderson were sure that Lardner would be forgotten, even with his talent. Donald Elder argues that Lardner "wanted to be in places where people were, but he still felt himself an alien,"[38] and it is hard to imagine Lardner the toiling writer, the talented craftsman, living in the same body as the man who never bothered to keep his stories in case others wanted to collect them, like other writers trying to make a legacy. More importantly, why did Lardner refuse to confirm the overriding consensus that he was sitting on the talent to create comic novels of great cultural value? Much like Anderson, Noverr concludes that Lardner's greatest talent as a writer was his masking: "But underneath the surface of [*You Know Me Al*] is a human personal drama of a simple and uncomplicated person dealing with the pressures to succeed in big-time baseball and with the anomie of early twentieth century urban life and its confusions and uncertainties."[39] Lardner's best stories deal with the pressures of success, whether they be small time or significant. In lampooning prefaces for his Scribner's titles, he merged every complex anxiety that was in him, chief among them the anxiety of being unable to work anymore. The first preface satirizes writing manuals, showing he is both within and removed from the literary hierarchy, depending on how one reads the preface. Either way, the pose keeps his work read. The second preface goes further, as he writes about his own death (and the death of his narrator) with striking and prophetic clarity. In his prefaces he writes about being remembered, even if it is masked beneath layers of nonsense, comedy, and satire.

Ring Lardner, imbued with endless talent and aware always of his survival, took the opportunity to forward his career by publishing collections with Scribner's. He entered the big leagues, working with the man who would become the most famous literary editor in America, encouraged by the author of, arguably, the great American novel, and the recipient of a major New York publisher's affections and attention. Through it all, he resisted succumbing to the pitfalls and promises of a serious writer, choosing to measure success by another more instinctual means: surviving as the writer he had willed himself to become, and hoping he would be remembered for it.

HOW TO WRITE SHORT STORIES (WITH SAMPLES) (1924)

Scribner's attempted to recast Lardner by publishing *How to Write Short Stories (with Samples)*, an ambitious collection of the author's best known stories, on 9 May 1924. Leading up to publication editor Max Perkins sent Lardner several letters outlining his intentions—as well as his reservations—with the firm's new literary property. His introductory letter inquired about Lardner's willingness to "form a volume" around "The Golden Honeymoon."[40] While simple and straight forward, the editor mentions F. Scott Fitzgerald at three different points: he claims Scott recommended "The Golden Honeymoon" to him; he alleges that Scott persuaded him to write to Lardner; and finally, he defers to Scott's judgment concerning Lardner's possible decision.[41] In all, this introductory letter prefaces the relationship Lardner, Perkins, and Fitzgerald would forge for the remainder of the 1920s, with Lardner reluctantly—at times— acquiescing to Perkins's requests. By 15 January 1924, Lardner had sent Perkins a preface to his first collection, which Perkins dubbed "excellent."[42] Perkins had taken the initiative and placed *How to Write Short Stories* on the Spring list, though he had never formally asked Lardner for permission. His 1 February letter points to the editor's propensity for action, as he assured Lardner, "we felt that the best thing to do was to act immediately and get out a volume." Lardner agreed and told Perkins the next day that "the arrangement and terms are satisfactory to me" before inviting him out to his home in Great Neck.[43]

Unlike the oftentimes contentious correspondence from Hemingway or Fitzgerald to Perkins, Lardner's letters were understated, calm, and professional, akin to his reputation within the writing profession. This reputation made his relationship with Perkins rather simple; case in point, when Perkins recommended Lardner include short introductory notes between stories due to a "weakness in the title,"[44] the author responded, "I think the preface idea is a good one."[45] Lardner was always willing to hear Perkins's requests, though often he would oftentimes benignly disregard his editor. He allowed Perkins to collect and publish his stories, but the money earned never approached the sums reached from his magazine work. However, the new volumes did bring him significant publicity and critical attention. Beginning with a collection of already published stories, Perkins knew full well he had to create a different kind of book for readers. Lardner's preface and commentaries featured a persona already established within the writer's canon and public reputation. So established was his authority that the preface was reworked from one of his "Weekly Letter" segments for the Bell Syndicate, which allowed Lardner to transition his persona seamlessly from magazine to trade publication with little interruption or effort. Even with his recycled preface, the most successful and innovative of Lardner's volumes proved to be *How to Write Short Stories (with Samples)*, with its "new" preface and short introductory commentaries garnering much critical and popular attention.

The purpose of Lardner's preface was to send up the use of writing manuals in the writing profession, which had been in vogue since the nineteenth century. H. L. Menken recognizes the purpose of Lardner's preface immediately in his review: "The present collection has a buffoonish preface on the art of writing short stories—a devastating *reductio ad absur-dum* of the sort of bilge ladled out annually by Prof. Dr. Blanche Colton Williams and other such self-constituted experts."[46] Knowing that his persona had garnered him a significant following, and that the same persona had brought him to the attention of Perkins and Scribner's, Lardner reinforced his intention to keep his readers—and himself—in as stable a state as possible. However, a Scribner's *The New York Times* display advertisement from 1 June 1924 declared Lardner, "an extraordinary humorist, who, like Mark Twain, puts far more than fun into his stories. Compassion follows laughter; amusement gives way to a sense of infinite pathos. Authenticity and veracity are the first qualities of the stories in this volume."[47] With Twain front and center as a literary antecedent, the ad suggests that Lardner makes good on his early promise, since Twain was equally known for short stories and for novels. Further, by insisting that Lardner's stories exhibited as much compassion and pathos as they did laughter and amusement, it was clear Scribner's wanted Lardner to evolve. The ad continues with quotes from critic Burton Rascoe, who compares Lardner to Sherwood Anderson, Katherine Mansfield, and Willa Cather. Perkins wanted Lardner to become the next Mark Twain, and early advertisements made this point clear to the reading public. As both a new and established author, Lardner had to attract readers in order to make his new publisher's investment worthwhile, and he used prefatory manipulation as a means to amplify and maintain an established authorial persona.

Biographer Jonathan Yardley refers to the preface and notes to *How to Write Short Stories* as "offhand" and "self-mockery,"[48] with each piece providing a satiric slant on established literariness and training. Early on in his preface Lardner attacks "correspondence schools that learns you the art of short-story writing" and the ineffectiveness of such schools.[49] He claims that "the most of the successful authors of the short fiction of today never went to no kind of a college, or if they did, they studied piano tuning or the barber trade," concluding "they could of got just as far in what I call the literary game if they had of stayed home those four years and helped mother carry out the empty bottles."[50] Lardner separates the mind from the act, with his ideal writer making the most out of realistic experience and judgment rather than engaging in an intellectual exercise. Lardner recognized that his immense readership's response to a non-intellectual, non-literary writer would be positive rather than negative. He plays to the sensibility of a simpler reader, calling the trade a "game" and referring to intellectual novice writers as "boys or gals who had win their phi beta skeleton keys at this or that story-writing college."[51] Rather than spend money and time being taught how to write, Lardner insists that "you can't find no operation up to date, whether it be a general institution of learning or a school that specializes in story writing, which can make a great author out of a born druggist."[52] If taken seriously Lardner's preface would lose all effectiveness, but this comment rings true even today. His critique of authorship centers on talent and work ethic. Lardner possessed both the talent to create a unique perspective and the work ethic to regularly produce printable copy. Talent and work are required to successfully write for the public, and his satire of this duality makes the point even clearer.

Lardner's first three paragraphs are simple on the surface, but beneath that surface is the efficiency of a hard-working professional writer. More effective is the preface's appearance in a Scribner's book rather than a periodical for mass publication. If he was to refine his authority and write a serious introduction to the art of the short story, his readers may have responded with either dismissal or puzzlement. Inversely, Edmund Wilson was puzzled at the authorial reversal; as referenced earlier, the critic expected an evolution in Lardner's persona. Wilson inquired, "is all this an idea of the publishers, who do not want to forfeit the prestige of Lardner's reputation as a humorist, or is it due to Mr. Lardner, who is timid about coming forward in the role of serious writer?"[53] The Scribner's label altered Lardner's ability to completely get away with his satiric sentiments, though he continued to mine them for the remainder of his association with the firm. Lardner maintained a persona consistent with his magazine work, playing for laughs more so than enlightenment. At no point could he be categorized as timid, though complications were bound to arise because he chose Scribner's. Both his preface and the mini-introductions that accompanied each story in the collection generated a divided reaction. "The nonsense of his introductions," writes Wilson, "is so far below his usual level that one suspects him of a guilty conscience at attempting to disguise his talent for social observation and satire. ... For, aside from a very few things ... *How to Write Short Stories* is a series of studies of American types almost equal in importance to those of Sherwood Anderson and Sinclair Lewis."[54] Wilson recognizes the resistance, listing two major novelists to whom Lardner's work *should* be equaling but will not, due in large part to Lardner's introductions.

Suffice it to say, Lardner's preface does instruct readers on composition, editing, and publication, though the instruction is cloaked with ridicule. He notes that "the first thing I generally always do is try and get hold of a catchy title, like for instance, 'Basil Hargrave's Vermifuge,' or 'Fun at the Incinerating Plant,'" before looking "cock-eyed" at colored pencils and blank paper.[55] The humor of his titles obviates the authority of a serious author, for the catchiness of those titles outweighs their meaning. "Vermifuge" sounds better than its definition ("an agent used to expel parasitic worms"), and Basil's use of vermifuge on himself or others offers readers an initial conceit. Likewise, one generally does not have fun at incinerating plants, though the curiosity of what fun could be had promotes the title's main goal: catch the reader. Similarly, he utilizes double speak to poke fun at the writing professional: "How to begin—or, as we professionals would say, 'how to commence'—is the next question. It must be admitted that the method of approach ('L'approchement') differs even among first class fictionists."[56] Lardner recognizes the duality of authority (personal and public), and he shows how his work differs from others while maintaining a link to a similar professional mindset. He would never have signed with Scribner's if he had not understood the possibility of professional gain, but because his preface was written prior to the publication of the text for an altogether different medium, Lardner can again position himself between literary and popular, serious and silly. His explanation of beginning a story continues this duality, for he offers helpful commentary and self-effacing posturing in equal measure.

When Lardner observes that "the reading public prefers short dialogues to any other kind of writing," he means it.[57] His circulation and prosperity rested on short work, and his reputation promoted condensation rather than expansion. The less we know about the "real" Ring Lardner the better, and his preface maintained his vigil against over-emphasizing anything other than the writer his readers would surely recognize. At this point in the preface one expects Lardner to get on with the specifics of writing and promote a semi-serious tutoring service for his volume's readers. His fabricated sample plot makes sense, with two girls at a resort looking for famous autographs and narrowly escaping a forger, which would certainly have embarrassed them. He then begins writing "with haphazard dialogue" to see where his plot might go.[58] Of course it goes nowhere, which leads Lardner to scrap his plot and "take up the life of a mule in the Grand Canyon," who watches trains go by and "keeps wondering who is going to ride him."[59] Lardner then writes of strangers on a train who end up playing and listening to the same composer (Chopin) outlined in the original plot. Both musical pieces mentioned do not exist; the first is the 121st

fugue for bass drum, while the other is the 12th sonata for flute and cus-
pidor (spittoon). Aware of his readers' expectations, and sounding rather
like Mark Twain, Lardner plays up the farce, and it is this comedy that
drives the preface, the collection, and his will to survive in the face of elevated expectations.

With his farcical approach, Lardner uses the form to resist, rather than
promote, authorial posturing. Lardner's stories were his own, and when
he finished them he gave them to the public for their entertainment. He
neither edited a story nor revised an existing piece for Perkins and
Scribner's; instead, Lardner let his stories live on their own. "Personally I
have found it a good scheme to not even sign my name to the story,"
Lardner concludes, "and when I have got it sealed up in its envelope and
stamped and addressed, I take it to some town where I don't live and mail
it from there. The editor has no idea who wrote the story, so how can he
send it back? He is in a quandary."[60] Putting one's name on a story grants
that writer authority over the material, and authority was never Lardner's
game. To this point, it is evident that Lardner never required all of Perkins's
attention. He dealt with Lardner as he was and encouraged his writing
throughout their relationship, while Lardner's reading public provided a
buffer between the writer's sensibilities and his new firm's more serious
literary intentions.

To conclude his preface, Lardner mentions how his collected stories
"will illustrate in a half-hearted way what I am trying to get at."[61] The
preface forms one singular conclusion: literary pretention deserves to be
skewered. Pretension leads to false representation, and falsehood further
separates writers from readers. Lardner's preface and notes lead readers
down back alleys and rabbit holes, poking fun at other writers who direct
their readers under the guise of authority. He knew his readers would
laugh rather than engage in thought-provoking critical dialogue, and by
refusing to put a square peg in a round hole, Lardner maintained his carefully constructed magazine persona throughout the preface and its accompanying text. Like his preface, the short commentaries introducing each
story in-text relinquish any serviceable authorial function in favor of
humor. Each selection offers humorous asides for the reader. "The Facts"
was "written on top of a Fifth Avenue bus, and some of the sheets blew
away, which may account for the apparent scarcity of interesting situations."[62] "Some Like Them Cold" was "a story written from a title, the
title being a line from Tennyson's immortal 'Hot Cross Buns.'"[63] Lardner
thanks Chief Justice William Howard Taft for the "slang employed" in

"Alibi Ike."[64] "The Golden Honeymoon" is preceded by a single-phrase preface—"a story with 'sex appeal'"—ironic in that it is a story about two septuagenarians who dislike each other.[65] "Champion" is "an example of the mystery story. The mystery is how it came to get printed."[66] And "Horseshoes," Lardner writes, "is the kind of story which the reader can take up at any point and lay down as soon as he feels like it."[67] Lardner chose to do away completely with traditional notions of prefacing, which results in pieces as true to their writer as any other. For Perkins, adding a preface and notes meant expanding Lardner's loosely connected stories into a serviceable volume, since prefaces typically provide authors with a forum for explanation, conversation, and reader engagement. However, since Lardner maintained an air of post-composition negligence with his own work, one can assume that his prefaces and notes meant about as much to him as if they were written by someone else.

THE LOVE NEST AND OTHER STORIES (1926)

In an uncharacteristic move, Lardner wrote an original piece for the preface to *The Love Nest and Other Stories*. How it was written proves important for two reasons. One, Lardner wrote the piece as a space-filler at the behest of Perkins, who was concerned the book lacked size compared to other collections. He asked Lardner, "will you write the preface—And the longer you make it, the better. Please do make it long if you can without forcing it. Say anything you want to. The stories add up to 46,200 words. I suppose the preface could easily make it 50,000, but even that is much shorter than the book. It will do, however.—"[68] Two, Lardner may have written it as a response to Perkins's persistence regarding novel writing. Again, in his preface Lardner resists authorial refashioning and offers a cynical approach to the publishing industry, which proves that he recognized the effect of his material on a readership already dedicated to his writing. Composed of recently published short stories, the collection was released at Lardner's peak with Scribner's, which begs a question about his preface. Why not choose a straightforward model to present newer work and maintain momentum within the firm? Lardner was never one to bend to demands or conventions, and because of the duality inherent in his preface—he writes from the fictional Sarah E. Spooldripper's perspective, a maid and wolf-caretaker for Lardner—we can trace a noticeable authoritative move. He literally removes himself from his own preface, choosing instead to write from a fake maid's point of view. Lardner actively resists serious authority in the Spooldripper preface by making himself a character and then having his maid mock and eventually eulogize him.

Both of Lardner's biographers define the preface in a similar fashion. Elder sees the piece as "a burlesque of all introductions, of intimate memoirs, of literary scholarship,"[69] and Yardley adds that Lardner "outdid himself in self-mockery" and wrote a "charmingly nonsensical" piece.[70] While Yardley sees the humor in the piece, Elder categorizes the targets of Lardner's preface correctly: authorship, criticism, and the publishing industry. Lardner tells readers in a footnote that Spooldripper "knew all there was to know about Lardner, and her mind was virtually blank. It was part of her charm," and she characterizes Lardner as "perhaps not loveable, but certainly irresistible. There was an impishness in him that fascinated. It was part of his charm."[71] She goes on to describe literary rivalries, with Lardner, Fitzgerald, and "Opie Reade"[72] [sic] pining over "the love of Lily Langtry."[73] When Lily is asked to rise and toast her favorite, "the muscles of Fitzgerald and Reade were taut; Lardner's were very flabby." Accordingly, each "swain" was affected by Lily's toast: "Reade arose and told the story of the two half-breeds, Seminole and Deminole. Lardner and Fitzgerald took up rotation pool, and weighed themselves once a week. Every so often they became maudlin, or, better still, inaudible."[74] Choosing between hearing the authors' self-pitying and drunken sentimentality or silence shows Lardner's comedic spirit regarding his close friend Fitzgerald. It is all the more ironic that Lardner is effectively "silent" throughout the preface, as his maid does all the talking for him.

Spooldripper then takes readers on "a preposterous introductory tour" of the collection's stories.[75] The doctor in "Haircut" was "Lardner's favorite among all his fictional characters, or as he called them, 'my puppets'" (*Love Nest* ix). Lardner had used "puppets" to describe manipulation of character in the preface to *How to Write Short Stories*, though using the term for "Haircut" takes on greater meaning. Doc Stair covers up the crime at the center of the story, effectively making a puppet out of the narrator Whitey, who remains oblivious to any foul play. In a story told by someone who doesn't have all the information, though throughout his story the truth comes clearly into view for the listener, Lardner perfects the style we was known for, and Whitey becomes the ultimate puppet.[76] For "Reunion," Spooldripper recalls a golf anecdote featuring the mayor of New York, in which "Lardner could not remember whose turn it was to drive first. 'Your honor?' he said to the Mayor. 'Yes?' the Mayor replied.

'What can I do for you?' It is incidents like this that paint the man in his true colors. He was forever blowing bubbles. It amounted to a whim."[77] Though populated with a relatively cheap joke ("Your honor," your honor), this episode sums up much of Lardner's artistic temperament and reminds readers of his skill with language.[78] "Zone of Quiet" came to *Cosmopolitan* editor Ray Long during the "equinoctial gales" after "every other sheet of copy was blown away or destroyed by stray dogs" (xii). No matter, for "Mr. Long thought this all for the best as he was crowded that month" (xiv). Lardner's straightforward reduction of magazine publishing and editing practices characterizes Ray Long as an editor looking for printable copy rather than a thoughtful artistic expression, which adequately sums up the magazine market of the early twentieth century. James L. W. West III notes that "writing for the magazines took patience, adaptability, and thick skin. ... The work could be frustrating, but the potential financial rewards were large."[79] Lardner possessed all of the traits needed to be successful in the magazine market, and he reaped the rewards of his efforts. He had earned the right to write about editors and their fluctuating needs, since he had always been the kind of patient professional that editors needed to further their magazines. The short explications in his preface provide each story a nonsense history while critiquing various publishing standards, and Lardner's ability to play with both farce and criticism marks a considerable advancement in his preface writing. He was serious about helping readers see how ridiculous the industry he had mastered had become.

Spooldripper eventually concludes that "the Master is gone and the next question is who will succeed him? Perhaps some writer still unborn. Perhaps one who will never be born. That is what I hope."[80] Veiled references to Lardner's own death throughout the piece finally reach their zenith, and some critics and readers believed Spooldripper's account.[81] Lardner even kills off Spooldripper and notes "the joke is on Miss Spooldripper, for she is gone too. Two months ago she was found dead in the garage, her body covered with wolf bites left there by her former ward, who has probably forgotten where he left them."[82] By killing off not one but two preface writers, Lardner takes a significant jab at the various functions of publishing and performs the ultimate act of authorial resistance: he kills himself in print. Though he wrote another Spooldripper piece for his fake autobiography the following year (*The Story of a Wonder Man*), his work for *The Love Nest* shows a keen eye for prefaces of all kinds. His work satisfies the core requirements of an authorial preface: he provides the genesis of his stories, offers an outside perspective of the author, eulogizes his own work by faking death, and positions his work amidst the current standards of the day.[83] The moment where these ideas collide occurs immediately before his conclusion, when Spooldripper references "the invention and perfection of the radio" as the leading cause of Lardner's penchant for short stories.[84] The radio provided short, consumable programming, akin to Lardner's writing. After Lardner builds his own and installs it "in the suit of pajamas which he habitually wore nights," Spooldripper describes his final days:

> He was always trying to tune in on Glens Falls, N.Y., and it was only in his last illness that he found out there was no broadcasting station at that place. His sense of humor came to his rescue in this dilemma. 'Junior,' he said to his wife, 'they tell me there is no broadcasting station at Glens Falls.' 'Am I to blame for that?' retorted the little Nordic, quick to take umbrage. 'No,' he answered. 'It's Glens Falls.'[85]

Somewhat sad, these lines give the introduction an added immediacy, for Lardner had contracted tuberculosis prior to the publication of *The Love Nest*, and during that period Yardley notes: "as the twenties moved on and the thirties neared, as Ring's health declined and his work became routine and repetitive, he must have looked at his life's work, and in doing so, he may well have reached a stern judgment."[86] This judgment makes an appearance in the preface, for by separating his perspective and adding the fictional Spooldripper, Lardner doubly controls his own authority. Instead of speaking for himself, he indirectly creates a mixed reaction to his supposed death, calling more for continued indifference than a eulogy. However, Lardner offers a possible judgment of his skills by creating the dialogue between himself and his wife, Ellis. His sense of humor had driven him his entire creative life, and through that humor even he can't find blame outside of the simplest of answers: "It's Glens Falls."[87] One can read the interaction as Lardner coming to terms with his supposed failure to advance beyond the writer he had always been, and Yardley, among others, sees an opportunity to imply regret. Lardner certainly had regrets, but if read carefully, the prefaces he wrote for Scribner's help us see the game he was playing all along. We want him to feel regret so that we can amplify what could have been, as Americans relish opportunity and exposure in equal measure. Lardner took advantage of both without ceding any of his authority in the process, making any regret the product of critics' imaginations. He might have known his work would receive less attention than some of his contemporaries after his death, but in his lifetime he was known, and he was successful. There is no tragedy in that.

STEPPING IN

The prefaces for *How to Write Short Stories (with Samples)* and *The Love Nest and Other Stories* provide a meaningful way to investigate the authorial resistance Lardner undertook throughout his time with Charles Scribner's Sons. To paraphrase Genette, rather than turning his back on his carefully cultivated persona, Ring Lardner stepped into it. "Ring Lardner seems to have imitated nobody," wrote Edmund Wilson, "and nobody else could reproduce his essence."[88] In what Clifford Caruthers deduces was Lardner's final letter,[89] the ailing writer responded to a Long Island woman who had written him about whether or not he cared for his characters. Clifton Fadiman, in a 1933 essay titled "Ring Lardner and the Triangle of Hate" for *The Nation*, advanced the theory that Lardner hated his characters, and that "Except Swift, no writer has gone further on hatred alone."[90] Wilma Seavey, having defended Lardner around the dinner table, wanted to know what he thought. He responded with a fair assessment of his intentions, closer than either of his Scribner's prefaces get to understanding the real Ring Lardner: "I don't suppose any author either hates or loves all his characters. I try to write about people as real as possible, and some of them are naturally more likeable than others. ... I cannot remember ever having felt any bitterness or hatred toward the characters I have written about." He ends his letter prophetically: "I am grateful to you for your defense of me."[91] Sherwood Anderson had recognized not only the tragedy brewing behind Lardner's mask but also the bustling creativity and sincerity with which he went about his business. H. L. Mencken and Virginia Woolf praised his originality, and even Edmund Wilson lauded his realism while denouncing his presentation. "Ring Lardner writes about you and me," Mary Rennels wrote in a piece for *Cleveland Topics*. "He makes us as ridiculous as we are—and he counterbalances the ridicule with the pathos, the pain and the joy that make up our life time. In fact he makes us live on paper."[92] With defenders and detractors, Ring Lardner resisted the serious literary life by remaining just outside of it, surviving and succeeding on his own terms rather than acquiescing to the expectations of literary greatness.

NOTES

1. Sherwood Anderson, "Meeting Ring Lardner," in *No Swank* (Philadelphia, PA: Centaur Press, 1934). Reprinted in *The Sherwood Anderson Reader*, ed. Paul Rosenfeld (Boston, MA: Houghton Mifflin Company, 1947), 301.
2. H. L. Mencken, "The Library: Ring W. Lardner," *American Mercury* vol. 2 (May–August 1924): 377.
3. Clifford M. Caruthers, ed. *Letters of Ring Lardner* (Alexandria, VA: Orchises Press, 1995), 221.
4. Carruthers, *Letters of Ring Lardner*, 222. All inflation adjustments were made using the Consumer Price Index (CPI) Inflation Calculator, provided by the United States Bureau of Labor Statistics, https://www.bls.gov/data/inflation_calculator.htm.
5. C. Edgar Grissom, *Ernest Hemingway: A Descriptive Bibliography* (New Castle, DE: Oak Knoll Press, 2011), 109.
6. See James Hutchisson, *The Rise of Sinclair Lewis, 1920–1930* (University Park, PA: Pennsylvania State University Press, 1996), 192.
7. Jonathan Yardley, *Ring: A Biography of Ring Lardner* (New York: Random House, 1977), 225.
8. Virginia Woolf, "American Fiction," *The Saturday Review of Literature* 2, no. 1 (1925). Reprinted in *The Moment and other Essays* (New York: Harcourt, Brace and Company, 1948), 113–127.
9. Dorothy Parker, "Hero Worship," *The New Yorker* (April 27, 1929). Reprinted in *The Portable Dorothy Parker*, ed. Marion Meade (New York: Penguin, 2006), 514.
10. See Yardley, *Ring: A Biography of Ring Lardner*, 189–190.
11. The novel in progress became *Tender Is the Night* (1934). See John Kuehl and Jackson R. Bryer, eds., *Dear Scott/Dear Max: The Fitzgerald-Perkins Correspondence* (New York: Charles Scribner's Sons, 1971), 149.
12. Matthew J. Bruccoli, ed., with the assistance of Robert W. Trogdon, *The Only Thing That Counts: The Ernest Hemingway-Maxwell Perkins Correspondence* (Columbia, SC: University of South Carolina Press, 1996), 224.
13. Carruthers, *Letters of Ring Lardner*, 163.
14. Ring Lardner (RL) to Max Perkins (MP), 2 December 1924. Carruthers, *Letters of Ring Lardner*, 168.
15. Clifford M. Caruthers, ed. *Ring Around Max: The Correspondence of Ring Lardner & Max Perkins* (DeKalb, IL: Northern Illinois University Press, 1973), 97.
16. Carruthers, *Ring Around Max*, 125.
17. Kuehl and Bryer, *Dear Scott/Dear Max*, 141.
18. Kuehl and Bryer, *Dear Scott/Dear Max*, 156.

19. Edmund Wilson, "Ring Lardner's American Characters," *The Dial* (July 1924). Reprinted in *The Shores of Light: A Literary Chronicle of the Twenties and Thirties* (New York: Farrar, Strauss and Young, Inc., 1952), 97.
20. Wilson, "Ring Lardner's American Characters," 98.
21. Wilson, "Ring Lardner's American Characters," 98.
22. Wilson, "Ring Lardner's American Characters," 98.
23. Charles S. Holmes, "Ring Lardner: Reluctant Artist." In *A Question of Quality: Popularity and Value in Modern Creative Writing*, ed. Louis Filler (Bowling Green OH: Bowling Green State University Popular Press, 1976), 29.
24. Even Lardner's "autobiography"—*The Story of a Wonder Man*—was initially serialized in *Cosmopolitan* from 11 July 1926 to 9 January 1927. The book was then published soon after in March 1927.
25. Gerard Genette, *Paratexts: Thresholds of Interpretation*. 1987. Trans. Jane E. Lewin (New York: Cambridge University Press, 1997), 221.
26. Sandra Spanier and Miriam B. Mandel, eds., *The Letters of Ernest Hemingway (1929–1932)* (New York: Cambridge University Press, 2017), 94.
27. Douglas A. Noverr, "The Small Town and Urban Midwest in Ring Lardner's *You Know Me Al*," *MidAmerica* 25 (1998): 76.
28. Ring W. Lardner, *You Know Me Al: A Busher's Letters*. 1916. Reprinted in *Ring Lardner: Stories & Other Writings*, ed. Ian Frazier (New York: Library of America, 2013), 10.
29. Lardner, *You Know Me Al*, 116.
30. Mencken, "The Library: Ring W. Lardner," 377.
31. Woolf, "American Fiction," 123.
32. RL to Hewitt Howland, 14 March 1921. Carruthers, *Letters of Ring Lardner*, 131.
33. RL to MP, 2 February 1924. Carruthers, *Letters of Ring Lardner*, 151.
34. Mencken, "The Library: Ring W. Lardner," 377.
35. Anderson, "Meeting Ring Lardner," 302.
36. Anderson, "Meeting Ring Lardner," 304–305.
37. Anderson, "Meeting Ring Lardner," 302.
38. Donald Elder, *Ring Lardner: A Biography* (New York: Doubleday & Company, Inc., 1956), 226.
39. Noverr, "The Small Town," 69.
40. MP to RL, 2 July 1923. Carruthers, *Ring Around Max*, 2–3.
41. Carruthers, *Ring Around Max*, 2–3.
42. Carruthers, *Ring Around Max*, 7.
43. Carruthers, *Ring Around Max*, 9–10.
44. MP to RL, 17 March 1924. Carruthers, *Ring Around Max*, 14.
45. RL to MP, 22 March 1924. Carruthers, *Ring Around Max*, 17.

46. Mencken, "The Library: Ring W. Lardner," 377. Blanche Colton Williams wrote two mainstream short-story manuals: *A Handbook on Story Writing* (1917) and *How to Study "The Best Short Stories"* (1919). Lardner sends up both in his preface to (and title for) *How to Write Short Stories (with Samples)*.
47. Display Ad 51. No Title. *New York Times.* 1 June 1924. *ProQuest Historical Newspapers: The New York Times (1851–2010)*, BR 27.
48. Yardley, *Ring: A Biography of Ring Lardner*, 275–276.
49. Ring W. Lardner, *How to Write Short Stories (with Samples)* (New York: Charles Scribner's Sons, 1924), v.
50. Lardner, *How to Write Short Stories*, v.
51. Lardner, *How to Write Short Stories*, v.
52. Lardner, *How to Write Short Stories*, v–vi.
53. Wilson, "Ring Lardner's American Characters," 94.
54. Wilson, "Ring Lardner's American Characters," 94–95.
55. Lardner, *How to Write Short Stories*, vi.
56. Lardner, *How to Write Short Stories*, vi–vii.
57. Lardner, *How to Write Short Stories*, vii.
58. Lardner, *How to Write Short Stories*, viii.
59. Lardner, *How to Write Short Stories*, ix.
60. Lardner, *How to Write Short Stories*, x.
61. Lardner, *How to Write Short Stories*, x.
62. Lardner, *How to Write Short Stories*, 1.
63. Lardner, *How to Write Short Stories*, 45.
64. Lardner, *How to Write Short Stories*, 79.
65. Lardner, *How to Write Short Stories*, 113.
66. Lardner, *How to Write Short Stories*, 143.
67. Lardner, *How to Write Short Stories*, 317.
68. MP to RL, 23 December 1925. Carruthers, *Ring Around Max*, 85.
69. Donald Elder, *Ring Lardner: A Biography*, 235.
70. Yardley, *Ring: A Biography of Ring Lardner*, 294.
71. Ring W. Lardner, *The Love Next and Other Stories* (New York: Charles Scribner's Sons, 1926), v.
72. Opie Read (not "Reade") was a popular comic writer and founder of the *Arkansas Traveler* magazine.
73. Lardner, *The Love Nest*, vi.
74. Lardner, *The Love Nest*, vii.
75. Yardley, *Ring: A Biography of Ring Lardner*, 295.
76. See Lardner, "Haircut," *The Love Nest*, 31–54.
77. Lardner, *The Love Nest*, xii.
78. Lardner reworked "I'm Forever Blowing Bubbles" during the 1919 World Series (the Black Sox Scandal) to read: "I'm forever blowing ball games/

Pretty ball games in the air." See Yardley, *Ring: A Biography of Ring Lardner*, 214. The scene was also made famous in John Sayles's 1988 film, *Eight Men Out*, featuring Sayles as Lardner.

79. James L. W. West III, *American Authors and the Literary Marketplace since 1900* (Philadelphia, PA: University of Pennsylvania Press, 1988), 113.
80. Lardner, *The Love Nest*, xvi. This is a possible allusion to novelist Henry James, known as "The Master" during his prolific career.
81. Both of Lardner's biographers reference various examples in regard to the initial publication of *The Love Nest*. See Yardley, *Ring: A Biography of Ring Lardner*, 295; and Elder, *Ring Lardner: A Biography*, 234.
82. Lardner, *The Love Nest*, xvi.
83. See Genette, *Paratexts*, for a full discussion.
84. Lardner, *The Love Nest*, xiv.
85. Lardner, *The Love Nest*, xiv–xv.
86. Yardley, *Ring: A Biography of Ring Lardner*, 284.
87. Lardner, *The Love Nest*, xv.
88. Wilson, "Ring Lardner's American Characters," 96.
89. See Carruthers, *Letters of Ring Lardner*, 286.
90. Clifton Fadiman, "Ring Lardner and the Triangle of Hate," *The Nation*, CXXXVI (22 March 1933), 315.
91. RL to Wilma Seavey, 24 August 1933. Carruthers, *Letters of Ring Lardner*, 286.
92. Mary Rennels, "The Road to Genius," *Cleveland Topics*, August 23, 1924. Ring Lardner Papers, Modern Manuscripts and Archives, Newberry Library, Chicago, IL.

BIBLIOGRAPHY

Anderson, Sherwood. "Meeting Ring Lardner," *No Swank*. 1934. Reprinted in *The Sherwood Anderson Reader*, edited by Paul Rosenfeld, 301–305. Boston, MA: Houghton Mifflin Company, 1947.

Bruccoli, Matthew J., ed., with the assistance of Robert W. Trogdon. *The Only Thing That Counts: The Ernest Hemingway-Maxwell Perkins Correspondence*. Columbia, SC: University of South Carolina Press, 1996.

Caruthers, Clifford M., ed. *Letters of Ring Lardner*. Alexandra, VA: Orchises Press, 1995.

———. *Ring Around Max: The Correspondence of Ring Lardner & Max Perkins*. DeKalb, IL: Northern Illinois University Press, 1973.

Display Ad 51. No Title. *New York Times*. 1 June 1924. *ProQuest Historical Newspapers: The New York Times (1851–2010)*, BR 27.

Elder, Donald. *Ring Lardner: A Biography*. New York: Doubleday & Company, Inc., 1956.

Fadiman, Clifton. "Ring Lardner and the Triangle of Hate," *The Nation*, CXXXVI (22 March 1933), 315–317.

Genette, Gerard. *Paratexts: Thresholds of Interpretation*. 1987. Jane E. Lewin, trans. New York: Cambridge University Press, 1997.

Grissom, C. Edgar. *Ernest Hemingway: A Descriptive Bibliography*. New Castle, DE: Oak Knoll Press, 2011.

Holmes, Charles S. "Ring Lardner: Reluctant Artist." In *A Question of Quality: Popularity and Value in Modern Creative Writing*, edited by Louis Filler, 26–39. Bowling Green, OH: Bowling Green State University Popular Press, 1976.

Hutchisson, James. *The Rise of Sinclair Lewis, 1920–1930*. University Park, PA: Pennsylvania State University Press, 1996.

Kuehl, John, and Jackson R. Bryer, eds. *Dear Scott/Dear Max: The Fitzgerald-Perkins Correspondence*. New York: Charles Scribner's Sons, 1971.

Lardner, Ring W. *How to Write Short Stories (with Samples)*. New York: Charles Scribner's Sons, 1924.

———. *The Love Nest and Other Stories*. New York: Charles Scribner's Sons, 1926.

———. *You Know Me Al*. 1916. Reprinted in *Ring Lardner: Stories & Other Writings*, edited by Ian Frazier, 1–132. New York: Library of America, 2013.

Mencken, H. L. "The Library: Ring W. Lardner," *American Mercury* 2 (May–August 1924): 376–377.

Noverr, Douglas A. "The Small Town and the Urban Midwest in Ring Lardner's *You Know Me Al*." *MidAmerica* 25 (1998): 64–77.

Parker, Dorothy. "Hero Worship," *The New Yorker* (April 27, 1929). Reprinted in *The Portable Dorothy Parker*, edited by Marion Meade, 513–514. New York: Penguin, 2006.

Rennels, Mary. "The Road to Genius." *Cleveland Topics*, August 23, 1924. Ring Lardner Papers. Modern Manuscripts and Archives. Newberry Library, Chicago, IL.

Robinson, Douglas. "Ring Lardner's Dual Audience and the Capitalist Double Bind." *American Literary History* 4, no. 2 (1992): 264–287.

Spanier, Sandra, and Miriam B. Mandel, eds. *The Letters of Ernest Hemingway (1929–1932)*. New York: Cambridge University Press, 2017.

West, James L. W., III. *American Authors and the Literary Marketplace since 1900*. Philadelphia, PA: University of Pennsylvania Press, 1988.

Wilson, Edmund. "Ring Lardner's American Characters." *The Dial* (July 1924). Reprinted in *The Shores of Light: A Literary Chronicle of the Twenties and Thirties*, 94–98. New York: Farrar, Strauss and Young, Inc., 1952.

Woolf, Virginia. "American Fiction," *The Saturday Review of Literature*, 2, no. 1 (1925). Reprinted in *The Moment and other Essays*, 113–127. New York: Harcourt, Brace and Company, 1948.

Yardley, Jonathan. *Ring: A Biography of Ring Lardner*. New York: Random House, 1977.

CHAPTER 4

Inhibiting Signposts: F. Scott Fitzgerald and Authorial Anxiety

Drunk at 20, wrecked at 30, dead at 40.
—F. Scott Fitzgerald[1]

In the summer of 1920, F. Scott Fitzgerald wrote in a preface to the third printing of his debut novel, *This Side of Paradise* (1920): "to write it took three months; to conceive it—three minutes; to collect the data in it—all my life."[2] Early in his career, Fitzgerald manufactured a glib and facile persona, markedly different from his actual writing life; by flippantly emphasizing the ease and speed with which he wrote, he gave readers the impression that he cared little for craft, that his talent was effortless, not carefully honed. No piece represents this flippancy more obviously than his table of contents to *Tales of the Jazz Age* (1922), which reads as more of a comic introduction to the work than a traditional listing of stories. However, he wrote *The Great Gatsby* (1925) yearning for critical (as well as popular) acceptance and shifted from this initial authorial pose. Although he noted in his preface to *Paradise* that "an author ought to write for the

Parts of this chapter appeared originally as "My Own Personal Public: Fitzgerald's Table of Contents in *Tales of the Jazz Age*." *F. Scott Fitzgerald Review* 13 (2015): 130–145, and "Alone and Alone: Defense, Justification, and Apology in Fitzgerald's Late Prefaces." *F. Scott Fitzgerald Review* 15 (2017): 51–71. I wish to thank Pennsylvania State University Press, as well as managing editor Kirk Curnutt, for permission to reprint portions of those essays in this book.

© The Author(s), under exclusive license to Springer Nature Switzerland AG 2021
R. K. Tangedal, *The Preface*, New Directions in Book History,
https://doi.org/10.1007/978-3-030-85151-4_4

youth of his generation, the critics of the next, and the schoolmasters of ever afterward,"[3] he wanted his writing to mature. He told his Scribner's editor Maxwell Perkins in April 1924 that his new book represented "a consciously artistic achievement,"[4] and on 27 October he lamented to Perkins that he was "tired of being the author of *This Side of Paradise* and I want to start over."[5] Fitzgerald did not express this longing in mid-1920s essays or interviews, however, so what readers knew of his identity remained the early glibness, not his professionalism. When *The Great Gatsby* appeared, that levity tainted the critical response,[6] and Fitzgerald resolved to move beyond the persona he himself created with his next novel.

Although he produced lucrative magazine fiction after *Gatsby*, he struggled with what became *Tender Is the Night* well into the 1930s. Writing to Ernest Hemingway on 9 September 1929, he joked, "Here's a last flicker of the old cheap pride:—the <u>Post</u> now pay the old whore $4000. a screw. But now its because she's mastered the 40 positions—in her youth one was enough." Fitzgerald's pessimism regarding his ability to write novels had reached a climax; in that same letter, he said his work up to that point "may have taken all I had to say too early, adding that all the time we were living at top speed in the gayest worlds we could find."[7] Hemingway's reply reads as advice and admonishment: "(They never raise an old whore's price—She may know 850 positions—They cut her price all the same—So either you arent old or not a whore or both) The stories arent whoreing, they're just bad judgement—you could have and can make enough to live on writing novels. You damned fool. Go on and write the novel."[8]

During the next decade, after finally completing *Tender Is the Night* in 1934, Fitzgerald wrote two complete prefaces, one published (an introduction to The Modern Library edition of *The Great Gatsby*, 1934) and one unpublished (a short foreword to *Taps at Reveille*, 1935). These pieces epitomize his authorial frustrations and reveal the opposite of the youthful author of *Tales of the Jazz Age*, whose table of contents stands in stark opposition to the late-career prefaces. Gerard Genette contends that the choice of public regarding an introduction or preface is crucial, for "it is not always wise to cast one's net too wide, and authors often have a fairly specific idea of the kind of reader they want, or the kind they know they can reach."[9] By defining his readership early on as "my own personal public"[10] in his earlier table of contents to *Tales of the Jazz Age*, Fitzgerald maintained direct access to a group of loosely defined consumers he knew he could reach. These readers, as the author saw them, wished to have their Fitzgerald fiction presented a certain way, with a certain tone and style. But Genette insists that once an introduction has been published the reader "will have to make an effort to circumvent this inhibiting signpost, which won't be that easy to do."[11] After appearing to cast off his table for *Tales* relatively quickly, Fitzgerald's struggled with his late prefaces, partly due to his inability to settle on one group of readers to reach, which may help us understand why he cut one of the "inhibiting signposts" under investigation prior to publication.

I begin with an examination of his table of contents for *Tales of the Jazz Age*, which peddled the image of Scott the celebrity hobbyist rather than Fitzgerald the serious writer. The prefaces that follow suggest the degree to which his reputation had waned by the mid-1930s. Designed partially as apologies and correctives, the 1930s prefaces highlight Fitzgerald's desire to be recognized as a craftsman and his doubts that he ever would. An introduction to the Modern Library edition of *The Great Gatsby* provides a cogent, insightful, and ultimately sad window into an author only fourteen years into his professional career. His unpublished three-sentence foreword to *Taps at Reveille* reminds readers of the author's goal: to create fiction out of his own material and unique perspective, regardless of time, place, or circumstance. Scholars rarely discuss these pieces, much less analyze them in sequence for how they illuminate Fitzgerald's glittering beginnings and career disappointments. Together, these prefaces amplify the anxiety of a writer at odds with himself, his artistic choices, and eventually, his own talent.

TALES OF THE JAZZ AGE (1922)

Coming off of the surprise success of his debut novel, *This Side of Paradise* (1920), and in the final stages of finishing his much-anticipated follow-up, *The Beautiful and Damned* (1922), Fitzgerald knew full well the power of presentation. His short stories, for better or for worse, made him money, but only as magazine pieces. Story collections, historically, do not sell well compared to novels, and this was certainly true throughout Fitzgerald's career. Nonetheless, as with many Scribner's authors under the care of editor Maxwell Perkins, authors would follow a novel with a story collection, with the collection's primary goal to keep the author's name and work in the public while he or she completed a new novel. Ernest Hemingway, Thomas Wolfe, and other Scribner's authors followed this pattern throughout the 1920s and 1930s, as did Fitzgerald. Between 1920 and 1925, Fitzgerald published five books (three novels and two story collections), as well as scores of essays and short stories for magazines. His second collection, he determined, would need something new, leading him to consider calling his new manuscript "Sideshow" or "A Sideshow."[12]

What was produced was *Tales of the Jazz Age*, a miscellany of stories representing different genres and approaches. Fitzgerald is dexterous yet immature in many of the stories, some of which originated as pieces he wrote while an undergraduate at Princeton. While it features two classic stories ("The Diamond as Big as the Ritz" and "May Day"), what ties the collection together is an innovative table of contents, a document James L. W. West III believed Fitzgerald wrote to promote "an appearance of unity,"[13] appearance being the key word. While the table features offhand remarks, flippant asides, and bald-faced lies, it was a new kind of writing, a genre in and of itself, more so than any other preface included in this study. In his search for presentation, Fitzgerald crafted a table of contents tailor made for his new readers, those who "read as they run and run as they read."[14] Whether or not critics showered the book with praise was an afterthought. Fitzgerald knew what he had, and how to sell it, inscribing his copy to influential critic H. L. Mencken, "Please read the Table of Contents,"[15] and telling Perkins, "the stories will be reviewed a great deal, largely because of the *Table of Contents*."[16] Once Fitzgerald enclosed his revised proofs for the table of contents to Perkins in July 1922, he mentioned that "with the title, the jacket + the table of contents the Jazz Age will get a lot of publicity and may sell ten or fifteen thousand copies." In the same letter, he observed: "I don't suppose such an assorted bill-of-fare as these eleven stories, novellettes, plays + 1 burlesque has ever been served up in one book in the history of publishing."[17] Although the future was unknowable to Fitzgerald, the table of contents cost him as much as it buoyed him. He wanted readers to read the book quickly, ignore its drawbacks, and recognize his ingenuity with the table of contents; the table is an inhibiting signpost in every sense of the phrase. Without it the collection would have had to be read on its own, but read with it, Fitzgerald accounted for and redirected reading tastes, a practice he found necessary in creating a new book out of old material.

The table, at just over four pages, is laid out with story titles immediately preceding italicized mini-prefaces, ranging in length from 100 to 150 words. Some are dialogues, while others are narrative paragraphs ranging from humorous to more serious. Self-critique remains throughout the table of contents, as each successive commentary shifts between humor and self-deprecation, confidence and sincerity. In his first commentary, Fitzgerald writes of the "strange circumstances" under which "The Jelly-Bean" was written, naming his wife, Zelda, as a collaborator. He goes so far as to say, "finding that I was unable to manage the crap-shooting episode, I turned it over to my wife, who, as a Southern girl, was presumably an expert on the technique and terminology of that great sectional pastime." This deferral plays directly into the debonair pose Fitzgerald wanted to establish, at least in the table of contents. Fitzgerald was happy to include his wife in the revelry, as she too played a public role as Mrs. Fitzgerald. He also refers to the many letters "from all over the South denouncing me in no uncertain terms."[18] Starting a collection with a story that allegedly garnered a large number of Southern denunciations, as well as a gloss from his wife's hand, placed the author somewhere between self-doubt and brazen ingenuity.

The comments on "The Camel's Back" find the author relegating himself to a camel's "latter part" by their end. Leading up to this punch line, Fitzgerald regards the genesis of his story, writing: "I suppose that of all the stories I have ever written this one cost me the least travail and perhaps gave me the most amusement."[19] Staying true to his pose, Fitzgerald subdues the truth, in which he labored long and hard over "The Camel's Back"; West's "Record of Variants" for the Cambridge Edition[20] includes over five full pages of changes made between the serial and first Scribner's printing.[21] Fitzgerald's habits of revision were sound, though he recalls:

> As to the labor involved, it was written during one day in the city of New Orleans, with the express purpose of buying a platinum and diamond wrist watch which cost six hundred dollars. I began it at seven in the morning and finished it at two o'clock the same night. It was published in the "Saturday Evening Post" in 1920, and later included in the O. Henry Memorial Collection for the same year. I like it least of all the stories in this volume.[22]

The posturing put everything on the line: Fitzgerald's writing habits and his self-judgment. If readers saw the effort, perhaps they would discount the talent. Bryant Mangum argues that Fitzgerald "became the specialist in upper class life—an historian of the wealthy who could make his chronicles as amusing to the average citizen as they were sometimes, perhaps, tragic to him."[23] This persona, created in order to satiate both popular and critical publics, began with his *Saturday Evening Post* stories, of which "The Camel's Back" was one. Fitzgerald was quick to disregard both the artistic labor and staying power of his story—it being his "least favorite" in the collection. Even so, the commentary finds Fitzgerald firmly entrenched in the *Post* story persona Mangum identifies, the persona he intended to display in *Tales of the Jazz Age*.

Fitzgerald tones down his irreverence in favor of sincerity in introducing "May Day." The story, he says, "relates a series of events which took place in the spring of the previous year" and explains that "in my story I have tried, unsuccessfully I fear, to weave them into a pattern—a pattern which would give the effect of those months in New York as they appeared to at least one member of what was then the younger generation." Even as he poses as the off-the-cuff huckster of stories written for wristwatches, he can still create an "effect," and he seeks to offer more with his "somewhat unpleasant tale" focused on "the general hysteria of that spring which inaugurated the Age of Jazz."[24] West, Bruccoli, and Mangum elevate "May Day" above other stories in the collection,[25] and Fitzgerald does the same. Written for *The Smart Set* and sold in March 1920, "May Day" represents an evolving Fitzgerald. In his initial letter to Perkins outlining his new collection, Fitzgerald placed "The Camel's Back" after "May Day," a somewhat innocuous point easily overlooked.[26] However, placement of stories within a collection was extremely important to Fitzgerald, and he worked hard on the construction of his collection.[27] That being said, Fitzgerald produces a jarring tonal shift by placing "May Day" after "The Camel's Back." Both stories involve parties, miscommunication, and accidental marriages, but the force of one ("May Day") outweighs the farce of the other ("The Camel's Back"). Fitzgerald wanted readers to take "May Day" seriously. Narrative balance, ingenuity, and character development highlight "May Day," which showed readers a writer interested in chronicling his time, even if that writer also sold silly stories about men in camel costumes. Always one to embrace versatility, Fitzgerald directs his readers like the patterns in his introduction and forces them to accept not only the stories of a flapper historian but a serious social historian as well, side by side.

But such a choice also has its drawbacks. The sublime power of "May Day" is immediately flushed by the breezy, ridiculous "Porcelain and Pink." Entirely tongue-in-cheek, the commentary on the story consists of a dialogue between the author and a female reader clearly unhappy with the material in the play as well as with the publication in which it appeared. According to the woman, *The Smart Set* publishes "stuff about girls in blue bathtubs, and silly things like that!"—a nod to the story.[28] Although editors H. L. Mencken and George Jean Nathan would certainly have objected to *The Smart Set* publishing "silly things," Fitzgerald's use of a disgruntled reader attacking the magazine only elevates it. Since both "Porcelain and Pink" and "May Day" were published in *The Smart Set*, Fitzgerald could not help but demonstrate the range of the magazine's offerings, in essence praising Mencken and Nathan for their editorial judgment. Fitzgerald cared about Mencken's opinion throughout his career, and here he appears to tip his cap to one of his earliest champions.

Fitzgerald's section labeled "Fantasies" begins with commentary on "The Diamond as Big as the Ritz," which was "designed utterly for my own amusement" while "in that familiar mood characterized by a perfect craving for luxury."[29] Whether or not the story was created under those circumstances we cannot tell, though it does contain some of Fitzgerald's most telling passages about wealth, and his correspondence with Harold Ober indicates that they had great difficulty in getting what was then titled "The Diamond in the Sky" published. After considering several options (including *McCall's*, *Scribner's Magazine*, and *The Smart Set*), Fitzgerald concluded in a 5 February 1922 letter, "In short I realize I can't get a real good price for the three weeks work that story represents—so I'd much rather get no price but reap the subtle, and nowadays oh-so-valuable dividend that comes from Mencken's good graces."[30] A far cry from being an amusement, the genesis of "Diamond" left Fitzgerald "rather discouraged that a cheap story like The Popular Girl written in one week while the baby was being born brings $1500.00 + a genuinely imaginative thing into which I put three weeks real entheusiasm [sic] like The Diamond in the Sky brings not a thing."[31] Clearly, the realities of Fitzgerald's working habits were subsumed by the persona he wished to project in his commentary. He finishes his comments on "The Diamond as Big as the Ritz" with a disclaimer: "to tamper slightly with Lincoln: If you like this sort of thing, this, possibly, is the sort of thing you'll like."[32] Perhaps readers would bristle at the story's genre, a far cry from the *Post* stories that readers had come to admire; or maybe the story's Western setting was too great a stretch for his urban flappers and philosophers to make. Whatever the reason, Fitzgerald chooses to downplay one of his best stories, and that pose affects the stories and causes one to read "Diamond" with marked caution rather than "entheusiasm."[33]

Bryant Mangum notes that Fitzgerald's experiments with naturalism, fantasy, and what *Metropolitan* magazine called a "realistic gift" influenced his early story writing. With experimentation comes risk, and Fitzgerald's popularity following *This Side of Paradise* allowed him to test "the limits of the popular reading public to see how far he could go without offend-ing them."[34] Although first rejected by *Metropolitan* and later published by *Collier's*, "The Curious Case of Benjamin Button" falls under experi-mentation, and Fitzgerald's commentary offers a slick, roundabout expla-nation for the genesis and clever conceit of the story. He claims that the story was "inspired by a remark of Mark Twain's to the effect that it was a pity that the best part of life came at the beginning and the worst part at the end." He doubts his treatment of Twain's idea, for "By trying the experiment upon only one man in a perfectly normal world I have scarcely given his idea a fair trial." He admits to plagiarizing Samuel Butler's *Notebooks*, which includes "an almost identical plot." Finally, he quotes a letter from an "anonymous admirer," who refers to the story and its author as "the biggest peice [sic]" of cheese he or she has ever read.[35] There are times when a writer knows that a story is what it is: Benjamin Button ages backward; that is the story. Therefore, Fitzgerald credits his influences and quotes an alleged fan rather than analyze or complicate the conceit, for that is all "Benjamin Button" is: the conceit at its core.

"Tarquin of Cheapside" provides a window into the author's early career, as the story, in which Shakespeare commits an actual rape before composing "The Rape of Lucrece" to commemorate it, was originally published in the *Nassau Literary Magazine* in 1917 and revised for *The Smart Set* in 1921. Fitzgerald's commentary on it is historical rather than pedagogical; he accounts for the weakness of the story as "a product of undergraduate days at Princeton."[36] The story acts as filler and, despite Perkins's objections, was included solely because early reviewers "tickled" him and the story with public praise for the first time.[37] However, Fitzgerald claims that his final fantasy, "'O Russet Witch!,'" resulted from a "feeling that there was no ordered scheme to which I must conform" following the drafting of *The Beautiful and Damned*. Telling readers that "none of the characters need be taken seriously,"[38] he accepts a strange defeat, suggesting that the structure, style, and tone of the story may in fact be counter to the tastes of his reading public. Whereas "Tarquin of Cheapside" could be dismissed due to its author's youth and inexperience as a writer, the comments on "'O Russet Witch!'" express confidence and criticism simultaneously. Consequently, Mangum defines it as one of the author's "near-fantasies," a comment largely based on the ambiguous time element within the story;[39] this is the same item about which Fitzgerald concludes in his commentary: "After due consideration, however, I have decided to let it stand as it is, although the reader may find himself somewhat puzzled at the time element."[40] Fitzgerald recognizes, as he did with "Benjamin Button," the inherent flaw of the story—Grainger's aging so rapidly throughout the narrative—and admits it to the reader before the latter has read it. Indeed, part 4 begins, "The years between thirty-five and sixty-five revolve before the passive mind as one unexplained, confusing merry-go-round," following Grainger's "gradual withdrawal from life."[41] Although the story addresses the rapid progression of Grainger's age from part to part, much of it finds the character either in his twenties or his sixties, a forty-year gap Fitzgerald alludes to in his commentary. Grainger's aging can also be read as a metaphor for *Tales of the Jazz Age*, since Fitzgerald felt he required a unifying entity to combat the "unexplained, confusing merry-go-round" that the collection was. A fitting final piece to his fantasies, the story and its commentary relate the intentionality of style and narrative, and how an author's governing voice can make or break a prospective reading.

Going into his final section, he notes that "The Lees of Happiness" "will be accused perhaps of being a mere piece of sentimentality, but, as I saw it, it was a great deal more." He follows his table's well-worn path: he implies a weakness in the story and employs the words of a fake observer to make his point. As in his introductions to "Porcelain and Pink" and "The Curious Case of Benjamin Button," a fictional observer lays out a "Jamesian" paragraph introducing the action, Fitzgerald's play on "stark melodramas," and his tongue-in-cheek reference to one of his early idols, Henry James. This is the core of his authorial pose, the "flapper historian" doubling as critic and hack, as well as professional and natural. While he seems to dote on "Lees," his introductions for "Mr. Icky" and "Jemina" give very little insight, though "Mr. Icky," according to Fitzgerald, "has the distinction of being the only magazine piece ever written in a New York hotel," and "Jemina" follows the technique of Stephen Leacock (the noted Canadian humorist of the early twentieth century), for which he apologizes. The three final tales amount to minor works, though one of the most telling passages of the table of contents concludes the commentary on "Jemina," where Fitzgerald sums up his legacy: "['Jemina'] seems to me worth preserving a few years—at least until the ennui of changing fashions suppresses me, my books, and it together."[42] The final line proves prophetic, as the author diagnoses his future correctly in terms of the decline of his popular appeal. His youthful assertion amplifies the downward turn his career took, even if he felt his popularity would endure. Such a pose highlights the anxiety Fitzgerald exhibited toward critical treatment, even if his table of contents played to a fad (flappers) he helped create. Fitzgerald spends more time denouncing his work in his table of contents then he does praising it, suggesting for readers (and critics) that a more mature writer will come around, a writer that Fitzgerald always knew he would become. What he showed his readers was not really him, but the staying power of that persona overpowered any attempt by him in the decade that followed to embody the image of the mature public writer he really wanted to be.

THE GREAT GATSBY (MODERN LIBRARY, 1934)

Twelve years after the publication of *Tales of the Jazz* Age, Fitzgerald's reputation was in decline, the fashions having changed dramatically in American writing. While not suppressed entirely—he continued to make good money writing short stories for various magazines—the celebrity status brought by his first novel had faded. He had spent nine years on the follow-up to *The Great Gatsby*, and both he and Perkins were hoping for a grand reentry into the literary market with his fourth novel, *Tender Is the Night*. The Modern Library reissue of *Gatsby* was supposed to follow *Tender* as the second part of a one-two punch. As early as 30 April 1932, Fitzgerald insisted to Perkins that a demand existed for his third novel seven years after its original publication:

> *Gatsby* is constantly mentioned among memorable books but the man who asks for it in a store on the basis of such mention does not ask twice. Booksellers do not keep such an item in stock & there is a whole new generation who cannot obtain it. This has been on my mind for two years and I must insist that you give me an answer that doesn't keep me awake nights wondering why it possibly benefited the Scribners to have me represented in such an impersonal short story collection as that of *The Modern Library* by a weak story.[43]

Great Modern Short Stories, edited by Grant Overton and published two years earlier, had included Fitzgerald's "At Your Age," a *Post* story that netted Fitzgerald $4000 in 1929.[44] Most critics regard "At Your Age" as one of the "weakest, most sentimental stories in the canon."[45] Fitzgerald was displeased with its inclusion in a supposedly "great" short story collection because it reinforced the perception that he was a purveyor of "popular" fiction. The fact that the Modern Library had published the Overton collection made all the more pressing the imperative of seeing *Gatsby* reissued under that prestigious imprint.

Perkins agreed with the desire to reissue *Gatsby*. Yet he informed Fitzgerald of the preference of Cerf, who edited the Modern Library, "to wait until another novel had been published, or another book of some kind, which would bring you forward again."[46] Fitzgerald replied respectfully but with marked pessimism: "Thanks about the *Modern Library*. I don't know exactly what I shall do. Five years have rolled away from me and I can't decide exactly who I am, if anyone."[47] When Cerf agreed to the new edition in 1934, Fitzgerald's anxieties about his authorial identity took center stage in the commentary he composed to reintroduce *Gatsby*.

According to Bruccoli, "The published introduction, written after the bitterly disappointing reception of *Tender Is the Night*, provides Fitzgerald's response to the critics of both novels, without mentioning the later one."[48] Indeed, this introduction says more about the critical reception *Tender Is the Night* received than it tries to contextualize *The Great Gatsby* itself for a new readership. Fitzgerald's comments drip with negativity, lamentation, and overt cynicism regarding the profession of literature in the 1930s. Throughout, he refers to contemporary critics as "jackals," cowards, and "dinosaurean"[49]—yet he also holds up H. L. Mencken as the standard-bearer for book reviewing, despite the unacknowledged fact that Mencken panned *Gatsby* as "a glorified anecdote" in the *Baltimore Evening Sun* in 1925.[50] The reason for his respect is that Mencken's opinions exuded "bravery" and "a tremendous and profound love of letters" that some columnists briefly emulated, thereby creating in metropolitan newspapers and magazines a realm for debating aesthetics and educating mass audiences in matters of art. Writers of the 1920s, Fitzgerald insists, "were spoiled in that regard, living in generous days when there was plenty of space on the page for endless ratiocination about fiction."[51]

With the coming of the Great Depression, however, reviewing fiction became less a celebration of "the world of imagination" than worldly matters. Fitzgerald rails against critics whose literary values are forged by their political ideology: "If the present writer had seriously to attend some efforts of political diehards to tell him the values of a métier he has practised since boyhood—well then, babies, you can take this number out and shoot him at dawn."[52] He also insists that one reason *Gatsby* went uncelebrated a decade earlier was because it was not "concerned with farmers (who were the heroes of the moment)." The agrarian theme is a reference to *Samuel Drummond*, a novel by Fitzgerald's former St. Paul friend and protégé Thomas Boyd that Scribner's also published in 1925, and whose merits Fitzgerald had viciously impugned.[53] Writing to Perkins at the time, Fitzgerald lampooned the trend of writing novels about "the simple inarticulate farmer and his hired man" and likened Boyd's novel to "dressing up a few heart throbs in overalls."[54]

In effect, the Modern Library introduction presents the critical neglect of *The Great Gatsby* in 1925 as a foreshadowing of the fate that had befallen contemporary criticism in the 1930s. The growing influence of politics and social issues in literary criticism led to "easy judgment" that "had nothing to do with criticism but was simply an attempt on the part of men who had few chances of self-expression to express themselves."[55] Fitzgerald's language is vague and indicative of the lashing out at imprecise targets that characterizes the disorderly argument of his introduction. Nevertheless, blaming the critical reception of *Gatsby* (and, by implication, *Tender*) on critics ill-trained to appreciate his artistic sensibility leads to a passionate defense of his work:

> Now that this book is being reissued, the author would like to say that never before did one try to keep his artistic conscience as pure as during the ten months put into doing it. Reading it over one can see how it could have been improved—yet without feeling guilty of any discrepancy from the truth, as far as I saw it; truth or rather *equivalent* of the truth, the attempt at honesty of imagination. I had just re-read Conrad's preface [to *The Nigger of the 'Narcissus'*], and I had recently been kidded half hay-wire by critics who felt that my material was such as to preclude all dealing with mature persons in a mature world.[56]

His plea for understanding culminates with the introduction's most vulnerable exclamation: "But, my God! it was my material, and it was all I had to deal with." The assertion then leads to Fitzgerald's main point—namely, that a book should be measured by a writer's aim, not the critic's taste. In an age when reviewers lack "any appreciation of the world of imagination in which they (the writers) have been trying, with greater or lesser success, to live," however, authors are doomed to be misunderstood. As an example par excellence of a victim of such obtuseness, Fitzgerald declares himself his own best critic: "I think [*Gatsby*] is an honest book," he insists, "that is to say, that one used none of one's virtuosity to get an effect, and, to boast again, one soft-pedalled the emotional side to avoid the tears leaking from the socket of the left eye, or the large false face peering around the corner of a character's head." However biased, his opinion is at least more informed than that of a particularly irksome detractor—"a woman, who could hardly have written a coherent letter in English"— who "described [*Gatsby*] as a book that one read only as one goes to the movies around the corner."[57] But one cannot ignore the unconscious reference to his own novel, whereby narrator Nick Carraway assures readers that he is one of the most honest people he has ever known.[58]

Fitzgerald segues abruptly into an odd list of the "intimate explorations" writers confident in their intent will assert to convey their conviction in their vision:

— Look—this is here!
— I saw this under my eyes.
— *This* is the way it was!
— No, it was like this.
"Look! Here is that drop of blood I told you about."
— "Stop everything! Here is the flash of that girl's eyes, here is the reflection that will always come back to me from the memory of her eyes."[59]

At this point, a reader might feel that Fitzgerald has lost control of his introduction. Yet this sequence culminates in a passage that states, explicitly, the main point that reviewers should evaluate fiction according to the author's motivating ambition, not their own: "If [a writer] chooses to find that face again in the non-refracting surface of a washbowl, if one chooses to make the image more obscure with a little sweat, *it should be the business of the critics to recognize the intention*" (emphasis added). Given reviewers' negligence to this obligation, the only consolation prize seems a line Fitzgerald proffers in an earlier paragraph: "If there is a clear conscience, a book can survive—at least in one's feelings about it."[60]

At strategic points in the introduction, Fitzgerald presents his lament in the form of advice to emerging writers. In some passages his "I" slips into the more impersonal "one" to avoid sounding too bitter or self-pitying: "To one who has spent his professional life in the world of fiction the request to 'write an introduction' offers many facets of temptation."[61] In other moments, the formality of "one" gives way to the more direct, instructional "you." Encouraging writers to cultivate "a healthy cynicism toward contemporary reviews," Fitzgerald insists the artist must don "a suit of chain mail" to survive the slings and arrows of uninformed commentary: "Your pride is all you have, and if you let it be tampered with by a man who has a dozen prides to tamper with before lunch, you are promising yourself a lot of disappointments that a hard-boiled professional has learned to spare himself."[62] The introduction's final line makes a direct appeal to the sad young literary man whose pride has been tampered with: "But remember, also, young man: you are not the first person who has ever been alone and alone."[63] Here Fitzgerald almost seems to speak to himself, trying to reassure himself that just because artists who live in the imagination might be misunderstood does not mean that they have to remain isolated. He is long removed from 1922, when he was living at top speed.

Two days after the Modern Library edition of *Gatsby* was published on 13 September 1934, Fitzgerald frantically mailed Bennett Cerf a plea. The introduction's organization was a mess, he wrote, its tone too self-pitying: "I do not like the Preface. Reading it over it seems to have both flipness and incoherence [sic], two qualities which the story that succeeds it manages to avoid."[64] He wanted to cut one paragraph and amend certain sentences, although he does not specify which. Cerf's reply on 17 September suggests he was likewise underwhelmed by the introduction but had no interest in stressing further over it. It was "thoroughly O. K."[65]

Fitzgerald had good reason to worry over the reception of the introduction. In a 20 September column in *The New York Times*, John Chamberlain gently rebuked him for his unfavorable attitude toward reviewers: "There were two really penetrating reviews of 'Tender Is the Night,'" Chamberlain reminded readers, "one by C. Hartley Grattan in *The Modern Monthly*, and one by Malcolm Cowley in *The New Republic*, neither of which was 'cowardly' in its defense of phases of Fitzgerald's work. ... And it seems to me that many critics have been extremely discerning and loyal about 'The Great Gatsby.' Gilbert Seldes is forever talking about it, and there are others who have not been far behind."[66] Cerf mailed a copy of the column to Fitzgerald that very day, perhaps not realizing it would upset him. Soon afterward, Fitzgerald replied: "The preface *is* incoherent. I am not even going to revise it, but simply do it over again."[67] Cerf never gave him the chance. The 6000 copy print run was not selling.

There was one additional insult to the injury Fitzgerald never knew about. For his "thoroughly O. K." preface he was paid a mere $50 (roughly US $1000 in 2021).[68] Three years earlier William Faulkner had received four times that amount (nearly US $4000 in 2021) for a controversial introduction to the Modern Library edition of *Sanctuary*. A year after that, Random House offered to publish a collector's edition of *The Sound and the Fury*, since the novel's original publisher, Cape and Smith, had gone into receivership. Cerf offered $500 (or roughly US $10,000 in 2021) for a new introduction. Momentarily flush with Hollywood money, Faulkner declined. "Why not wait until better times," he replied slyly, "when you can pay me a thousand or fifteen hundred?"[69] Fitzgerald should have been so lucky. Random House made no such offer for *The Great Gatsby*. In 1939, citing poor sales, Cerf discontinued the Modern Library edition of the novel.[70]

TAPS AT REVEILLE (1935)

As Fitzgerald corresponded with Cerf throughout September and October 1934, he simultaneously assembled stories for what would be the last book published in his lifetime, the story collection *Taps at Reveille*. Fretting over the order of the contents and the jacket design, he apologized to Perkins on 20 November: "Excuse me for being so finicky but in the pressure of doing many things at once I am slipping into the old psychology that if I don't do it myself it will be all wrong—a fault that *you*, young man, are inclined to share with me. This Lee biography is shooting me in that direction. Again and again his weakness in trusting others, when he carried only the main scheme in his head, is emphasized."[71] He refers here to Douglas Southall Freeman's biography of Robert E. Lee, equating its depiction of the Confederate general with the thesis of his Modern Library introduction that authors should trust no one but themselves when assessing their work. The truly amateurish dust jacket Scribner's commissioned for *Taps* confirmed his wariness toward relying on others. "I don't know who Miss Doris Spiegal [sic] is," he complained to Perkins, referring to the jacket's artist, "but it's rather discouraging to spend many hours trying to make the creatures in a book charming and then have someone who can't draw as well as Scottie cover five square inches with daubs that make them look like morons."[72]

Despite his dissatisfaction with the published Modern Library introduction, Fitzgerald decided to begin the book with an authorial note. The idea seems to have begun with Perkins, who rather ambivalently suggested the previous June that Fitzgerald should contextualize the stories within reflections on the 1920s: Fitzgerald "could write a short preface which would explain that all the stories dealt with this period. I doubt if this would be right, but I thought I might speak of it."[73] Whether the modest size of the resulting foreword reflects Fitzgerald's restraint or his lack of enthusiasm is uncertain. Regardless, he limited himself to a three-sentence statement:

> Before the last of these stories were written the world that they represented passed. In consequence the reviewer may be tempted to apply the title harshly to the fate of the collection. Yet almost all these stories, the winnowing of fifty odd, meant a great deal to the author at the time of writing: all of them tried for an arduous precision in trying to catch one character or one emotion or one adventure—which is all that one can do in the length of a short story.[74]

The note echoes the Modern Library introduction in several ways, not the least of which is his defensive certainty that reviewers would denounce the volume as outdated and out of touch with the present Great Depression. The antecedent for his core assertion may be a 30 July 1934 letter to Perkins in which Fitzgerald insists that he, Hemingway, and Thomas Wolfe attempted to "recapture the exact feel of a moment in time and space exemplified by people rather than by things—that is, an attempt at what Wordsworth was trying to do rather than what Keats did with such magnificent ease, an attempt at a mature memory of a deep experience."[75] "Arduous precision" and "exact feel" suggest, again, the artist's devotion to what in the Modern Library introduction he calls "the honesty of the imagination,"[76] the clear conscience that comes with not showing off one's stylistic dexterity and expressing an experience so purely that the words recreate the emotion in the reader that the artist felt. The key word in the letter is "mature." Although it does not appear in the foreword, one senses its implications in Fitzgerald's declaration of intent: the stories were meaningful to him as signs of his commitment to craft, the true sign of a mature writer. The showy young apprentice of *Tales of the Jazz Age* has been replaced with the mature, experienced writer, which is neither a pose nor an imagined persona. This is the real F. Scott Fitzgerald.

Two elements undermine this point, though. One concerns genre: the phrase "all that one can do in the length of a short story" seems once more to belittle short fiction and imply that it suffers aesthetic limitations unknown to the novel. The dismissiveness toward the short story likely reflects yet again Fitzgerald's anxiety about being perceived as a writer of commercial fiction rather than as a novelist. Even so, introducing a story collection whose back cover insists one's "fame as a writer rests quite as securely on his short fiction as his novels"[77] with a qualification of said genre seems at best contradictory and at worst self-defeating. More important are the implications of the opening line about "the world" that the stories represent having "passed." The phrase conjures the stereotypical image of Fitzgerald as the nostalgic chronicler of the Roaring Twenties, implying, as the dust jacket makes explicit, the stories "portray various phases of American life from the beginning of the aureate twenties to the bitter end of the age of gold."[78] In fact, the claim is inaccurate. Perhaps Fitzgerald was thinking of the eight Basil and Josephine stories that begin the collection.[79] They are, however, set in the 1910s, although that era would, in 1934–1935, certainly seem remote from a post-crash perspective. Yet the other ten stories in the collection are not nostalgic for the "age of gold." The best of the stories, "Babylon Revisited," *critiques* nostalgia. Like "Babylon," which famously takes place in the post-crash economy, other selections—"Crazy Sunday," "Family in the Wind," and "One Interne"—are either based on incidents from the early 1930s or are set during them. Stories that date back to the 1920s, whether "The Last of the Belles" or "A Short Trip Home," are far cries from "flapper and philosopher" or even "sad young men" tales.[80] Another story, "The Night at Chancellorsville," is a dramatic monologue by a prostitute set during the Civil War, thoroughly unlike any story Fitzgerald had ever written before. What may be the most overlooked selection in the collection, "The Fiend," is a neo-Gothic doppelgänger story about a man's obsession with the killer of his wife and child, akin to something Hawthorne or Poe might have written.

Taps at Reveille is not the fictional equivalent of "Echoes of the Jazz Age" (1931), Fitzgerald's contemporaneous eulogy for the 1920s. *Taps at Reveille* is, rather, a diverse gathering of stories—some better than others, certainly—that highlights its author's underappreciated diversity and proficiency. Fitzgerald's melancholic insistence that they reflect a bygone world seems, rather, an expression of his anxiety that to readers *he* is a relic of that period. Where *Tales of the Jazz Age* suffers from its merry-go-round, hodgepodge, scattershot approach, *Taps at Reveille* serves as a showcase for Fitzgerald's breadth, with a higher number of quality stories filling its pages. Despite this fact, he appears to grasp for the same defense he offered of *Gatsby* in his more recent introduction: the stories are valuable because they "meant a great deal to the author at the time of writing." And what they meant to him was that "in trying to catch one character or one emotion or one adventure"[81] he was pursuing his craft, not reveling in atmosphere, like he had done a decade earlier in *Tales*. This was mature writing from a mature writer.

For better or worse, Fitzgerald decided that his note would not sell a $2.50 book in the middle of the Depression. Though the foreword survived through the second galleys, in December 1934, Fitzgerald asked Perkins to cut it:

> Zelda didn't like it and her taste is usually good in such things and it doesn't read well to me. It has a kind of snappy-snooty sound which I intruded into the preface of Cerf's publication of "The Great Gatsby." If you can, without undue fermentation, arrange this, I think the fortunes of the book will be furthered.[82]

When published three months later in March 1935, *Taps at Reveille* failed to meet critical or commercial expectations. Did the absence of the foreword negatively influence the book's fortunes? Of course not. Although Fitzgerald wanted desperately to reintroduce himself to audiences as a newly refreshed F. Scott Fitzgerald—the "serious novelist"—rather than the unfulfilled Scott Fitzgerald—the "Jazz Age oracle"—his two late-career prefaces find him exposing his insecurities while standing his aesthetic ground. They reveal the anxiety brought on by the vulnerable position every writer experiences when faced with rejection in the marketplace after a brief period of success. In his last letter to Perkins, he added that he had "been doing a lot of ruminating as to what this whole profession is about,"[83] an ironic exercise given his twenty years in the business. As such, his table of contents to *Tales of the Jazz Age*, the introduction to the Modern Library edition of *The Great Gatsby*, and the draft foreword to *Taps at Reveille* enhance our sympathy for the worries all authors feel when they say, "Go, little book! In faith I send thee forth."[84] And even more importantly, they show us what it means to be an author with an uncertain future in a business where certainty does not exist. The significance of the table of contents, the introduction, and the foreword is tied not to sales, but rather to what each piece reveals about F. Scott Fitzgerald and his career; that the profession of authorship, while capable of high water marks and personal triumphs, is equally proficient at scuttling ambition and curtailing artistic promise.

Notes

1. F. Scott Fitzgerald, *The Notebooks of F. Scott Fitzgerald*, ed. Matthew J. Bruccoli (New York: Harcourt Brace Jovanovich/Bruccoli Clark, 1972), 189.
2. Reprinted in Matthew J. Bruccoli, *F. Scott Fitzgerald: A Descriptive Bibliography* (Pittsburgh, PA: University of Pittsburgh Press, 1987), 19.
3. F. Scott Fitzgerald, *This Side of Paradise*, 1920, ed. James L. W. West III (New York: Cambridge University Press, 1996), 19.
4. John Kuehl and Jackson R. Bryer, eds., *Dear Scott/Dear Max: The Fitzgerald-Perkins Correspondence* (New York: Charles Scribner's Sons, 1971), 70.
5. Kuehl and Bryer, *Dear Scott/Dear Max*, 80.
6. See Jackson R. Bryer, *F. Scott Fitzgerald: The Critical Reception* (New York: Burt Franklin, 1978).
7. Matthew J. Bruccoli, ed., *F. Scott Fitzgerald: A Life in Letters*, (New York: Charles Scribner's Sons, 1994), 169. Fitzgerald published eight short stories in 1929 (four of which earned him US $4000, or $63,000 in 2021, per story), netting him $27,000 (roughly US $425,000 in 2021) after the agent's commission. Sales of his published books combined (including *Gatsby*) netted the author $31.77 that same year. See Fitzgerald, *F. Scott Fitzgerald's Ledger: A Facsimile*, ed. Matthew J. Bruccoli (Washington, D.C.: Bruccoli Clark/NCR Microcard, 1973), 65.
8. Sandra Spanier and Miriam B. Mandel, eds., *The Letters of Ernest Hemingway (1929–1932)* (New York: Cambridge University Press, 2017), 94.
9. Gerard Genette, *Paratexts: Thresholds of Interpretation*, 1987, trans. Jane E. Lewin (New York: Cambridge University Press, 1997), 212.
10. Kuehl and Bryer, *Dear Scott/Dear Max*, 59.
11. Genette, *Paratexts*, 224.
12. Kuehl and Bryer, *Dear Scott/Dear Max*, 51.
13. James L. W. West III, "Introduction" to Fitzgerald, *Tales of the Jazz Age*, 1922, ed. James L. W. West III (New York: Cambridge University Press, 2002), xii.
14. F. Scott Fitzgerald, *Tales of the Jazz Age*, 1922, ed. James L. W. West III (New York: Cambridge University Press, 2002), 9.
15. Matthew J. Bruccoli, and Margaret M. Duggan, eds., with the assistance of Susan Walker, *Correspondence of F. Scott Fitzgerald* (New York: Random House, 1980), 116.
16. Kuehl and Bryer, *Dear Scott/Dear Max*, 51.
17. Bruccoli and Duggan, *Correspondence*, 111.
18. F. Scott Fitzgerald, *Tales of the Jazz Age*, 5.

19. Fitzgerald, *Tales of the Jazz Age*, 5.
20. West, in *Tales of the Jazz Age*, 407–498.
21. West, in *Tales of the Jazz Age*, 412–417.
22. Fitzgerald, *Tales of the Jazz Age*, 5.
23. Bryant Mangum, *A Fortune Yet: Money in the Art of F. Scott Fitzgerald's Short Stories* (New York: Garland, 1991), 31.
24. Fitzgerald, *Tales of the Jazz Age*, 6.
25. See West, in *Tales of the Jazz Age*, xvii; Matthew J. Bruccoli, *Some Sort of Epic Grandeur: The Life of F. Scott Fitzgerald*. (2nd rev. ed. Columbia, SC: University of South Carolina Press, 2002), 166; Mangum, *A Fortune Yet*, 45.
26. Kuehl and Bryer, *Dear Scott/Dear Max*, 54.
27. West, in *Tales of the Jazz Age*, xvi, xx.
28. Fitzgerald, *Tales of the Jazz Age*, 6.
29. Fitzgerald, *Tales of the Jazz Age*, 6.
30. Matthew J. Bruccoli, ed., with the assistance of Jennifer McCabe Atkinson, *As Ever, Scott Fitz—: Letters Between F. Scott Fitzgerald and his Literary Agent Harold Ober, 1919–1940* (Philadelphia, PA: Lippincott, 1972), 35–36.
31. Bruccoli, *As Ever, Scott Fitz—*, 36.
32. Fitzgerald, *Tales of the Jazz Age*, 7.
33. Bruccoli, *As Ever, Scott Fitz—*, 36.
34. Mangum, *A Fortune Yet*, 44.
35. Fitzgerald, *Tales of the Jazz Age*, 7.
36. Fitzgerald, *Tales of the Jazz Age*, 7.
37. Kuehl and Bryer, *Dear Scott/Dear Max*, 62.
38. Fitzgerald, *Tales of the Jazz Age*, 7.
39. Mangum, *A Fortune Yet*, 42.
40. Fitzgerald, *Tales of the Jazz Age*, 7–8.
41. Fitzgerald, *Tales of the Jazz Age*, 225.
42. Fitzgerald, *Tales of the Jazz Age*, 8–9.
43. Kuehl and Bryer, *Dear Scott/Dear Max*, 175.
44. Fitzgerald, *Ledger*, 65.
45. For instance, see Mangum, *A Fortune Yet*, 95.
46. Kuehl and Bryer, *Dear Scott/Dear Max*, 175.
47. Kuehl and Bryer, *Dear Scott/Dear Max*, 177.
48. The preface to the Modern Library edition is reprinted in F. Scott Fitzgerald, *The Great Gatsby*, 1925, ed. Matthew J. Bruccoli (New York: Cambridge University Press, 1991), 222–225.
49. Fitzgerald, *The Great Gatsby*, 223.
50. Quoted in Bryer, *The Critical Reception*, 211. Andrew Myers suggests that Fitzgerald paid tribute to Mencken because "in these very days, and nights

[of late summer 1934] Scott was making a nuisance of himself as a frequently unravelled [sic] caller at Mencken's apartment in Baltimore." See
Myers, "'I Am Used to Being Dunned': F. Scott Fitzgerald and the Modern
Library," *Columbia Library Columns* 25 (February 1976): 34.
51. Fitzgerald, *The Great Gatsby*, 222–223.
52. Fitzgerald, *The Great Gatsby*, 223.
53. See Fitzgerald, in Bruccoli, *A Life in Letters*, 120, 127.
54. Kuehl and Bryer, *Dear Scott/Dear Max*, 110–111.
55. Fitzgerald, *The Great Gatsby*, 223.
56. Fitzgerald, *The Great Gatsby*, 224.
57. Fitzgerald, *The Great Gatsby*, 224.
58. Fitzgerald, *The Great Gatsby*, 48.
59. Fitzgerald, *The Great Gatsby*, 224–225.
60. Fitzgerald, *The Great Gatsby*, 224.
61. Fitzgerald, *The Great Gatsby*, 223.
62. Fitzgerald, *The Great Gatsby*, 223.
63. Fitzgerald, *The Great Gatsby*, 225.
64. Fitzgerald, quoted in *The Great Gatsby*, 222.
65. Bennett Cerf, quoted in Myers, "Fitzgerald and the Modern Library," 36.
66. John Chamberlain, "Books of the Times," *The New York Times*, Sept.
    20, 1934.
67. Myers, "Fitzgerald and the Modern Library," 36.
68. All inflation adjustments were made using the Consumer Price Index
    (CPI) Inflation Calculator, provided by the United States Bureau of Labor
    Statistics, https://www.bls.gov/data/inflation_calculator.htm.
69. Joseph Blotner, ed. *Selected Letters of William Faulkner* (New York:
    Random House, 1977), 69.
70. Fitzgerald, *The Great Gatsby*, 222.
71. Kuehl and Bryer, *Dear Scott/Dear Max*, 212.
72. Kuehl and Bryer, *Dear Scott/Dear Max*, 217. Scottie was Fitzgerald's
    daughter.
73. Maxwell E. Perkins, Letter to F. Scott Fitzgerald, 19 June 1934. Archives
    of Charles Scribner's Sons; Box 74, Folder 19. Manuscripts Division,
    Department of Rare Books & Special Collections, Princeton University
    Library, Princeton, NJ.
74. F. Scott Fitzgerald, *Taps at Reveille*, 1935, ed. James L. W. West III (New
    York: Cambridge University Press, 2014), 402.
75. Kuehl and Bryer, *Dear Scott/Dear Max*, 203–204.
76. Fitzgerald, *The Great Gatsby*, 224.
77. Quoted in Mary Jo Tate, *F. Scott Fitzgerald A to Z: The Essential Reference
    to His Life and Work* (New York: Checkmark Books, 1998), 238.
78. Quoted in Tate, *F. Scott Fitzgerald A to Z*, 238.

79. Fitzgerald included only eight of the thirteen total Basil and Josephine stories published by the *Saturday Evening Post* in *Taps at Reveille*. Because the Cambridge edition of the *Basil, Josephine, and Gwen Stories* published the entire group together in 2009—a precedent set by Jackson R. Bryer and John Kuehl's original 1973 collection of them—the 2014 Cambridge *Taps* does not include the eight from the original 1935 Scribner's edition.
80. I refer here to two of Fitzgerald's earlier story collections: *Flappers and Philosophers* (1921) and *All the Sad Young Men* (1926).
81. Fitzgerald, *Taps at Reveille*, 402.
82. Bruccoli and Duggan, *Correspondence*, 396.
83. Kuehl and Bryer, *Dear Scott/Dear Max*, 268.
84. Robert Southey, *The Lay of the Laureate*. In *The Poetical Works of Robert Southey* (Paris: Galignani, 1827), 509–517.

BIBLIOGRAPHY

Blotner, Joseph, ed. *Selected Letters of William Faulkner*. New York: Random House, 1977.

Bruccoli, Matthew J. *F. Scott Fitzgerald: A Descriptive Bibliography*. Pittsburgh, PA: University of Pittsburgh Press, 1987.

———. *Some Sort of Epic Grandeur: The Life of F. Scott Fitzgerald*. 1981. 2nd Revised Edition. Columbia, SC: University of South Carolina Press, 2002.

Bruccoli, Matthew J., ed. *F. Scott Fitzgerald: A Life in Letters*. New York: Simon and Schuster, 1994.

Bruccoli, Matthew J., ed., with the assistance of Jennifer McCabe Atkinson. *As Ever, Scott Fitz—: Letters Between F. Scott Fitzgerald and his Literary Agent Harold Ober, 1919–1940*. Philadelphia, PA: Lippincott, 1972.

Bruccoli, Matthew J., and Margaret M. Duggan, eds., with the assistance of Susan Walker. *Correspondence of F. Scott Fitzgerald*. New York: Random House, 1980.

Bryer, Jackson R. *F. Scott Fitzgerald: The Critical Reception*. New York: Burt Franklin, 1978.

Chamberlain, John. "Books of the Times," *The New York Times* (Sept. 20, 1934).

Fitzgerald, F. Scott. *F. Scott Fitzgerald's Ledger: A Facsimile*. Matthew J. Bruccoli, ed. Washington, D.C.: Bruccoli Clark/NCR Microcard, 1973.

———. *The Great Gatsby*. 1925. Matthew J. Bruccoli, ed. New York: Cambridge University Press, 1991.

———. *The Notebooks of F. Scott Fitzgerald*. Matthew J. Bruccoli, ed. New York: Harcourt Brace Jovanovich/Bruccoli Clark, 1972.

———. *Tales of the Jazz Age*. 1922. James L. W. West III, ed. New York: Cambridge University Press, 2002.

———. *Taps at Reveille*. 1935. James L. W. West III, ed. New York: Cambridge University Press, 2014.

———. *This Side of Paradise*. 1920. James L. W. West III, ed. New York: Cambridge University Press, 1996.

Genette, Gerard. *Paratexts: Thresholds of Interpretation*. 1987. Jane E. Lewin, trans. New York: Cambridge University Press, 1997.

Kuehl, John, and Jackson R. Bryer, eds. *Dear Scott/Dear Max: The Fitzgerald-Perkins Correspondence*. New York: Charles Scribner's Sons, 1971.

Mangum, Bryant. *A Fortune Yet: Money in the Art of F. Scott Fitzgerald's Short Stories*. New York: Garland, 1991.

Myers, Andrew. "'I Am Used to Being Dunned': F. Scott Fitzgerald and the Modern Library," *Columbia Library Columns* 25 (February 1976): 28–39.

Perkins, Maxwell E. Letter to F. Scott Fitzgerald, 19 June 1934. Archives of Charles Scribner's Sons; Box 74, Folder 19. Manuscripts Division, Department of Rare Books & Special Collections, Princeton University Library, Princeton, NJ.

Southey, Robert. *The Lay of the Laureate*. In *The Poetical Works of Robert Southey*. 509–517. Paris: Galignani, 1827.

Spanier, Sandra, and Miriam B. Mandel, eds. *The Letters of Ernest Hemingway (1929–1932)*. New York: Cambridge University Press, 2017.

Tate, Mary Jo. *F. Scott Fitzgerald A to Z: The Essential Reference to His Life and Work*. New York: Checkmark Books, 1998.

CHAPTER 5

The Will to Control: Ernest Hemingway and the Action of Writing

I'm just a God-damned writer.
—Ernest Hemingway to Maxwell Perkins[1]

[Critics] can't tell literature from shit and I have no more illusions on that
score, nor any of fairness, nor any idea but what they want to put you out of
business. Nor will I ever again notice them, mention them, pay any attention
to them, nor read them. Nor will I kiss their asses, make friends with them,
nor truckle to them. Am going to work by myself, for myself and for the long
future as I have always done.
—Ernest Hemingway to Maxwell Perkins[2]

In 1949, Ernest Hemingway was writing *Across the River and Into the Trees* when he agreed to write an introduction to a reprint of an obscure Italian novel, Elio Vittorini's *In Sicily* (originally published in 1941). In his introduction he casts literary critics as dust upon the earth, an "Academic" America/Italy that "periodically attacks all writing like a dust storm and is always, until everything shall be completely dry, dispersed by

Parts of this chapter appeared in different forms originally in "Excuse the Preface: Hemingway's Introductions for Other Writers," Copyright 2015, The Ernest Hemingway Foundation. All Rights Reserved. Originally Published in *The Hemingway Review*. Volume 34, Number 2. I wish to thank the Ernest Hemingway Foundation, as well as editor Suzanne del Gizzo, for permission to reprint portions of that essay in this book.

© The Author(s), under exclusive license to Springer Nature Switzerland AG 2021
R. K. Tangedal, *The Preface*, New Directions in Book History,
https://doi.org/10.1007/978-3-030-85151-4_5

115

rain."[3] He characterizes New York literary reviews (and reviewers) as "dry and sad, inexistent without the water of their benefactors, feeding on the dried manure of schism and the dusty taste of disputed dialectics, their only flowering a desiccated criticism as alive as stuffed birds, and their steady mulch the dehydrated cuds of fellow critics"; opposed to these reviewers are the "good writers," made of "knowledge, experience, wine, bread, oil, salt, vinegar, bed, early mornings, nights, days, the sea, men, women, dogs, beloved motor cars, bicycles, hills and valleys, the appearance and disappearance of trains on straight and curved tracks, love, honor and disobey." These natural elements bring life to the dry country, creating for Hemingway a stimulant which encourages literary growth. He heralds Vittorini for "his ability to bring rain with him when he comes if the earth is dry and that is what you need" and assures readers that "if there is any rhetoric or fancy writing that puts you off at the beginning or the end just ram through it. Remember he wrote the book in 1937 under Fascism and he had to wrap it in a fancy package. It is necessarily wrapped in cellophane to pass the censor." Since Hemingway finds Vittorini's politics "honorable," he rewards the author with a preface that promotes life over death, growth over stagnation, writing over criticism.

Hemingway had critiqued fakery and dishonest writing in his African safari travelogue *Green Hills of Africa* a decade earlier, calling New York writers (and critics) "angleworms in a bottle, trying to derive knowledge and nourishment from their own contact and from the bottle."[4] They suffer from writing "when there is nothing to say or no water in the well."[5] Criticism feeds on art and exerts pressure on authors, and those authors "read the critics and they must write masterpieces. The masterpieces the critics say they wrote. They weren't masterpieces, of course. They were just quite good books. So now they cannot write at all. The critics have made them impotent."[6] Critics render the natural writing process sterile, and given the upcoming publication of *Across the River and Into the Trees* (1950), we can read his introduction to *In Sicily* as preparation for critical reaction. Hemingway's first book of any genre since the bestselling blockbuster *For Whom the Bell Tolls* (1940), *Across the River and Into the Trees* was critically dismissed. The novel was "a parody by the author of his own manner—a parody so biting that it virtually destroys the mixed social and literary legend of Hemingway that has now endured for nearly three decades," Philip Rahv wrote in *Commentary*. "It is greatly to be hoped that in his future work the man recedes and the artist regains control."[7] J. Donald Adams, having surveyed eleven contemporary reviews of the book for *The New York Times*, was saddened "because a great talent has come, whether for now or forever, to such a dead end."[8] Even the positive notices were tempered. Novelist John O'Hara, while not as dismissive as Rahv or Adams, offered the following neutral endorsement: "What matters is that Ernest Hemingway has brought out a new book."[9] We have no way of knowing if Hemingway could forecast the critical drubbing his novel would endure, but we can read the preface to *In Sicily* as a piece on par with his other work critical of literary critics. Rain and growth must win out over dryness and death, his active, natural metaphors populating pages in the face of critics' unnatural, artificial tomes. The organic force of writing combats any critical onslaught, and the rain inevitably comes and nourishes the dry country. In a preface to an out-of-print Italian paperback, America's most famous writer took aim at critics in response to a novel he hadn't released yet.

In his dual role as author and literary celebrity, Ernest Hemingway wrote prefaces throughout his career. As a writers' writer, he often commented on the constraints put upon writers in the literary marketplace. Robert O. Stephens argues that "Hemingway's approach to preface writing was highly personal and at first glance either ignorant of or indifferent to the several conventions comprising the art of the preface."[10] Stephens even developed a formula for Hemingway's prefaces: a citation of the artist's credentials, personal expertness, significance of the work's appearance or inception, struggle with his own status as a man of letters, comments on quality, and finally, positioning the work within an artistic tradition. With his prefaces to specific works, Hemingway produced a deliberately controlled persona that enhanced his authority, granted him greater public exposure, and allowed him to defend his positions on good writers and writing. The preface, one of many "instruments of authorial control,"[11] gave him the space to highlight the action of writing, akin to his letters for *Esquire* in the 1930s. However, his will to control went beyond persona. He cared deeply for writers, whom he favored over the critic. Writing meant action, while critiquing meant passivity; his prefaces reinforce this dictum.

KIKI OF MONTPARNASSE (KIKI, 1929)

Hemingway's prefaces for others demonstrate the author's business acumen, his views on form, style, and criticism, and his willingness to publicly advise other writers. Moreover, the history of these pieces attests to the importance of prefatory material for attracting readers. Jimmie Charters and his editor Morrill Cody insisted that Hemingway's introduction would carry *This Must Be the Place* (1934). In fact, Charters went so far as to write Hemingway that he was "a thousand times more proud of" the introduction than his own book.[12] Similarly, editor Maxwell Perkins asked Hemingway to preface Jerome Bahr's *All Good Americans* (1937), knowing that it was important to have an established persona introduce the book and its author to the reading public. Hemingway had begun manipulating his public writing persona in 1929 following the successful publication of *A Farewell to Arms*, when the author set out to denounce criticism of his work and become the pre-eminent writer of his time. John Raeburn contends that "the critics had made him champion with their early enthusiasm, and by creating a public personality and thereby enlarging his reputation, he was trying to make certain that what the critics had done they could not easily undo."[13] Hemingway's many articles reflect a conscious attempt to defend his positions as an established literary icon of his day and the consummate stylist of contemporary fiction. This effort required careful placement of printed material, both primary and prefatory, throughout the 1930s. Hemingway's articles for *Esquire*, for example, demonstrate his effort to manage his persona, intentionally bolstering the image of Hemingway as "rugged, virile, and self-confident" and "in complete control of himself, capable of the appropriate response in any situation."[14] But Stephens points out that Hemingway also "had to accept the responsibilities of a recognized man of letters," and become "a man of prefaces" as much as a man of letters.[15] During this period, which includes Hemingway's first attempts at preface writing, he became "more renowned for his personality than for his accomplishments, however substantial those might be."[16] While little has been documented concerning the relationship between Hemingway and Kiki, Hemingway's first introduction, which has more to do with his image than with Kiki's text, provides an initial glimpse into the author's use of prefatory materials to create, sustain, and manipulate a public writing persona in tandem with his many dispatches, articles, and fiction.

Published in 1929, *Kiki of Montparnasse* collects the reminiscences of French art model and sometime prostitute Kiki (real name Alice Prin). Known primarily as modernist artist Man Ray's muse and the subject of his *Le Violon d'Ingres* (which depicts a nude Kiki with violin f-holes painted on her naked back), Kiki was a prominent figure in expatriate Paris during the 1920s. Hemingway certainly would have known Kiki, but his introduction to her memoir lacks a clear purpose as he plays with several themes, offering advice on "big writing," "Eras," and "the workers."[17] What emerges clearly is Hemingway's attempt to position himself in relation to writing and popular ideas about artistic work ethic. Early on, he notes the habit of some writers (including Kiki) to enact a specific type of "big writing" and claims that "the essential in big writing is to use words like the West, the East, Civilization, etc., and very often these words do not mean a damned thing but you cannot have big writing without them." Big writing produces hollow "Eras," since "no one knows when they begin, at least not at the time, and the ones that are noted and advertised at the start usually do not stand up very long."[18] Hemingway considers Montparnasse in the 1920s one of these eras. The similarity to Frederic Henry's denunciation of "abstract words such as glory, honor, courage, or hallow"[19] in *A Farewell to Arms* is clear. While Henry is testifying to the gross overuse of "proclamations" in favor of truth in warfare, Hemingway sees fit to establish a similar continuum in his introduction, insisting that "you can write very big putting those words in capitals but it is very liable not to mean anything."[20] At various times throughout his career, Hemingway was prone to reusing material, as many writers did, and many of his introductions take the tone and substance of a concurrent text. Here, the connection to the recently published *A Farewell to Arms* leads readers to establish a comfortable relationship with Hemingway's introduction, a comfort he could cultivate and sustain, and one that reinforced his image as a writer with a discernible style.

Hemingway continues to position himself, while also compensating for the questionable character and reputation of his introduction's subject (Kiki), by focusing on the work ethic of real artists. He defines Kiki's Montparnasse as "the cafes and restaurants where people are seen in public. It does not mean the apartments, studios and hotel rooms where they work in private." Despite the negative tone, Hemingway reminds readers that work often came before the revelry, but it also allows Hemingway to critique artistic culture as he saw it and differentiate between "workers" and "bums."[21] Hemingway had rehearsed this cultural critique seven years prior in his 25 March 1922 *Toronto Star* article "American Bohemians in Paris," in which he described the "loafers expending the energy that an artist puts into his creative work in talking about what they are going to do and condemning the work of all artists who have gained any degree of recognition."[22] Eager to stress the importance of writing and writing faculties, Hemingway offers a distinction between writers and bums:

> In the old days the difference between the workers and those that don't
> work was that the bums could be seen at the cafes in the forenoon. A real
> writer, having finished his work for the day, goes to the café with the lone-
> someness that a writer or painter has after he has worked all day and does
> not want to think about it until the next day but instead see people and talk
> about anything that is not serious and drink a little before supper. And
> maybe during and after supper, too, depending on the individual.[23]

Separating those that create (workers) from those that consume (bums)
characterizes the ironic conclusion of an era which "passed along with the
kidneys of the workers who drank too long with the bums."[24] However,
Hemingway assures us that with Kiki, "we do not have to worry about her
kidneys," and segues back to the book which, at this point, he has spent
little time introducing. Hemingway finally praises Kiki as a woman who
"never had a Room of Her Own, but I think a part of it will remind you,
and some of it will bear comparison with, another book with a woman's
name written by Daniel Defoe."[25] The playful tone and references to
Virginia Woolf and *Moll Flanders* are his concession to the expectation
that he will offer a critical framework; nonetheless, he mostly begs off
since "the people who tell me which books are great lasting works of art
are all out of town so I cannot make an intelligent judgment."[26] Hemingway
is a writer, not a critic, and he likes knowing that critics will read what he
says about them. After all, he is in active pursuit of craft and the work it
takes to achieve it. Although he informs readers that "this is the only book
I have ever written an introduction for and, God help me, the only one I
ever will,"[27] Hemingway would return to the well again and again throughout the 1930s.

GREEN HILLS OF AFRICA (1935)

In many ways, *Green Hills of Africa* was a complex dual experiment for
Hemingway. He wanted to dismiss critics (as he had done with his introduction to *Kiki*), but he still hoped that they would praise his experimentation. His foreword claims to present a "writer" attempting something
new, and *Green Hills of Africa* condenses so much of Hemingway's
authority into a complex text that our understanding of his 1930s persona
relies on its unpacking. In his three-sentence foreword to the American
edition and a short "Dedicatory Letter to Mr. J.P." for the first English
edition, Hemingway prepares his readers for action while challenging his

critics. Robert E. Fleming points out that with *Green Hills*, along with his other books from the decade, "Hemingway seems both concerned and troubled about the possible failures of a writer, potential heresies against the faith that had informed his whole life."[28] *Green Hills*—much like *Death in the Afternoon* (1932)—is as much about writing and authorship as it is about the natural world, and as he wrote Perkins on 30 April 1934: "my idea of a career is never to write a phony line, never fake, never cheat, never be sucked in by the y.m.c.a. movement of the moment, and to give them as much literature in a book as any son of a bitch has ever gotten in the same number of words."[29] Hemingway's prefaces to *Green Hills of Africa* represent the author's wish to comment on reading and critical tastes, a position he would continue to mine in various public pieces for the rest of his life.

Hemingway's shortest and most subtle preface, the foreword to *Green Hills* encapsulates authorial and pedagogical intention simultaneously, which results in clarity of purpose. The foreword reads in its entirety:

> Unlike many novels, none of the characters or incidents in this book is imaginary. Any one not finding sufficient love interest is at liberty, while reading it, to insert whatever love interest he or she may have at the time. The writer has attempted to write an absolutely true book to see whether the shape of a country and the pattern of a month's action can, if truly presented, compete with a work of the imagination.[30]

In terms of function, the foreword reads as a distillation of Wordsworth's "Preface to the *Lyrical Ballads*," which opens: "It was published, as an experiment, which, I hoped, might be of some use to ascertain, how far, by fitting to metrical arrangement a selection of the real language of men in a state of vivid sensation, that sort of pleasure and that quantity of pleasure may be imparted, which a Poet may rationally endeavour to impart."[31] Wordsworth's mixing of real language and vivid sensation pairs with Hemingway's desire to blend true action with the imagination, the latter asking the reader to accept the writer's imparted "quantity of pleasure." Genette argues that a preface that deploys a "contract of fiction" "profess[es] the work's fictiveness."[32] He cites Hemingway's foreword as a "humorously reversed"[33] example of the contract function, since Hemingway goes out of his way to profess the work's *non*fictiveness; it is an "absolutely true book" rather than a work of fiction. But we know better, and Hemingway trains his readers to know better. The first sentence is a play on legal disclaimers, specifically ones found in *A Farewell to Arms* and *In Our Time* (1925, 1930), when Hemingway and Perkins were concerned with libel dating back to *The Sun Also Rises* (1926).[34] His first novel, though critically acclaimed, still received some blowback for Hemingway's apparent reportage. Was he a creator or a chronicler? He wrote Perkins on 17 November 1933: "95 per cent of The Sun Also was pure imagination. I took real people in that one and I controlled what they did—I made it all up."[35] He controlled real people in his fiction, and that will to control became a natural part of his 1930s nonfiction. But even so, his foreword warns readers that this book is not like the others, even if it is "pure imagination."

The second sentence is a veiled crack at his novel writing, for his preceding novels included romantic relationships and were advertised that way. Though *Green Hills* charts a month in Hemingway's marriage to Pauline Pfeiffer, the relationship is secondary to the narrative, which operates on landscape and action rather than romance. He calls instead for readers "while reading" to include some if they wish, a comic aside which forces readers to recognize the author's shift in focus. The final sentence of the foreword outlines the three main tenets of the book: truth, landscape, and action. Hemingway's role as "writer" rather than "author" is important. The act of writing takes precedence over authorial posturing. The word "author" does not appear once in *Green Hills of Africa*, whereas derivations of "writer" appear over forty times. Needless to say, the writer of *Green Hills* takes precedence over the author, a splitting of functions Hemingway had played with in *Death in the Afternoon* three years earlier.[36] By designing his work to "compete with a work of the imagination," Hemingway directs readers to his earlier fiction, works of the imagination that led him to write the book in readers' hands. The competition, centered on creating something from real lived experience that has the ability to strike similar emotional and visceral notes usually found in fiction, represents Hemingway's desire to upend critical neglect. They would read his book, and they would understand what he had done. When Perkins considered publishing pictures with the book Hemingway replied, "I don't think pictures help the book. I make the pictures."[37] The foreword is also similar to Perkins's 30 August 1935 directive to Hemingway, where "All you have to do is follow your own judgment, or instinct, + disregard what is said ... the utterly real thing in writing is the only thing that counts, + the whole racket melts down before it."[38] Perkins wanted Hemingway to complete the book as he saw fit, and he allowed his author to risk his (for the first time) uncertain critical reputation in favor of artistic integrity. The preface is a harbinger for what he expects readers to see. Without the foreword the book, certainly, still achieves its author's goals, but Hemingway wanted more than to achieve his stated claim of a fourth or fifth dimension of writing; he controls how we read the book. If we miss it, that is our misfortune. After all, he told us (and his critics) what to do.

While critiquing Fitzgerald's *Tender Is the Night*, Hemingway noted that "you can make up every word, thought, and action. But you must make them up truly. Not fake them to suit your convenience or to fit some remembered actions. And you must know what things are about."[39] He basically summarizes the idea of honest depiction he intended with *Green Hills of Africa*, even if those depictions were presented to a reading public ill-equipped to recognize their importance (i.e., *Death in the Afternoon*). Hemingway wanted to force the issue, a trend throughout his career. Much of his correspondence leading up to the publication of *Green Hills of Africa* links writing ideology to fiction, in which Hemingway acts out what he had rehearsed with Perkins. These correlations lead to the foreword—a clear evocation of Hemingway's desire for control. The rehearsal is key to understanding Hemingway's text. Writing Perkins on 16 November 1934, Hemingway asserted: "you know why your geniuses stall so long and are afraid to publish may very well be because they have a big fear inside of them that it's phoney instead of being a World Masterpiece and are afraid somebody will find it out."[40] Referring to Thomas Wolfe and F. Scott Fitzgerald, Hemingway calls the title to a recent Wolfe story ("Dark in the Forest, Strange as Time") "the most Christ-awful grandiloquent title of anything I ever read," before referencing his "overassed and underbrained contemporaries, your World Geniuses." He continues, "It's better to write good ones one at a time and let the critics jump on what they don't like and have orgasms about what they do like and you know they're good yourself and write them and get them out and not give a good God-damn about what anybody says." He feels that "the only way you can do that is not to fake and most of the boys, if they don't fake, would be starved to death by Wednesday next."[41]

Hemingway writes something similar in *Green Hills*, when he informs Kandisky that economics and critics destroy American writers: "if they believe the critics when they say they are great then they must believe them when they say they are rotten and they lose confidence."[42] "Others are ruined by the first money," he continues, "the first praise, the first attack, the first time they find they cannot write, or the first time they cannot do anything else, or else they get frightened and join organizations that do their thinking for them."[43] Once Kandisky asks Hemingway about the "damn serious subject," he defines "the kind of writing that can be done. How far prose can be carried if any one is serious enough and has luck. There is a fourth and fifth dimension that can be gotten … it is a prose that has never been written. But it can be written, without tricks and without cheating."[44] He asks readers and critics in his preface to insert a love story if necessary, but action propels his narrative, not the ornamentation of a "masterpiece"; his directive gives readers clear instructions. The attention to the "shape" and "pattern" of the landscape echoes his desire to shape and pattern the book itself. Hemingway wrote Perkins, "there's no feeling, Max, like knowing you can do the old stuff, even though it makes you fairly insufferable at the time to your publisher."[45] "The old stuff" is a reference to Hemingway's "Big Two-Hearted River," the story to which he frequently compared *Green Hills*. Readers will get their money's worth, since Hemingway makes his intentions clear to them, as clear as he had to Kandisky and Perkins.

The complicated experiment that fuels *Green Hills of Africa* generates from the author's foreword, which begins a chain reaction of dual ideas played out amidst a landscape few had experienced. He displays the tools it will take to read his text properly.[46] Though the foreword to the first American edition adds to the duality and establishes a firm (albeit tricky) ground for readers to begin, his "Dedicatory Letter to Mr. J. P." for the first English edition the following year—3 April 1936—complicates matters further. Reynolds notes the negative reviews *Green Hills* received upon its publication. "For a writer desperately wanting his work to be well received," he argues, "Hemingway was almost daring the reviewers to trash *Green Hills*," and "to seek unqualified praise from the very critics his book professed to despise was, he now saw, a game he was bound to lose. No one, it seemed, wanted natural history from a novelist whose last novel was published six years ago."[47] Critical indifference led to Hemingway omitting his initial dedication—"To Philip, to Charles, and to Sully"—and replacing it with a single letter to Mr. J. P.[48] In doing so, Hemingway utilizes the foreword to respond, yet again, to critical standards he fought to defy. Hemingway instructs Mr. J. P.:

> Just tell them you are a fictional character and it is your bad luck to have a writer put such language in your speeches. We all know how prettily the best

brought up people speak but there are always those not quite out of the top drawer who have an 'orrid fear of vulgarity. You will know, too, how to deal with anyone who calls you Pop. Remember *you* weren't written of as Pop. It was all this fictional character. Anyway the book is for you and we miss you very much.[49]

Reynolds reads the new letter as a response to New York critics like John Chamberlain, who felt the book was "spoiled by characters all speaking in Hemingway's pidgin English. ... Could people really speak this way, and would they keep asking the narrator to lecture them?"[50] As usual, Hemingway responded quickly and omitted his foreword in exchange for this letter only months after the American edition appeared. He did not want to explain himself, especially when it came to his writing, and he disapproved of American critics and readers evaluating his work against current popular trends. For example, Granville Hicks, reviewing *Green Hills* for *The New Masses*, felt that Hemingway should "write a novel about a strike ... not because a strike is the only thing worth writing about, but because it would do something to Hemingway. ... If he would just let himself look squarely at the contemporary American scene, he would be bound to grow."[51] Similar to the derision Fitzgerald lobbed at critics pining for more work about the social issues of the day, Hemingway allegedly told his brother, Leicester, that in England "you can write about the non-competitive sports and they'll call it literature if that is what it is. Over here they see the subject matter and say, 'You can't write seriously about stuff like that.' Over here you have to write about strikes or a social uplift movement or they don't even know if you can write."[52] In the face of mounting pressure to "grow," Hemingway instead leaned into his persona, and his book on Africa and big game hunting does exactly what his foreword says it will do. The prefaces for *Green Hills of Africa* show Hemingway developing beyond the young architect of omission into the combative man of letters who fought to protect the storyteller rather than the critic.

All Good Americans (Jerome Bahr, 1937)

Sometime later, Perkins asked Hemingway about new Scribner's author Jerome Bahr's role as a first-time author, especially one who was publishing a short story collection as his first book. Short story collections were rarely best sellers, and Perkins encouraged his writers to begin their careers with a novel rather than a collection. Perkins sees the issue coming: "of course there will be the objection that stories, a first book of them, are almost impossible to sell, but the man has to get started."[53] Hemingway mirrors Perkin's concern in his eventual preface to Bahr's book, as he reminds readers that for a young writer, "the only way you can get a book of stories published now is to have some one with what is called, in the trade, a name write a preface to it."[54] Earlier Hemingway had satirized the idea of being a literary property in "The Sights of Whitehead Street: A Key West Letter" for *Esquire* (April 1935), in which he tells an unnamed visitor, "the name's sort of like a trade-mark."[55] The difficulty of selling short fiction as a first book offers Hemingway to comment publicly on the difficult mechanism of publication. Should a name be offered, Bahr's stories have a better chance at selling. If he were to write a novel first, the name, though helpful, would not be necessary, for novels carried more weight than a collection of short fiction. Given this reality, the book's first edition dust jacket (created by Hemingway's friend Waldo Peirce) prominently featured the words "Introduction by Ernest Hemingway," and in the preface, Hemingway explains that the publication of new authors presents a range of economic issues rarely recognized by the general reading public.

Hemingway's finished preface reads as a microcosm of the publishing industry and his own composition process following the disappointing sales of several works in the mid-1930s. Perkins consistently pushed for Hemingway to produce a novel following the relatively dismal sales of *Death in the Afternoon* (1932), *Winner Take Nothing* (1933), and *Green Hills of Africa* (1935), two nonfiction books and a short story collection. As he wrote the introduction for Bahr's book, Hemingway was continuing work on what would become *To Have and Have Not* (1937), an experimental book which he characterized as "that thing the pricks all love—a novel."[56] Hemingway's dissatisfaction with the publication expectations of a professional author (even one as popular as him) inevitably led to his attitude throughout the Bahr preface, an attitude he had partially rehearsed in his letters for *Esquire*. Although he begins his preface with an admonishment of prefaces ("These stories need no preface"), Hemingway constructs an analytical frame where he gives readers insight into the mechanisms and considerations behind the rough business of publishing, including the need to have a recognized author recommend new work and the dangers of beginning a literary career with a short story collection. After reading and approving Hemingway's preface, Perkins wrote on 18 February 1937: "the preface for Bahr seemed to me excellent,—much better than if it had all been given over to high praise of the stories.—And what you said about them carries conviction. It should be much more effective than a eulogy."[57] The preface relies more on economics than literary praise, a theme set up early on with his preface to *Kiki*. Hemingway's concerns are business in action and professional writing in action. For him, "a novel, even if it fails, is supposed to sell enough copies to pay for putting it out. If it succeeds, the publisher has a property, and when a writer becomes a property he will be humored considerably by those who own the property."[58] Hemingway had given similar literary advice earlier in "Monologue to the Maestro: A High Seas Letter," which appeared in *Esquire* (October 1935): "Most live writers do not exist. Their fame is created by critics who always need a genius of the season, someone they understand completely and feel safe in praising, but when these fabricated geniuses are dead they will not exist."[59] Authors (and their books) are created through compromise and criticism, which tends to swallow up younger writers, as "many natural, good story writers lose their true direction by having to write novels before they are ready to if they want to earn enough at their trade to eat; let alone to marry and have children."[60] Hemingway's cogent distillation of the profession fits into William Charvat's definition of professional authorship some thirty years later, in which professional writing "provides a living for the author, like any other job; that it is a main and prolonged, rather than intermittent or sporadic, resource for the writer."[61] Hemingway shows readers how the sausage gets made, and he adds literary credibility to Jerome Bahr's first crack at being a published writer.

Hemingway knows that a writer will be humored by his publisher "as long as he continues to make them money, and sometimes for a long time afterwards on the chance that he will produce another winner."[62] Hemingway wrote *To Have and Have Not* with the hope that it would rebound his somewhat floundering literary reputation in the mid-1930s, a hope Perkins shared. Author and editor perceived its release as a failure, although Robert W. Trogdon notes that "a sale of over 37,000 copies within seven months was very good for the 1930s."[63] Even so, prior to the release of the novel, Hemingway's relative disillusionment with the process spilled over into his preface. We see this disillusionment in perhaps the most crucial metaphor of the introduction: Hemingway's comparison between publishing and boxing. In particular, he emphasizes the dangers to young fighters developing their skills: "the same system by which young prizefighters are overmatched and destroyed because their managers need the money that the fight, which the fighter does not yet know enough to win, will bring."[64] Comparing the writer to the boxer reinforces Hemingway's action writing mythos and his aversion to literary elitism. At the same time, Hemingway emerges as a practical artist, able to determine the value of art as product rather than celebrating art for art's sake. The system destroys as many writers as it creates, and Hemingway was keenly aware of his role in Bahr's publishing efforts: a creator, not a destroyer. In the end, Hemingway apologizes to Bahr's readers "for the economic necessity of pointing out qualities that would be perceived without any pointing" and asks them to "excuse the preface" altogether.[65] Categorizing his preface as a publishing need rather than a simple act of friendship shows the significance that Hemingway put on understanding the publishing industry and how that industry controlled its literary properties.

THE FIFTH COLUMN AND THE FIRST FORTY-NINE STORIES (1938)

Coming off the middling success of his 1937 novel *To Have and Have Not*,[66] Hemingway sought to publish and produce his first (and only) play, *The Fifth Column*, and put out an omnibus collection of short stories in the fall of 1938. Most of the correspondence between Perkins and Hemingway regarding these projects deals with two major issues: one, should the play be published separately from the stories or as part of the omnibus; and two, in what order should the stories be set for the collection? These questions lingered between the two for most of 1938, with each offering solutions, schemes, and compromises. However, a unifying factor was developed by 12 July, when Hemingway wrote Perkins: "the preface I would write, if you wanted a preface, would naturally be changed by whether the play was produced or not. Can write that in a day or two at the most at any time." He recommended publishing "the play as the first story. Then the forty eight others." He insisted on calling the book "The Fifth Column and the first forty eight short stories of Ernest Hemingway" and concluded: "put them all together and no matter how they damn them nor what happens I won't feel bad because I know that there is the work that I have done, there you can see what I have learned, and all the vitality of dialogue and action is there in the play, and it comes after all that solid body of work." His introduction to the collection would help explain the order in which pieces were written and result in a big book. Known for his shorter and middle-length novels and micro-stories, Hemingway claimed that "I'd like to have a pretty big one for a change."[67] He is concerned with structure and narrative, specifically the risk of packaging his short stories with a new play. If an introduction were necessary, Hemingway would utilize its pedagogical function more so than before. He had to teach his readers how to read his work, something he had rehearsed since the publication of *A Farewell to Arms.*

Always concerned with presenting the process and the place of writing, Hemingway's second letter to Perkins on 12 July lists places alongside certain stories in response to Perkins's communication with early Hemingway bibliographer Louis Cohn.[68] Believing Cohn's chronology "all preposterous" and "simply nonsense," Hemingway gives concrete composition locations for "Fifty Grand," "The Killers," "Today Is Friday," "A Banal Story," "A Canary For One," and "Hills Like White Elephants," before asserting, "so if they are not to be chronological let's have them in the order they were in the books which was always carefully worked out." Hemingway rebuffs Cohn's chronology in favor of his own inner order, both artistically and editorially, yet he usually disliked having to work too hard on story collections, especially ones composed of material he had already written and published. Whether his attitude toward ordering was genuine is up for debate, but his thoughts about the size of the book were real: "I could explain that by saying in introduction that some people complained that last novel was a little short so had decided that there should be plenty of reading matter in this book." Increasingly concerned with the size of his books, Hemingway wanted his book to contain "so much good reading, and so obviously good that you have them on quality and bulk anyway."[69] In fact the sales dummy referenced the "unmatched value" of the book, which contained stories "that thousands of readers will want to have in one book."[70] However, Hemingway finishes with a suggestion: "I could write a modest, straight, and I think interesting introduction about writing the stories and the play. There are some things which are rather impressive if just stated baldly about the play and there are some interesting things about the stories."[71] Within five weeks Hemingway had drafted a preface to his omnibus collection, an essay designed to situate the multiple genres in the collection and clarify the composition of each part.

The preface considers the play and the short stories separately, with his first nine paragraphs focused on *The Fifth Column.* Unlike previous prefaces, Hemingway produces a straightforward piece which chronicles the composition of the play, the difficulty in getting it produced, the significance of the title, and the greater implications of the play's subject matter. The play "was written in the fall and early winter of 1937 while we were expecting an offensive," and Hemingway recounts the shelling of his hotel, for "if it is a good play, perhaps those thirty some shells helped write it." He also alleges to have kept the play "slipped inside the inner fold of a rolled up mattress" while he went to the front. Important are the additions Hemingway made in typescript and galleys once the piece was drafted. A corrected carbon, dated 18 August 1938, features significant additions to the first half of the preface during drafting. Most apparent are Hemingway's added flourishes regarding war and its impact on readers. Paragraph seven—concerning the fates of the captured members of the Fifth Column—informs readers that "later they were to be tried and given prison or labor camp sentences or sentenced to execution depending upon the crimes they had committed against the Republic."[72] He added the following in typescript: "But in the early days they were shot. They deserved to be and expected to be."[73] He would clarify this further in galleys, adding "under the rules of war" to read: "they deserved to be, under the rules of war, and they expected to be."[74] Hammering home the immediacy of violence and judgment relates back to his *in our time* vignettes and *A Farewell to Arms*. The remainder of his changes were equal in weight and similar in structure, with many coming at the ends of various paragraphs to further modify his thematic immediacy. Hemingway wanted his readers to engage in the material as passionately as he had. After confessing that his play did not attempt to show "the nobility and dignity of the cause of the Spanish people," he added in typescript: "It will take many plays and novels to do that, and the best ones will be written after the war is over." Indeed, the publication of his bestselling novel *For Whom the Bell Tolls* two years later—which took as its subject "the nobility and dignity of the cause of the Spanish people"—made true his prophetic assertion that creative work would come from the conflict, especially his own. His final major addition calls directly to readers and critics by indirectly judging their inexperience in the face of his carefully laid out experience: "But if being written under fire makes for defects, it may also give a certain vitality. You who read it will have a better perspective on this than I have."[75] As with the *Green Hills* foreword, Hemingway knows his experience trumps that of his readers and critics, and rather than leave them to their own devices, he offhandedly reminds them of their vacancy in the face of his activity.

His short story section offers a catalogue of place names followed by a critique of his reception in the classroom, a critical move in the narrative of these materials. Before, Hemingway had little to say about the longevity of his fiction, but entering his fortieth year the author recognized the power his name now had in classrooms. He begins adroitly: "about the stories there is not much to say. The first four are the last ones I have written. The others follow in the order in which they were originally published." As he had assured Perkins, his preface would explain the ordering of his stories, but chronology meant little without context. He informs readers that "the first one I wrote was Up in Michigan, written in Paris in 1921. The last was Old Man at the Bridge cabled from Barcelona in April of 1938." He displays his worldliness and activity, cabling his last story from Spain only months before the collection was published. He then offers a list of writing locations and expands his cultured tone by mentioning Madrid; Paris; Key West, Florida; Cooke City, Montana; Kansas City; Chicago; Toronto; and Havana, Cuba.[76] His list speaks directly to his second 12 July letter to Perkins, where he mentions Schruns, Madrid, and Paris as composition locations for his stories. The overt concern with location rebuts his declaration to Perkins that "if you put me on the witness stand I could not tell exactly when each story was written. Nor do I give a good god-damn."[77] In *Green Hills of Africa*, Hemingway wanted readers to *feel* places, as if they had actually been there. Here, he does the opposite. He must prove to readers that he has traveled and worked in many places, and that the work of writing can be authenticated only by listing the places where it was written. The listing of place names in his preface to *The First Forty-Nine* grants him a dual authority: he has traveled to many places, both rough and refined, and like in his pieces for *Esquire* in the 1930s, those places are as much his home as any one location. Yet, he feels at home in those places only when working and writing.[78] He never strayed too far from his active persona, the one that left critics incapable of understanding the experience of real writing. The public Hemingway must associate the act of writing with the place of writing so that his readers (and, begrudgingly, his critics) will recognize the effort, his main concern.

After listing his favorite stories and referencing their usage in classrooms by teachers who "include them in story collections that their pupils have to buy in story courses, and you are always faintly embarrassed to read them and wonder whether you really wrote them or did you maybe hear them somewhere," he singles out "The Light of the World" as a story "which nobody ever liked." From this he concludes that "there are some others too. Because if you did not like them you would not publish them."[79] Throughout this section Hemingway deconstructs the difference between author and writer; this intentionally puts the author Hemingway—the one taught in schools—at odds with the writer Hemingway—the one cabling stories from Spain during a civil war. His dedication to approving his own material in the face of market demands references his somewhat derisive comments[80] regarding authors like Fitzgerald, who "is scared and builds up all sorts of defences like the need for making money with stories etc. all to avoid facing the thing through" and who "has ever had more talent or wasted it more."[81] Hemingway makes certain to elevate his work over his public persona and concludes with an oft-quoted metaphor concerning writing:

> In going where you have to go, and doing what you have to do, and seeing what you have to see, you dull and blunt the instrument you write with. But I would rather have it bent and dulled and know I had to put it on the grindstone again and hammer it into shape and put a whetstone to it, and know that I had something to write about, than to have it bright and shining and nothing to say, or smooth and well-oiled in the closet, but unused.[82]

Here is Hemingway the creator, the sculptor of prose—a pose he performs in service to his fiction. He uses the almost childlike metaphor of putting one's instrument to the grindstone to simplify his process for readers. By publishing the collection near the end of a critically and commercially difficult decade, Hemingway reinforces work ethic and craft. He wants readers to know that he has not stopped working, even in the face of critical disappointment. Selling a play and stories with a long, cumbersome title required something direct from Hemingway, so direct that he concludes: "now it is necessary to get to the grindstone again. I would like to live long enough to write three more novels and twenty-five more stories. I know some pretty good ones."[83] If ever Hemingway pleaded with his public to stay with him regardless of critical reception, this is it. And he plans on returning to the grindstone, the signifier for one who works.

CONTROLLING THE ACTION

Ernest Hemingway exemplifies the writer at work, a popular artist fighting with public persona, critical ebbs and flows, and the threat of authorial extinction. He defended his work and the work of other writers, and he always bet on himself, the one thing he knew he could control. But unlike Fitzgerald, whose rejection permeated his late career, Hemingway was never wholly rejected, neither critically nor popularly. There was always a sense of something more, something new, and important. The 1930s ended with the publication of *For Whom the Bell Tolls*, and 1952 saw the publication of *The Old Man and the Sea*, reigniting the angleworms in bottles who had denounced his work immediately prior to the publication of those books. Though he took every opportunity to impugn the integrity of those who, according to Fitzgerald, tampered with the prides of writers, Hemingway reserved some of his best criticism of the business of literature for his prefaces, which provide one roadmap for how to look at the career of a writer who made his legacy on action and experience, and bringing rain to the dry country.

NOTES

1. 16 November 1934. See Matthew J. Bruccoli and Judith S. Baughman, eds., *The Sons of Maxwell Perkins: Letters of F. Scott Fitzgerald, Ernest Hemingway, Thomas Wolfe, and Their Editor* (Columbia, SC: University of South Carolina Press, 2004), 183.
2. 20 April 1936. See Matthew J. Bruccoli, ed., with the assistance of Robert W. Trogdon, *The Only Thing That Counts: The Ernest Hemingway-Maxwell Perkins Correspondence* (Columbia, SC: University of South Carolina Press, 1996), 243.
3. Ernest Hemingway, "Introduction to *In Sicily*." By Elio Vittorini. 1949. Reprinted in *Hemingway and the Mechanism of Fame*, eds. Matthew J. Bruccoli and Judith S. Baughman (Columbia, SC: University of South Carolina Press, 2006), 102.
4. Ernest Hemingway, *Green Hills of Africa* (New York: Charles Scribner's Sons, 1935), 21.
5. Hemingway, *Green Hills of Africa*, 23.
6. Hemingway, *Green Hills of Africa*, 24.
7. Philip Rahv, "Into, the Trees and Out of Sight," *Commentary*, October 1950, https://www.commentarymagazine.com/articles/philip-rahv/across-the-river-and-into-the-trees-by-ernest-hemingway/.
8. J. Donald Adams, "Speaking of Books," *The New York Times*, September 24, 1950, https://archive.nytimes.com/www.nytimes.com/books/99/07/04/specials/hemingway-speaking.html.
9. John O'Hara, "The Author's Name is Hemingway," *The New York Times*, September 10, 1950, https://archive.nytimes.com/www.nytimes.com/books/99/07/04/specials/hemingway-river.html.

10. Robert O. Stephens, *Hemingway's Nonfiction: The Public Voice* (Chapel Hill, NC: University of North Carolina Press, 1968), 135.
11. Gerard Genette, *Paratexts: Thresholds of Interpretation*. 1987. Trans. Jane E. Lewin (New York: Cambridge University Press, 1997), 221.
12. Jimmie Charters, Letter to Ernest Hemingway, 23 January 1934. Ernest Hemingway Collection. John F. Kennedy Library, Boston, MA.
13. John Raeburn, *Fame Became of Him: Hemingway as Public Writer* (Bloomington, IN: Indiana University Press, 1984), 35.
14. Raeburn, *Fame Became of Him*, 35.
15. Stephens, *Hemingway's Nonfiction*, 13; 135.
16. Stephens, *Hemingway's Nonfiction*, 37.
17. Ernest Hemingway, "Introduction to *Kiki of Montparnasse*." By Kiki (Alice Prin). 1929. Reprinted in *Hemingway and the Mechanism of Fame*, 15.
18. Hemingway, "Introduction to *Kiki of Montparnasse*," 15.
19. Ernest Hemingway, *A Farewell to Arms* (New York: Charles Scribner's Sons, 1929), 184.
20. Hemingway, "Introduction to *Kiki of Montparnasse*," 15.
21. Hemingway, "Introduction to *Kiki of Montparnasse*," 15.
22. Ernest Hemingway, *Dateline Toronto: Hemingway's Complete Dispatches for* The Toronto Star, *1920–1924*, ed. William White (New York: Charles Scribner's Sons, 1985), 115.
23. Hemingway, "Introduction to *Kiki of Montparnasse*," 15–16.
24. Hemingway, "Introduction to *Kiki of Montparnasse*," 16.
25. Hemingway, "Introduction to *Kiki of Montparnasse*," 17.
26. Hemingway, "Introduction to *Kiki of Montparnasse*," 16.
27. Hemingway, "Introduction to *Kiki of Montparnasse*," 17.
28. Robert E. Fleming, *The Face in the Mirror: Hemingway's Writers* (Tuscaloosa, AL: University of Alabama Press, 1994), 67.
29. Bruccoli, *The Only Thing*, 208.
30. Hemingway, *Green Hills of Africa*, vii.
31. William Wordsworth, "Preface to the *Lyrical Ballads*." 1800. Reprinted in *Prefaces and Prologues: To Famous Books*, vol. 39, ed. Charles W. Eliot (New York: P.F. Collier & Son, 1909–1914), 1.
32. Genette, *Paratexts*, 215.
33. Genette, *Paratexts*, 217.
34. Audre Hanneman notes that Hemingway insisted on adding a legal disclaimer to the second American printing of *A Farewell to Arms*, though it ceased to run with the novel after that printing. See Audre Hanneman, *Ernest Hemingway: A Comprehensive Bibliography* (Princeton, NJ: Princeton University Press, 1967), 24.
35. Bruccoli, *The Only Thing*, 203.

36. *Death in the Afternoon* features a long middle section devoted to a dialogue between "Old Lady" and "Author," where Hemingway steps out of his writerly persona in order to characterize and subtly lampoon authority itself. See Hilary K. Justice, *The Bones of the Others: The Hemingway Text from the Lost Manuscripts to the Posthumous Novels* (Kent, OH: Kent State University Press, 2006), 92–118.
37. Ernest Hemingway, Letter to Maxwell Perkins, ca. 14 April 1935. Archives of Charles Scribner's Sons, Box 770, Folder 15; Manuscripts Division, Department of Rare Books and Special Collections, Princeton University Library, Princeton, NJ.
38. Bruccoli, *The Only Thing*, 224.
39. Bruccoli, *The Only Thing*, 209.
40. Bruccoli, *The Only Thing*, 214.
41. Bruccoli, *The Only Thing*, 214.
42. Hemingway, *Green Hills of Africa*, 23.
43. Hemingway, *Green Hills of Africa*, 24.
44. Hemingway, *Green Hills of Africa*, 26–27.
45. Bruccoli, *The Only Thing*, 214.
46. He had done this earlier in the decade with his "Introduction by the Author" to the 1930 reissue of *In Our Time* (which became the story "On the Quai at Smyrna"). See Ross K. Tangedal, "Breaking Forelegs: Hemingway's Early Prefaces," *Hemingway Review* 37, no.1 (2017): 67–84.
47. Michael S. Reynolds, *Hemingway: The 1930s* (New York: W.W. Norton, 1997), 205; 215.
48. Jackson Phillips in the book, based on Philip Percival, the white hunter who accompanied the Hemingways on their safari in 1933.
49. Ernest Hemingway, *Green Hills of Africa*. 1935 (London: Jonathan Cape, 1936), 7.
50. Reynolds, *Hemingway: The 1930s*, 214.
51. Granville Hicks, review of *Green Hills of Africa*, *The New Masses*, xvii (November 19, 1935), 23.
52. Quoted in Leicester Hemingway, *My Brother, Ernest Hemingway* (Cleveland, OH: World Publishing, 1962), 182.
53. Maxwell E. Perkins, Letter to Ernest Hemingway, 9 May 1936. Ernest Hemingway Collection. John F. Kennedy Library, Boston, MA.
54. Ernest Hemingway, "Preface." *All Good Americans*. By Jerome Bahr (New York: Charles Scribner's Sons, 1937), vii.
55. Ernest Hemingway, *By-Line: Ernest Hemingway*, ed. William White (New York: Charles Scribner's Sons, 1967), 195.
56. Bruccoli, *The Only Thing*, 244. Reynolds refers to *To Have and Have Not* as "an ambitious, complicated plan, a *War and Peace* in miniature." See Reynolds, *Hemingway: The 1930s*, 233. Hemingway's preface to *All Good*

Americans reads, partially, as a reaction to complications arising from his own writing.

57. Maxwell E. Perkins, Letter to Ernest Hemingway, 18 Feb 1937. Ernest Hemingway Collection. John F. Kennedy Library, Boston, MA.

58. Hemingway, "Preface," *All Good Americans*, vii.

59. Hemingway, *By-Line*, 218.

60. Hemingway, "Preface," *All Good Americans*, vii.

61. William Charvat, *The Profession of Authorship in America, 1800–1870*, ed. Matthew J. Bruccoli (New York: Columbia University Press, 1992), 3.

62. Hemingway, "Preface," *All Good Americans*, vii.

63. Robert W. Trogdon, *The Lousy Racket: Hemingway, Scribners and the Business of Literature* (Kent, OH: Kent State University Press, 2007), 185.

64. Hemingway, "Preface," *All Good Americans*, viii.

65. Hemingway, "Preface," *All Good Americans*, viii.

66. Unlike his earlier books of the decade, the novel sold well—over 37,000 copies, compared to 11,592 for *Green Hills*, 18,300 for *Winner Take Nothing*, 20,780 for *Death in the Afternoon*, and 4275 for the Scribner's *In Our Time*. See Trogdon, *Lousy Racket*.

67. Bruccoli, *The Only Thing*, 261–262.

68. Known as "Captain" Cohn for his service in the French Foreign Legion during WWI, he published *A Bibliography of the Works of Ernest Hemingway* (New York: Random House, 1931).

69. Bruccoli, *The Only Thing*, 263–264.

70. Reprinted in Trogdon, *Lousy Racket*, 195.

71. Bruccoli, *The Only Thing*, 264.

72. Ernest Hemingway, *The Fifth Column and the First Forty-Nine Stories* (New York: Charles Scribner's Sons, 1938), v–vi.

73. Ernest Hemingway, "Preface to *The Fifth Column and the First Forty-Nine Stories*." Corrected Carbon. Item 82B. 3pp. Ernest Hemingway Collection. John F. Kennedy Library, Boston, MA, 2.

74. Hemingway, *First Forty-Nine*, vi.

75. Hemingway, *First Forty-Nine*, vi.

76. Hemingway, *First Forty-Nine*, vi–vii.

77. Bruccoli, *The Only Thing*, 263.

78. Verna Kale contends that Hemingway's push and pull between parochial (a hard-working writer that can be appreciated by all kinds of readers) and cosmopolitan (well-traveled and cultured) personae comes through most effectively in his nonfiction. In *Death in the Afternoon*, he adopts "a self-consciously parochial understanding of the bullfighting practice," which for Kale is "the ultimate cosmopolitan turn as Hemingway presented himself as a well-travelled citizen of the world." Likewise, in his *Esquire* pieces and *Green Hills of Africa*, Hemingway "experienced the adventures that

the world had to offer and wrote about them ... so that his readers could glean this insider knowledge from the comfort of their own armchairs." A similar effect takes place in the preface to *The First Forty-Nine*, a well-worn traveler keying readers in to the generation of his work by telling them where he has been, and where the work was done. See Verna Kale, *Ernest Hemingway* (London: Reaktion Books, 2016), 86; 98.

79. Hemingway, *First Forty-Nine*, vii.
80. See the following letters in Bruccoli, *The Only Thing*: Hemingway to Perkins, 21 April 1928; Hemingway to Perkins, 11 October 1928.
81. Bruccoli, *The Only Thing*, 71; 82. Fitzgerald wrote many stories purely for profit, a point Hemingway disliked. However, Bruccoli notes that Fitzgerald disparaged his commercial work as much as Hemingway did. See Matthew J. Bruccoli, *Fitzgerald and Hemingway: A Dangerous Friendship* (Columbia, SC: Manly, Inc., 1999), 92.
82. Hemingway, *First Forty-Nine*, vii. Hemingway played with a similar idea in *Death in the Afternoon*: "Our bodies all wear out in some way and we die, and I would rather have a palate that will give me the pleasure of enjoying completely the Chateaux Margaux or a Haut Brion, even though excesses indulged in in the acquiring of it has brought a liver that will not allow me to drink Richebourg, Corton, or Chambertin, than to have the corrugated iron internals of my boyhood when all red wines were bitter except port and drinking was the process of getting down enough of anything to make you feel reckless." See Ernest Hemingway, *Death in the Afternoon* (New York: Charles Scribner's Sons, 1932), 11.
83. Hemingway, *First Forty-Nine*, vii.

BIBLIOGRAPHY

Adams, J. Donald. "Speaking of Books." *The New York Times*, September 24, 1950. https://archive.nytimes.com/www.nytimes.com/books/99/07/04/specials/hemingway-speaking.html.

Bruccoli, Matthew J. *Fitzgerald and Hemingway: A Dangerous Friendship.* Columbia, SC: Manly, Inc., 1999.

Bruccoli, Matthew J., and Judith S. Baughman, eds. *The Sons of Maxwell Perkins: Letters of F. Scott Fitzgerald, Ernest Hemingway, Thomas Wolfe, and Their Editor.* Columbia, SC: University of South Carolina Press, 2004.

Bruccoli, Matthew J., ed., with the assistance of Robert W. Trogdon. *The Only Thing That Counts: The Ernest Hemingway-Maxwell Perkins Correspondence.* Columbia, SC: University of South Carolina Press, 1996.

Charters, Jimmie. Letter to Ernest Hemingway, 23 January 1934. Ernest Hemingway Collection. John F. Kennedy Library, Boston, MA.

Charvat, William. *The Profession of Authorship in America, 1800–1870.* 1968, edited by Matthew J. Bruccoli. New York: Columbia University Press, 1992.

Fleming, Robert E. *The Face in the Mirror: Hemingway's Writers.* Tuscaloosa, AL: University of Alabama Press, 1994.

Genette, Gerard. *Paratexts: Thresholds of Interpretation.* 1987. Jane E. Lewin, trans. New York: Cambridge University Press, 1997.

Hanneman, Audre. *Ernest Hemingway: A Comprehensive Bibliography.* Princeton, NJ: Princeton University Press, 1967.

Hemingway, Ernest. *By-Line: Ernest Hemingway,* edited by William White. New York: Charles Scribner's Sons, 1967.

———. *Dateline Toronto: Hemingway's Complete Dispatches for* The Toronto Star, *1920–1924,* edited by William White. New York: Charles Scribner's Sons, 1985.

———. *Death in the Afternoon.* New York: Charles Scribner's Sons, 1932.

———. *A Farewell to Arms.* New York: Charles Scribner's Sons, 1929.

———. *The Fifth Column and the First Forty-Nine Stories.* New York: Charles Scribner's Sons, 1938.

———. *Green Hills of Africa.* New York: Charles Scribner's Sons, 1935.

———. *Green Hills of Africa.* 1935. London: Jonathan Cape, 1936.

———. "Introduction to *In Sicily.*" By Elio Vittorini. 1949. Reprinted in *Hemingway and the Mechanism of Fame,* edited by Matthew J. Bruccoli and Judith S. Baughman, 102–103. Columbia, SC: University of South Carolina Press, 2006.

———. "Introduction to *Kiki of Montparnasse.*" By Kiki (Alice Prin). 1929. Reprinted in *Hemingway and the Mechanism of Fame,* edited by Matthew J. Bruccoli and Judith S. Baughman, 14–16. Columbia, SC: University of South Carolina Press, 2006.

———. Letter to Maxwell Perkins, ca. 14 April 1935. Archives of Charles Scribner's Sons, Box 770, Folder 15; Manuscripts Division, Department of Rare Books and Special Collections, Princeton University Library, Princeton, NJ.

———. "Preface." *All Good Americans.* By Jerome Bahr. vii–viii. New York: Charles Scribner's Sons, 1937.

———. "Preface to *The Fifth Column and the First Forty-Nine Stories.*" Corrected Carbon. Item 82B. 3pp. Ernest Hemingway Collection. John F. Kennedy Library, Boston, MA.

Hemingway, Leicester. *My Brother, Ernest Hemingway.* Cleveland, OH: World Publishing, 1962.

Justice, Hilary K. *The Bones of the Others: The Hemingway Text from the Lost Manuscripts to the Posthumous Novels.* Kent, OH: Kent State University Press, 2006.

Kale, Verna. *Ernest Hemingway.* London: Reaktion Books, 2016.

O'Hara, John. "The Author's Name is Hemingway." *The New York Times*, September 10, 1950. https://archive.nytimes.com/www.nytimes.com/books/99/07/04/specials/hemingway-river.html.

Perkins, Maxwell E. Letter to Ernest Hemingway, 9 May 1936. Ernest Hemingway Collection. John F. Kennedy Library, Boston, MA.

———. Letter to Ernest Hemingway, 18 Feb 1937. Ernest Hemingway Collection. John F. Kennedy Library, Boston, MA.

Raeburn, John. *Fame Became of Him: Hemingway as Public Writer.* Bloomington, IN: Indiana University Press, 1984.

Rahv, Philip. "Into, the Trees and Out of Sight." *Commentary*, October 1950. https://www.commentarymagazine.com/articles/philip-rahv/across-the-river-and-into-the-trees-by-ernest-hemingway/.

Reynolds, Michael S. *Hemingway: The 1930s.* New York: W. W. Norton, 1997.

Tangedal, Ross K. "Breaking Forelegs: Hemingway's Early Prefaces," *Hemingway Review* 37, no.1 (2017): 67–84.

Trogdon, Robert W. *The Lousy Racket: Hemingway, Scribners and the Business of Literature.* Kent, OH: Kent State University Press, 2007.

Stephens, Robert O. *Hemingway's Nonfiction: The Public Voice.* Chapel Hill, NC: University of North Carolina Press, 1968.

Wordsworth, William. "Preface to the *Lyrical Ballads.*" 1800. Reprinted in *Prefaces and Prologues: To Famous Books*, vol. 39, edited by Charles W. Eliot. 1–14. New York: P.F. Collier & Son, 1909–1914.

CHAPTER 6

A Safe Distance: Robert Penn Warren's Introductions to *All the King's Men*

Historical sense and poetic sense should not, in the end, be contradictory, for if poetry is the little myth we make, history is the big myth we live, and in our living, constantly remake.
—Robert Penn Warren, *Brother to Dragons*[1]

Writers, generally, are afforded the opportunity to write about their work at some point in their careers, depending upon longevity and access to readers. Due to the prevalence of reprint editions in trade, mass market, and prestige formats, writers in the twentieth century witnessed a boom in making their personal meditations on writing, craft, memory, history, and so on, readily available to the public. Chapter 1 of this study highlights the development of several reprint options for writers, including the Book-of-the-Month Club, the Modern Library, and various trade editions. Few writers took advantage of the opportunities that reprint editions provided as assiduously as Robert Penn Warren. From the time that his novel, *All the King's Men* (1946), was published, up to the time of his death in 1989, Warren wrote five published introductions to the novel, four for American editions and one for an English edition. The count does not include a number of notes and other essays written for the play upon which the novel was based, *Proud Flesh*, or other translations, which Warren supplied at various points throughout his career. The novel won the Pulitzer Prize in 1947, catapulting Warren, who was then known primarily as a poet and co-founder (with Cleanth Brooks) of the "New Criticism" school of

141

R. K. Tangedal, *The Preface*, New Directions in Book History, https://doi.org/10.1007/978-3-030-85151-4_6

literary theory, to more widespread fame. For Warren, the novel was "one of the three I have to rest my case on, feel closest to," and offered him the chance to "eke out a living without teaching."[2] More importantly, the success of the novel stretched over several decades due to Warren's treatment of politics and the American character, resulting in several reprint editions; four of these American editions featured an introduction by Warren: the Modern Library (1953), Time, Inc. (1963), The Franklin Library (1977), and a Book-of-the-Month Club trade edition published concurrently with Harcourt Brace Jovanovich (1981).

The pieces live on in various incarnations—Warren's introduction for the Modern Library appeared first as "A Note on *All the King's Men*" in the *Sewanee Review* (Summer 1953); a revised version of the introduction to the Time, Inc. edition appeared simultaneously in *The Yale Review* (December 1963); and an adaptation of the introduction for the Book-of-the-Month Club edition appeared first in *The New York Times* as "In the Time of 'All the King's Men'" (31 May 1981). Warren wrote regularly about what he knew, and he knew his novel and its impact. "The great thing is to last and get your work done and see and hear and learn and understand," wrote Ernest Hemingway in *Death in the Afternoon* (1932), "and write when there is something that you know; and not before; and not too damned much after." Warren's longevity allowed for the continual reappraisal of his most celebrated novel, an activity of mind as much as it was an activity of economic gain. Hemingway concluded that "the thing to do is work and learn to make it,"[3] and Warren did both, thanks in large part to *All the King's Men*. The introductions are examples of a writer working through particular challenges, mainly how and why his novel was received the way it was, and what that reception meant for him. But they also feature histories—of composition, of intention, of character, of history—that inform the life of the novel. When asked to give advice to young writers, Warren insisted that "if he's honest and he works, advice is beside the point. He'll merely do what he must do, and that is everything."[4] The introductions reflect Warren's ethos, a combination of writer, poet, historian, teacher, and critic, yet figuring how to position them within his canon proves complicated.

While Warren displays the tools necessary to maintain a literary career *and* sustain a public for his book, he also compounds layers of meaning and storytelling with each introduction. His introductions become a genre of storytelling in and of themselves, and since so few writers wrote multiple introductions for a single work, Warren charts new territory. What would it mean for a writer to reassess one of their celebrated books every ten years and append an introduction to a new edition of that book? Prefaces that come later in a career, according to Gerard Genette, tend to project how "an author's tastes or ideas evolve—indeed, undergo a sudden conversion. More generally, a middle-aged or elderly writer, when the time has come to compile his Complete Works, sees a delayed preface as an opportunity to express his thoughts, at a safe distance, about some past work."[5] Yet, for Warren, he is not treating readers to introductions of his Complete Works. Only *All the King's Men* gets revisited, reassessed, and reborn this often, brought anew to readers in what appear to be particularly political times: 1953 (Dwight Eisenhower elected President); 1963 (John F. Kennedy's Camelot and his eventual assassination); 1977 (the aftermath of Richard Nixon and Watergate); 1981 (Jimmy Carter's "crisis of confidence"[6] and the election of Ronald Reagan). For a book that deals in power and politics, there is always a season for it, at least every four years or so. Yet the remarkable fact about the introductions is Warren's consistency. There are no sudden conversions or changes of heart, only the evolving resolve of an author's convictions. A new introduction builds on a previous one, and so on, until we are left with twenty-eight years' worth of story. In each introduction, Warren describes how and why he wrote the novel, and who and what inspired specific characters and scenes. There are conversations on front porches in Baton Rouge, days writing under olive trees and next to wheat fields in Italy, a library attic at the University of Minnesota, the composition of the verse play *Proud Flesh*, the invention of narrator Jack Burden, the rise of Fascism in Europe, the character of Talus from Edmund Spenser's *Faerie Queen*, and the complex of power and those who wield it.

His introductions also address the influence of Huey P. Long, populist Governor (1928–1932) and US Senator (1932–1935) from Louisiana, on Willie Stark, the fictional populist governor in the novel. Warren's view of Long and Stark (and earlier, Talos) forms the kind of interpretive exercise that Genette argues can only happen "at a safe distance"[7] from the original text, and Warren takes the many opportunities afforded him and his book to reflect on the intentions and integrity of story, myth, and history. Keith Perry, in his book-length study of Huey P. Long in American fiction, argues that Warren "creates a Huey Long figure more interested in the philosophical relationship between ends and means than illustrative of any particular political or social point of view."[8] Yet the "Hueys-who-aren't-Hueys"[9] that Perry investigates are "disguised composites who often live the life of Huey Long but, because of their creators' unique personal and political perspectives, also live lives unquestionably their own."[10] Though Robert H. Chambers refers to the novel as "one of American fiction's best examples of the making of art from the distortion of history,"[11] Warren spends a considerable amount of space dealing with what the editor of the Time, Inc. edition of the novel called "the 'Huey Long' side of the story,"[12] and in doing so, he shows readers what it takes to work with fiction and fact, even when the journalistic fact is sometimes more striking than the fiction. If read independently, each introduction does a utilitarian service to its narrative proper, providing a brief account of genesis and composition and relating the novel to its public reception. However, if read as a series, we begin to recognize Warren's pursuit, to maintain control of the text not to punish or impugn readers but to teach readers about story. His aim was not to distort history but to impart it with the fictional elements of story to create a human narrative about power, and what others do for it and because of it. "That's what makes power," he told Tom Vitale in 1985. "It's not being strong; it's knowing instinctively how to use other people, without thinking about it."[13] By denying Long's direct influence on Willie Stark, Warren elevates the nature of Long's influence and prolongs the life of his novel. In another denial of Long as Stark's immediate model, Warren told Frank Gado in 1966, "I know when water runs downhill; and if a bomb explodes, I know that someone lit the fuse. Events don't cause themselves. I saw the end products of Long and I know that men's motives and actions are triggered and operate in certain ways."[14] For Warren, Long was part of the long history of power, and his introductions attempt to frame the novel as more than a reportorial account of politics in Louisiana during the Great Depression. "Things don't come as clear options—" he told Gado, "rather, as aspects of a single complex process."[15] In the four introductions he wrote for American reprint editions[16] of *All the King's Men*, Robert Penn Warren provides the framework for how to write an effective introduction to a celebrated book—by highlighting the writer's responsibility to suggest rather than identify[17] and to make a story from the "'thinking and feeling'" of fact;[18] how origins, "in their infinite complexity, have no beginning; they are ultimately part of an ongoing process,"[19] and how "the drama of history" is "the old drama of power and ethics."[20] Genette estimates that "because a work's second edition (and, for that matter, each of its subsequent editions) addresses new readers, nothing prevents the author from adding to that second or subsequent edition a preface that is 'later' in date but 'original' for these new readers, to whom the author would tell the tale that, for one reason or another, he had originally thought could be dispensed with."[21] Warren told the tale of *All the King's Men*, and he told it consistently for nearly thirty years in introductions to new editions with different publishers, always at a safe distance with each opportunity.

Though he wrote William T. Bandy late in life that writing prefaces was "a job I abhor,"[22] Warren certainly produced a fair amount of them during his career, with *All the King's Men* receiving frequent treatment. The Modern Library reissue was in print from 1953 to 1971, with seventeen printings totaling 41,900 copies,[23] a strong sale for a reprint series. Given how other authors in the series were compensated, Warren would have received a flat fee for his introduction.[24] The Time, Inc. edition, produced in 1963 for members of the Time Reading Program, had gone through five printings totaling 155,000 copies by 1969.[25] Warren referred to the essay as "mandatory," though he expressed satisfaction after he "got into it" once he moved past the "so long ago, etc."[26] The Franklin Library first released a new edition without an introduction from Warren in 1976, but only a year later they released a signed edition featuring "A special message to subscribers from Robert Penn Warren." While sales information is not available, one can assume that the success of the first Franklin Library edition necessitated the second, a prestige volume sold for $39.00 per copy.[27] Several of Warren's letters from the latter half of 1976 reference the Franklin Mint, with its "vulgar"[28] and "extra flossy extra special editions"[29] that came with a "a very hefty advance."[30] He claimed to have told Random House editorial director Albert Erskine that "at the price I could stand any amount" of vulgarity,[31] and by 1977 he was asked to "do 20,000 to 25,000 signed sheets for an autographed edition of AKM, due out in spring, very deluxe, subscribed, etc."[32] He would make $2.00 per sheet for the first 20,000 and $3.00 per sheet thereafter, plus a royalty split.[33] "Lordie," he wrote Katherine Anne Porter, "what a man will do for money, but this is a lot and I can always use a lot."[34] If Warren's numbers are accurate, he would have made between $40,000 and $55,000 on the signed sheets alone (or between US $174,000 and $239,000 in 2021).[35] Finally, the 1981 Book-of-the-Month Club 35th-anniversary edition, released concurrently with a trade edition by Harcourt Brace Jovanovich, both featuring Warren's introduction, gave the novel another new life, after years of new lives. "Wallowing in recollections, trying to recover a lot of things that flowed into the making,"[36] Warren drafted what became his longest introduction to *All the King's Men*. He did what he termed "a vile thing" by sending Cleanth Brooks a draft of the introduction. "I had sort of written myself out on the subject, long back," he told Brooks. "But here is my try. I undertook to relate how certain things flowed into the background of the writing, this in a running sketch of Louisiana. ... I've depended on memory about Louisiana."[37] Warren's introductions are as much "tales" as they are documentary essays, exposing and revealing while also scaffolding and questioning. To get at Warren's introductions, I focus on his treatment of origins (both of the novel and of origins themselves), followed by a survey of Warren's "Huey," whose treatment drives, to a great extent, the success and staying power of the novel. "It is never too late to inform a new public,"[38] Genette notes, and Warren bridges the "many factors, and facts" that "flow strangely together"[39] as he remembers his book in and out of four decades.

Origins

Warren and his first wife Emma "Cinina" Brescia sailed to Italy in July 1939. He had received a Guggenheim Fellowship earlier in the year, making a stipend of $2250 along with a sabbatical leave from Louisiana State University, from which he earned a stipend of $2300.[40] The funds would give Warren the chance to write, and he began expanding a verse play that would eventually be called *Proud Flesh*, about a strong-willed governor who becomes corrupted by power. Biographer Joseph Blotner recounts the dangerous period immediately prior to World War II, when Warren and his wife "lived with uncertainty and anxiety" in Sirmione, "where the fall winds carried the tumble of artillery practice down from the lake."[41] Warren wrote Frank Owlsey on 11 November 1939 that the "radio began to give us bad dreams. For two or three weeks we had a very bad time ... we just sat quietly, and listened to the radio broadcasts, and occasionally had a moral collapse." "If things blacken up," he noted, "or if the Mediterranean is declared a war zone by the U.S. Congress, we'll just do the best we can."[42] He wrote author Katherine Ann Porter the same day, telling her, "As for our doings, there isn't a great deal to say. We stayed in Sirmione until the weather turned off on us—and had a lovely time of [it] there except when the radio gave us a turn, as it did almost daily. ... God help us to remain for some time to come, for if we do have to come back we haven't anyplace to go, and with the steamer fares so high now we would be painfully broke, for the war has played hell with our budget."[43] Two days later he wrote Brainard Cheney a similar letter: "As for the situation, we may be complete idiots. But it is possible that the situation looks more generally black from that distance than it does here. ... Sirmione is really a wonderful place; our hotel-pensione is a little place out in the country, on the peninsula, in an olive grove overlooking the lake, a wonderful place to work; but we spent a lot of our time gnawing our nails and waiting for the next broadcast."[44] Warren's narrative of struggle mounts with each letter, a struggle to maintain economic stability and a schedule for writing amidst the backdrop of impending war. Further letters outline the work he was doing, again connected to the threat of upheaval at any point. "Work is moving beautifully now," he wrote Porter on 12 December from Rome, "and if we have to be uprooted, it may be weeks, or months, before a routine can again be established."[45] Two days later he wrote friend Allen Tate, "Despite the alarums and excursions—and the fact that I can't get to work of a morning until I've gone out for the paper—I have managed to get a lot done. What it's like, I simply don't know. One day I feel pretty good about it, and the next I want to dump the whole thing in the Tiber."[46] Yet on 7 March 1940 he wrote Paul M. Hebert, then acting President of Louisiana State University, "The winter here has been very pleasant except for the vile weather and influenza and the newspapers. I have managed to go on pretty consistently with the work I have on hand. This is not exactly the year I would have chosen to be here, but in some respects the special circumstances are proving a good deal more instructive than those of more normal and happy times."[47] Taken together, Warren's letters preview how he created the origin story of *All the King's Men*, which began in Italy as much as it did in America, and which featured the more immediate shades of European war and fascism alongside those of the Great Depression.

Blotner reprints a note that Warren included at the outset of the manuscript for *Proud Flesh*: "Just as both realistic and non-realistic elements appear in the style of the play—prose at the level of fact and circumstance, verse at the level of interpretation and dramatic intensity—so the staging involves realistic and non-realistic elements."[48] As a metaphor for composition and artistic intention, and for movement between genres that David Madden calls Warren's "natural flow of creative energy,"[49] the note foreshadows Warren's decision to turn the project into a novel, though his poetic sensibility remained a critical component of the work. In the early days in Italy, he was writing a verse play, a heady mixture of fact and fiction with choruses of policemen and construction workers introducing the actions of Governor Strong, "a man who has the talent for gaining power and has never asked himself the question as to its meaning."[50] Blotner contends that Warren may have chosen drama (even one as poetic as the verse play) "in part for the promise of larger and quicker rewards than novels normally brought," but also to challenge himself by "trying his hand at this genre he had studied and taught for so long."[51] The social dramas of Robert E. Sherwood and Clifford Odets had garnered praise and success on the American stage, and though Warren may have felt the pull to do the same, the material eventually called for a different treatment. But in this early period are the beginnings, the initial stirrings, the origins that good stories, and stories about stories, come from.

In his introduction to the Modern Library edition (1953), Warren recalls getting "the notion of a verse play about a Southern politician who achieved the power of a dictator, at least in his home state, and who was assassinated in the Capitol which had been the scene of his triumphs. As well as I can recall, the notion began to take on some shape when, sitting one afternoon on the porch of a friend's cottage, I began to describe my intentions."[52] The first parts were written in Baton Rouge in the winter of 1937–1938, since Warren was teaching at Louisiana State University, followed by a trip to Italy in summer of 1938, where he "got a little more done, beginning the process … in the late afternoon, in a wheat field outside of Perugia." The rest was written back in Louisiana, "with a bit done after classes and on week-ends," he recounts, "but the bulk of the play was written in Rome, in the fall and winter of 1939, with the news of the war filling the papers and the boot heels of Mussolini's legionaries clanging on the stones."[53] Warren's marriage of war and writing suggests a more expansive narrative, one beyond the borders of Louisiana and beyond the trappings of American promise. "During that time I was deep in Machiavelli and Dante," Warren notes, and in *All the King's Men*, "Machiavelli found a place in the musings of Jack Burden, and Dante provided the epigraph."[54] A much more rounded conception of influence circles about the project, and Warren makes every effort to set up the non-Huey Long material and experiences that spurred on his early writing. After discovering the Jack Burden character, who would narrate the novel, Warren accounts for the time it took to turn the play into *All the King's Men*, as well as being "constantly interrupted, by teaching, by some traveling, by the duties of my job in Washington, by the study for and writing of a long essay on Coleridge."[55] He welcomed the interruptions, however, "for they meant the pot had to be pushed to the back of the stove to simmer away at its own pace," as the book was written in Minneapolis, Minnesota, 1943–1944; Washington,

D.C., 1944–1945; Connecticut, summer 1945; and finally, back in Minneapolis, "the last few paragraphs being written in a little room in the upper reaches of the Library of the University of Minnesota."[56] Similar to how Hemingway listed the names of places where he wrote the stories in *The Fifth Column and the First Forty-Nine Stories* (1938), Warren features Midwestern and East Coast states and cities, a far cry from Baton Rouge, Louisiana, where his first "notion of a verse play" took initial shape. Warren's attention to place universalizes his novel, releasing it from the strict confines of the "Southern" or "political" novel. His novel came from Dante and Machiavelli, from Baton Rouge and Connecticut, from wheat fields and university libraries.

With the introduction to the Time, Inc. edition (1963), Warren takes a different tack, clearly out of necessity. In the "Editor's Preface," the editors of *Time* frame the introduction narrowly: "Warren's gifts are most completely seen in *All the King's Men*. As he explains in a new introduction written for this special edition of the book, it was based on the career of Huey Long, the homespun dictator of Louisiana during the Depression years."[57] As far as inhibiting signposts, to borrow from Genette,[58] are concerned, the preface puts Warren in a bind, and he chooses to deal with "'the "Huey Long" side of the story'" before returning to the origin story of *Proud Flesh*. Following an extended section on Long (five and half of the introduction's seven pages), Warren recounts the novel's origins: "The first version of my story was a verse drama. The actual writing began in 1938, in the shade of an olive tree by a wheat field near Perugia."[59] He offers this account as proof that he did not "directly ... transpose into fiction Huey P. Long and the tone of that world," for "if you are sitting under an olive tree in Umbria and are writing a verse drama, the chances are that you are concerned more with the myth than with the fact, more with the symbolic than with the actual. And so it was."[60] There is a clearance that Warren hopes to achieve with his origin account, more so than in is first introduction for the Modern Library. "What I knew was the 'Huey' of the myth," he writes, "and that was what I had taken with me to Mussolini's Italy, where the bully-boys wore black shirts and gave a funny salute."[61] Removing the boundaries of the facts of Long and Louisiana politics, Warren asks readers to see more than they may want to see: "In 1942 I left Louisiana for good, and when in 1943 I began the version that is more realistic, discursive and documentary in spirit (though not in fact) than the play, I was doing so after I had definitely left Louisiana and the world in which the story had its roots."[62] Again, Warren strives to separate facts and fictions; his fiction can come from fact but does not necessarily have to depend upon those facts to achieve success, and one can write about a time and place without still being in that place—in Warren's case, Louisiana: "By now the literal, factual world was only a memory and therefore was ready to be absorbed freely into the act of the imagination. ... And however important was my acquaintance with Louisiana, it was far less important than my acquaintance with another country."[63] The experiences in Italy still hold Warren's interest, including the imagery of Benito Mussolini and the Black Shirts, even if he gives them a shorter treatment in 1963 than he did in 1953. Still, the country of his making proves to be the most interesting of all: "For any novel, good or bad, must report, willy-nilly, the history, sociology and politics of a country even more fantastic than was Louisiana under the consulship of Huey."[64] Warren made a country with the "thinking and feeling" of fact, suggesting rather than identifying. His novel comes to a "deeper and darker dialectic" of image and action than what he calls "the protracted dialectic between 'Huey' on the one side and me on the other."[65] The 1963 introduction sees Warren moving further into the territory of his own creation, a new country made "even more fantastic" than the real thing. As he told Frank Gado three years later, "I could bring to my surmises a certain body of feeling."[66]

The Franklin Library introduction (1977), printed as "A special message from Robert Penn Warren," reveals very little new information, though Warren appears to be more self-conscious about origins. "A word about origins," he begins. "In one sense origins, in their infinite complexity, have no beginning: they are ultimately part of an ongoing process."[67] He told Bill Moyers in a 1976 interview that the novel "grew out of circumstances. Grew out of a folklore of the moment where I was and I guess also because I was teaching Shakespeare and reading Machiavelli and William James. Everything flowed together."[68] Strands of memory and seemingly disparate moments spur on the "flow" of origin, a river moving swiftly and always changing, yet starting from somewhere: "But certainly in a book, to add to this complexity, we see two special strands of origin interesting. There is a writer who writes the book. He has his own story—largely unknown to him—of his origins; and he has the needs that sought fulfillment in the book. But he writes the book in a special context of subject and setting, often far beyond his choice."[69] Does the story take him away, or can he control the story? Earlier introductions do not offer a primer to Warren's idea of origins, they just begin. By introducing his

theory of origins, Warren offers a commentary on introductions themselves. Origins appear to come *after* the story has been written, as that
story is an ongoing one during composition. And if that story, still burgeoning and present, remains "largely unknown" to the writer, all they
have is the writing. Origins come later. Thirty years after the first publication of *All the King's Men*, Warren argues that "my book represents an
intersection of Louisiana, Huey P. Long, and me."[70] He never goes so far
as to admit any explicit reportage or biography, but Warren continues his
investigation into what Long meant for his book, directly and indirectly.

He had begun that work inadvertently in the Modern Library introduction by claiming that readers and critics "quickly equated" Willie Stark
with Long. While not a denial, Warren offers up a disclaimer: "For better
or for worse, Willie Stark was not Huey Long. Willie was only himself,
whatever that self turned out to be, a shadowy wraith or a blundering
human being."[71] The disclaimer turns into a treatment of Long and
Louisiana in the Time, Inc. introduction, where Warren admits, "I can be
sure that if I had never gone to live in Louisiana and if Huey Long had not
existed, the novel would never have been written."[72] Still stopping short
of reportage, Warren argues that rather than addressing "the factual world
of Governor, later Senator, Huey P. Long," his novel came from more
than that: "There were a thousand tales, over the years, and some of them
were no doubt literally and factually true. But they were all true in the
world of 'Huey'—that world of myth, folklore, poetry, deprivation, ran-
cor, and dimly envisaged hopes." Worlds collided in "a strange, shifting,
often ironical and sometimes irrelevant" manner, but they flowed together,
like the origins that Warren kept accumulating.[73] "So much for origins,"
he claims in 1976, after writing about Long, his time at Louisiana State
University, and Louisiana. He returns then to another origin story, the
one that began the Modern Library introduction: "One autumn afternoon in 1937, on the front porch of a cottage where I was visiting two
young graduate students, I began to talk about a play I had in mind, suggested by the Long story—or myth, if you will—trying to explain the
meaning it had for me. Before that, all had been shadowy."[74] The conversation on "a friend's porch"[75] in the Modern Library introduction was
followed by the explanation, and in the Time, Inc. introduction "the
actual writing began in 1938" in Italy.[76] Warren moves the "meaning" of
his work into different pockets of each introduction, expanding them in
the Time, Inc. introduction and contracting them in the Franklin Library
one. But the meaning is there. Warren still takes readers to Italy in 1938

and 1939, where he "could hear under my window the rhythmic bang of the heels of black-shirt infantry on the cobbles." The undertone of violence and myth begins early in the introduction, where Louisiana, "under the consulship of Huey," was "obsessive and violent" with "mythology growing before your eyes."[77] He still finishes the novel in Fall 1945, "in an attic room of the library of the University of Minnesota."[78] But he concludes with another strand, another persona that flows into the work and, until now, had not been featured in the earlier introductions: "But I must confess, many an intervening page was written in my office in the Library of Congress, where … I filled the post of the Consultant of Poetry. This is, I should imagine, a way of saying that poetry is not something you are consulted about all day long."[79] Should readers not know of Warren's status as a poet, they do now. Even in self-deprecation, Warren elevates the life of a working writer and the story that comes from the experience of writing as a profession. Warren was never just one kind of writer, though the kinds always flowed together, just like the origins of *All the King's Men*.

The Book-of-the-Month Club trade edition of *All the King's Men*, released concurrently with new edition from Harcourt Brace Jovanovich, features Warren's longest introduction. At over ten pages, the introduction cuts a much wider swath than the first three pieces, yet it follows a similar trajectory: origins, Louisiana State University, Louisiana, Huey, Italy, *Proud Flesh*, Mussolini, the attic room at the University of Minnesota. Warren's well-worn path gets its most complete treatment, with the writer more clearly committed to the piece than he was just four years earlier for the Franklin Library. His first paragraph is an examination of time and beginning, not unlike his more clipped opening paragraph on origins in 1977. Warren may also be at his most poetic, as the 1981 introduction features strong imagery and imaginative metaphors, especially concerning writing and memory. For all the defensiveness in 1953, the countering in 1963, and the more obvious examination of "origins" in 1977, the 1981 introduction can be termed complete, "with a certain kind of accuracy."[80] Warren takes the time to elaborate, to expand, and to illuminate, his phrasing more assured, his poetic sensibility on display from the outset:

Thirty-five years ago, *All the King's Men* was published and now, for this special edition, I am asked to say something about how it came to be. With any event in your life you know more after thirty-five years than after one. True, you may know less in some ways. Time does not necessarily improve memory. But in the course of time, strange odds and ends—or even fundamental facts not recognized in the noonday sun—may, out of blank idleness of a later mind, rise up, trailing God knows what, like a half-rotten log disturbed in a creek bed to rise dreamily up, trailing algae, patched with rotting moss, clung to by some strange, snail-like creatures, with a rusty length of barbed wire still nailed to it or embedded. What may rise so gratuitously out of the deep of time may be a set of relationships and connections of that you may not have been aware of when things were fresh. The unconscious thing may, years later, become startlingly conscious, seemingly by accident. That is why it is always hard to say precisely when and how a book—or anything else—'began.'[81]

Warren had been dealing with how his novel began for nearly thirty years by the time he made the previously quoted statement, and with somewhat assured consistency, his story had never changed. And it does not change in 1981. However, what does change is Warren's impressions about the beginnings, the connections he makes, and the conclusions he draws. Huey Long was always part of the novel, even when Warren downplayed the connection in 1953. The ghost of Long never let go, having grabbed on as something between the "strange odds and ends" and the "fundamental facts not recognized" that made up Warren's memory. He doesn't get to the geographical origins for awhile, diverging into Long and Louisiana, not unlike the 1963 introduction. "If you were living in Louisiana," he recounts, "you knew that you were living in history growing before your eyes. And you knew that you were not seeing a half-drunk hick buffoon performing an old routine, but were witnessing a drama which was a version of the current world's drama, and the drama of history, too, the old drama of power and ethics."[82]

He revisits the flowing together of performance and power that had been more distilled in 1953—"The book, however, was never intended to be a book about politics. Politics merely provided the framework story in which the deeper concerns, whatever their significance, might work themselves out."[83]—expanded upon and redirected in 1963—"Conversation in Louisiana always came back to the tales, to the myth, to politics; and to talk politics is to talk about power. So conversation turned, by implication at least, on the question of power and ethics, of power and justification, or means and ends, of 'historical costs.'"[84]—and distilled again in 1977— "But one thing is certain: power moves into a vacuum. And if the genteel regimes before Long had not been marked by political lethargy, contempt for the democratic process, for human needs and social good, and complacency based on a romantic dream of the past, then there would have been no Kingfish. Or at least one of a different kind."[85] In 1981, his origins more clearly involve Long, for under the shade of that olive tree in Umbria, Italy, in summer 1938, Warren "tried to get the speculations provoked by Huey organized into the play."[86] He journeys to Italy in summer 1939 on his Guggenheim money, "to gaze for a year at real Fascism in action,"[87] which connects back to Long, "as when Dante describes the vulgarity of new tyrants."[88] In Rome, with "Benito's Black Shirts clacking on the cobbles of Via Aurelia Safi," Warren finished a draft of his verse play, only to throw it in the same drawer he had introduced in 1953 ("I had taken the manuscript out of its cupboard"[89]). But it came out by 1943, and the manuscript was finished in 1945, just like the others. Yet, unlike the other introductions, Warren claims that "distance from the scene and time" gave him "perspectives," and that he wrote a portion of the book in New London, Connecticut, in the summer of 1945, "where on a couple of nights great fleets of bombers, returning from Europe and victory, shook the house, their lights like roaring, sky-filling constellations,"[90] prior to making it over to the attic room in the University of Minnesota library that fall. The added detail bridges the Italy period, where Mussolini and the Black Shirts clacked on cobbles, with Allied victory in World War II, a victory he had yet to account for in previous introductions. In the concluding sentences, Warren notes that the "first major review took [the novel] to be an apologia for Fascism. Well. Further the deponent saith not."[91] Warren had spent some time in the 1953 introduction positioning himself as neither a fascist nor a proponent of the "assassination of dictators," two positions that reviewers had accused him of taking.[92] He returns us to the first review, whose dismissal reduces Warren to simplicity, when the introduction that precedes the paraphrased review takes great pains to prove that the novel and Warren are anything but simple. So much for origins.

"HUEY"

Keith Perry surveys the ways in which Warren handled the "authorial side of the debate" surrounding *All the King's Men* and Huey Long. His analysis of the four introductions, as well as other essays and public pieces written by Warren, suggests that the debate was "often rephrased since 1953 but essentially unchanged since 1963."[93] After quoting liberally from the introductions, Perry concludes that Warren "did know what Long had done, though, and he did know what Long had said—and, as a result, Willie Stark not only does much of what Long did, says much of what Long said, but at times as much embodies what Warren referred to as the secrets of Long's soul inherent in those very words and deeds."[94] Warren battled with critics over the amount of influence Long had on him. In what follows, I chart how Warren introduces Long in each introduction, thereby focusing attention on Warren's focus, and how that focus shifted from piece to piece. Though slight, the shifts are only effective when reading the introductions as a unit, a practice that was certainly never intended but nevertheless possible given the existence of four books called *All the King's Men* by Robert Penn Warren, each with an introduction by the author. Building on Perry's work, what does it mean that Warren never caved to the pressure to just come out and say, "Willie Stark is Huey Long," and what, if anything, can we take away from his exercise in resistance?

Ladell Payne praises Warren's use of Long in *All the King's Men*, even if that praise is tempered due to Warren's refusal to admit direct influence: "For in the novel's sequence of events … so much is drawn directly from the publicly-known career, cohorts, and character of Huey Pierce Long that Warren's statements, while not false, nonetheless have been misleading."[95] Written after only the first two introductions by Warren were released, Payne's assessment, again, is one of praise for Warren's blending of fact and fiction, not a denunciation of the author's "misleading" statement. He concludes, "It is one of the marks of Warren's genius that he used the career of Huey Long as the source of such a wealth of meanings without doing violence either to what is known about Long or to the integrity with which the meanings are worked out: indeed, that he was able to alter so little as he imposed the order of art on the chaos of actuality."[96] Perry expands on Payne's position. "More than just a dry translation of fact into fiction," he argues, "*All the King's Men* is a novel that succeeds not because of the facts it appropriates from Long's life, but because of the fictional life that arises from—sometimes even in spite of—that same material."[97] But Warren's Modern Library introduction, while partially supporting Perry's reading, grates against it too. When Warren claims, without a shred of irony, that "Willie Stark was not Huey Long. Willie was only himself,"[98] he makes something more definite than he may have intended. Whether we choose to believe him in later introductions, where Long gets more credit (though still as myth, story, and folktale more than flesh and blood man) or not, is ultimately irrelevant. The novel will continue to be read with the image of Huey Long orbiting Warren, rather than Warren orbiting Long. "Long's biography becomes the means to something somewhere between fact and fiction," Perry argues, "but something that, at the same time, is also more than their mere combination: an intersection in which the fiction ... is just as inspired by, but paradoxically, is more independent of, the incorporated historical fact."[99] Perry's analysis could serve as the introduction to Warren's introductions, where the novel "amounts to an incorporation of detail from Long's biography into the story of a man who, although much like him, is at the same time as much unlike him."[100]

Given the obvious liminality at play, with Long, Warren, and the novel flowing strangely together, what can we make of Long's entrance into each introduction? While little changes from year to year, Warren's treatment of Long does evolve from a soft denial in 1953 to a more nuanced acceptance in the following years. Hugh Ruppersburg argues that Warren's Willie Stark "is a disillusioned Jeffersonian, a Great Man who answered the call to serve but discovered that good will and righteousness were not required for public service, were perhaps even counterproductive. ... And he lives in a world where a wholly moral man cannot survive."[101] William Bedford Clark indicates that Warren "recognized that the soul longs for completeness and communion, but these very longings may lead to the lusting after false gods,"[102] and he "believes that nations, not less than the men and women who compose them, must have 'myths' to live by,"[103] while John Burt believes that "the affirmation of *All the King's Men* is a fresh apprehension of value, not as a guide to action, but as an occasion for integrity in the face of one's inevitable failures to connect value and action."[104] Warren's introductions to *All the King's Men* treat the complication of "Huey," myth, and text as an evolving paradox, a center upon which things can hang but also a false center that dissolves under pressure. According to Jonathan Cullick, readers are empowered to "use stories to consider how we must act in the future. ... Stories serve as anchors for us, and in those anchors we are compelled to find applications for our current cultural moment."[105] The introductions are stories, as is Warren's thirty-five-year search for how best to describe the "Huey Long side of the story." Perry concludes his study on Long with a pertinent question: "How long will it be ... before Huey Long himself becomes a 'Huey-who-isn't-Huey? ... can we say with absolute certainty that, to at least some degree, he hasn't been one for decades?"[106] The myth and the man make appearances in Warren's introductions, and by examining Long's entrances into each piece, we see the shades of fact and fiction flowing together.

"Speaking in a voice that is neither jaded nor cynical, but open and enthusiastic," writes Charlotte Beck in *Robert Penn Warren, Critic,* "Warren reserves his anger and sarcasm for the reviewer or essayist who has been too quick to judge or has judged from benighted or misguided principles."[107] An excellent example of Beck's point lies in Warren's Modern Library introduction (1953). After spending four pages on the origins of the novel, Warren brings Huey Long in as a piece of critical and cultural controversy, rather than a direct influence on Willie Stark:

> One of the unfortunate characteristics of our time is that the reception of a novel may depend on its journalistic relevance. It is a little graceless of me to call this characteristic unfortunate, and to quarrel with it, for certainly the journalistic relevance of *All the King's Men* had a good deal to do with what interest it invoked. My politician hero, whose name, in the end, was Willie Stark, was quickly equated with the late Senator Huey P. Long, whose fame, even outside of Louisiana, was yet green in pious tears, anathema, and speculation.[108]

In line with his New Critical movement, Warren tangles with the initial critical response to the novel as nothing more than "a not-so-covert biography of, and apologia for, Senator Long, the author to be not less than a base minion of the great man." He refers to the reading as "innocent boneheadedness or gospel-bit hysteria," paraphrasing Louis Armstrong for effect: "there's some folks that if they don't know, you can't tell 'em."[109] Essentially, reading Stark as Long is a misreading for Warren in 1953. The scaffolded origin story from a friend's porch in Baton Rouge to Italy to Minneapolis plays a much larger role than the Kingfish, and readers approaching the novel for the first time could assume, as Perry suggests they did, that the novel had little to do with Long the man thanks to Warren's dismissal.[110] There was connection, but not direct influence.[111]

Open and enthusiastic, to borrow from Beck, Warren offers a more nuanced take on the Huey myth in the Time, Inc. introduction (1963), turning the late politician into less of a hindrance and more of a transformative force, yet still removed from Long the man:

> The editor of the series in which this edition of *All the King's Men* is an item has asked me to write an introduction that will touch on 'the "Huey Long"

side of the story' and have something to say 'about the whole thinking and feeling that led to the writing of the book.' As for the first part of the assignment, I can be sure that if I had never gone to live in Louisiana and if Huey Long had not existed, the novel would never have been written. But this is far from saying that my 'state' in *All the King's Men* is Louisiana, or that my Willie Stark is the late Senator. What Louisiana and Senator Long gave me was a line of 'thinking and feeling' that did eventuate in the novel.[112]

In what Perry calls a "'Huey' twice removed," Warren lays the groundwork for how he would address Long in future introductions. Huey Long was a story, in and of himself, and the myth surrounding his presence on the local and national scenes definitely contributed to Warren's work, yet the contribution was one of many, according to Warren, who listed Shakespeare, Dante, Machiavelli, William James, Mussolini, Guicciardini, Edmund Spenser, and American history as additional resources available to him. "Melodrama was the breath of life," Warren recounted. "In Louisiana people *lived* melodrama. They seemed to live, in fact, for it, for that strange combination of philosophy, humor and violence. Life was a tale that you happened to be living—and that 'Huey' happened to be living before your eyes."[113] "Huey" is not Huey P. Long, as much as Huey P. Long is not Willie Stark. Yet "Huey," like Basso's "Hueys-that-aren't-Hueys," allows Warren to separate enough from the "literal, factual world," which "was only a memory and therefore was ready to be absorbed freely into the act of imagination."[114] Myth, suggestion, essence, story, tale, thinking, and feeling—Warren had his "Huey" for future introductions.

The final two introductions follow a pattern that, according to Perry, Warren had set up in the Time, Inc. introduction: "an admission of inspiration, a qualification via disclaimer, an emphasis on intent, and a profession of interest in myth rather than fact."[115] The Franklin Library introduction (1977) establishes Long, at the end of the first paragraph, as a culmination of a "special context of subject and setting, often far beyond his choice. That is, my book represents an intersection of Louisiana, Huey P. Long, and me."[116] The introduction to the Book-of-the-Month Club edition (1981) locks Long into Warren's first Louisiana paragraph: "I might, with a certain kind of accuracy, be arbitrary, and say that the book began when, in September 1934, I moved to Baton Rouge, to teach at the Louisiana State University and thus entered the orbit of Huey P. Long, who had previously been for me an occasional headline."[117] From intersection to orbit, yet still myth and folktale, Huey Long comes first in Warren's latter introductions, or certainly closer to the beginning than the buried treatment he received in the Modern Library introduction. It is as if Long was an anecdote, something to be talked about and sometimes to be felt, rather than humanized. Warren was concerned with "the myth not the man"[118] in 1977, and he had "a great interest in what Huey did in his world, and a greater interest in Huey as a focus of myth" in 1981. "Without this gift for attracting myth," he argued, "he would not have been the power he was, for good and evil. And this gift was fused, indissolubly, with his dramatic sense, with his varying roles, and perhaps, ultimately, with the atmosphere of violence which he generated."[119] That atmosphere represented, as he called it, "the drama of history ... the old drama of power and ethics."[120]

By pushing further away from fact, and leaning ever inward to myth-making and myth reading, Warren stakes his claim over his "Huey." Really a textual diversion, began with his extended origin story in 1953 prior to even mentioning Long by name, the treatment of Long as myth more than man echoes what Hugh Ruppersburg suggests is part of Warren's regard for history as "an irresistible naturalistic process ... a mass of living individuals, tossed along involuntarily, moving with will and consciousness, bearing responsibility for their behavior in the flood which has swept them up."[121] "Huey" is part of Warren's flood of experience, the factors and facts that "flow strangely together,"[122] that "flowed more directly into my meditations,"[123] that "come alive, in shadowy distortions and sudden clarities,"[124] and that represent "the coiling, interfused forces that go into" literary decisions.[125] Even Perry concludes that the novel "succeeds, even excels ... because of the fictional character who is, not the historical figure who was."[126] Between 1953 and 1981, Warren turned Huey Long into "Huey," utilizing the effect of myth over the biography of a politician to, first, curtail charges of "minion" biography, and second, to clarify any writer's project: a writer has "his own story—largely unknown to him—of his origins; and he has the needs that sought fulfillment in the book. But he writes the book in a special context of subject and setting, often far beyond his choice."[127] "Huey" was subject, setting, suggestion, and sensation, "chaos in actuality,"[128] and an agent of the "convulsion of the world" which the novel's Jack Burden knows we must step out into.[129] "Huey," while being a shade of Huey P. Long, became more than *that* Huey to Warren. He became *his* "Huey."

Out of History Into History

In a corrected typescript of the introduction to the 1977 Franklin Library
edition of *All the King's Men*, Warren opens what is then titled a preface
with a paragraph not about origins or beginnings, but about results:

> First a few vital statistics. <u>All the King's Men</u> was published in 1946, received
> a rather mixed bag of reviews from enthusiastic praise to a savage contempt
> often charged with the conviction that the author was a fascist hireling of
> Huey Long. The book racked up a modestly gratifying sale in the first year,
> received the Pulitzer Prize in 1947, and since that time has appeared in vari-
> ous editions in English and in twenty odd translations, has sold over three
> million copies, has been transmorgrified [sic] into a movie and a TV version
> in the United States and, more recently, into another movie in Russia.[130]

Warren handwrote "Begin" in the margin to the left of the following paragraph, which would become the opening "origins" paragraph to the
introduction. The typescript features very few edits, the only major one
being the intended excision of the original opening. Warren's choice to
remove the "vital statistics" paragraph in favor of the "origins" paragraph,
whether that choice was his or the editor at the Franklin Library, preserves
the myth rather than the man. In a bit of metaphorical puckishness, Warren
removes the "vital statistics," like vital organs, in favor of a beginning
awash in imagination, about origins and promise, not reality. Regardless of
critical success (or critical misreading), sales figures, number of translations, or adaptations, Warren's concern in the introductions was always
story over statistics. But the draft first paragraph features one pearl between
the duller elements of his recollection: three million copies sold. None of
his introductions wielded that figure; in fact, none of them mention sales
in any way. It was always the beginning that mattered, then the legendry
and folktales, then the process of imagination after being "trapped in speculation"[131] and "living in history growing before your eyes."[132] Yet Warren
would have been well within his rights to recenter the narrative about *All
the King's Men* on its critical and popular success, rather than on whether
or not he used Huey Long for his own sculpting. But he chooses not to
muddy the flow of experience, which reads as a much greater height to
strive for (and evolve out of) than the constriction of success or royalties.
Or maybe that's what his editor told him would fly with the subscribers
buying the book for $39.00 per copy. Warren knew that vital statistics and
aesthetic origins must cohabitate for any writer to be able to write

introductions about either one. For instance, the first edition of *All the King's Men* provided Warren with a 12.5% royalty on the first 15,000 copies sold, and 15% thereafter.[133] The first edition went through eleven printings between 17 August 1946 and 11 November 1947, for a total of 54,755 copies.[134] The sale from those runs could have netted Warren $23,514.75 in royalties (nearly US $300,000 in 2021), and Harcourt executive S. Spencer Scott projected Warren's income from a number of sources in 1947 alone at approximately $92,000 (well over US $1,000,000 in 2021).[135] But numbers like these do not make it to readers, since books are outgrowths of inspiration and imagination first and goods to be purchased second, with a writer's remuneration rarely considered. The vital statistics matter a great deal to Warren, Harcourt, and booksellers. Readers want story.

Warren told C. Van Woodward that "the facts Jack Burden gets are deadly things," in reference to the "dirt" Burden gets on Judge Irwin, who is revealed to be his father before committing suicide. "Facts may kill," Warren concludes. "For one thing, they can kill myths."[136] Again, Warren's impression about the messy marriage between facts and fictions elevates the mythic origins of the novel and the fantastic orbit of Huey Long's Louisiana, the two elements he often returned to when asked about *All the King's Men*. He told Peter Stitt in 1977 that "All you have to cook up in a poem is to be honest with your feelings and your observation, somehow,"[137] and in a way, there is an honesty in the introductions that Warren maintains, or at least appears to maintain. He is diverting and somewhat allusive, mannered and folksy, never timid but clearly holding back from time to time, yet consistent with the story of his story. Warren's original opening (an alternative origin) to the novel, prior to Harcourt editor Lambert Davis suggesting it be cut, began: "The Boss was a son-of-a-bitch, and I will not deny it. He was a son-of-a-bitch of a purest ray serene. I will not deny it, for I do not wish to rob his name of its lustre." Front and center, the Boss enters, and Jack Burden has seen him: "I shore-God saw the Boss, plain as a pikestaff, and he was the son-of-a-bitch nonpareil, par excellence, and his belly was a sheaf of wheat set round with lilies, and violets sprung up in his footsteps. I have seen him, and Lord, let thy servant depart in peace."[138] Warren saw no need to kill the myth of his "Huey," neither its beginnings nor its effects, and in the introductions to *All the King's Men* we begin to see how he saw the story of his story.

NOTES

1. Robert Penn Warren, *Brother to Dragons: A Tale in Verse and Voices* (New York: Random House, 1953), xii.
2. William Kennedy, "Robert Penn Warren: Willie Stark, Politics, and the Novel," 1973, in *Conversations with Robert Penn Warren*, eds. Gloria L. Cronin and Ben Siegel (Jackson, MS: University Press of Mississippi, 2005), 85; 89.
3. Ernest Hemingway, *Death in the Afternoon* (New York: Charles Scribner's Sons, 1932), 278.
4. Roy Newquist, "Conversation: Eleanor Clark and Robert Penn Warren," 1967, in *Conversations with Robert Penn Warren*, eds. Gloria L. Cronin and Ben Siegel (Jackson, MS: University Press of Mississippi, 2005), 58.
5. Gerard Genette, *Paratexts: Thresholds of Interpretation*, 1987, trans. Jane Lewin (New York: Cambridge University Press, 1997), 253.
6. On 15 July 1979, President Jimmy Carter, in a nationally televised address to the nation, referred to the fundamental threat to American democracy as "a crisis of confidence. It is a crisis that strikes at the very heart and soul and spirit of our national will. We can see this crisis in the growing doubt about the meaning of our own lives and in the loss of a unity of purpose for our nation. The erosion of our confidence in the future is threatening to destroy the social and the political fabric of America." See Jimmy Carter, "Crisis of Confidence," 15 July 1979, PBS, https://www.pbs.org/wgbh/americanexperience/features/carter-crisis/.
7. Genette, *Paratexts*, 253.
8. Keith Perry, *The Kingfish in Fiction: Huey P. Long and the Modern American Novel* (Baton Rouge, LA: Louisiana State University Press, 2004), 42.
9. Perry references an article that American writer Hamilton Basso wrote for *Life* magazine about his and other depictions of what he called "Hueys-who-aren't-Hueys." See Perry, *The Kingfish in Fiction*, 32–33.
10. Perry, *The Kingfish in Fiction*, 42.
11. Robert H. Chambers, "Introduction," in *Twentieth Century Interpretations of* All the King's Men, ed. Robert H. Chambers (Englewood Cliffs, NJ: Prentice-Hall, Inc., 1977), 6.
12. Robert Penn Warren, *All the King's Men*. 1946 (New York: Time, Inc. 1963), xi.
13. Tom Vitale, "A Conversation with Robert Penn Warren." 1985, in *Conversations with Robert Penn Warren*, eds. Gloria L. Cronin and Ben Siegel (Jackson, MS: University Press of Mississippi, 2005), 222.

14. Frank Gado, "A Conversation with Robert Penn Warren," 1966, in *Conversations with Robert Penn Warren*, eds. Gloria L. Cronin and Ben Siegel (Jackson, MS: University Press of Mississippi, 2005), 38.
15. Gado, "A Conversation with Robert Penn Warren," 44.
16. Warren also wrote an introduction for an English edition of the novel in 1974. It does not necessarily strike out into any new territory; therefore, I restrict my analysis to the American edition introductions.
17. Robert Penn Warren, *All the King's Men*. 1946 (New York: Modern Library, 1953), vi.
18. Warren, *All the King's Men*, 1963, xi.
19. Robert Penn Warren, *All the King's Men*. 1946 (Franklin Center, PA: Franklin Library, 1977), vi.
20. Robert Penn Warren, *All the King's Men*. 1946 (New York: Harcourt Brace Jovanovich, 1981), xiii.
21. Genette, *Paratexts*, 239.
22. Robert Penn Warren (RPW) to William T. Bandy, October 2, 1983. See Randy Hendricks and James A. Perkins, eds., *Selected Letters of Robert Penn Warren: Toward Sunset, at a Great Height, 1980–1989* (Baton Rouge, LA: Louisiana State University Press, 2013), 183.
23. James A. Grimshaw, *Robert Penn Warren: A Descriptive Bibliography, 1922–1979* (Charlottesville, VA: University Press of Virginia, 1981), 38.
24. For more on the Modern Library, see Jay Satterfield, *The World's Best Books: Taste Culture, and the Modern Library* (Amherst, MA: University of Massachusetts Press, 2002) and Lise Jaillant, *Modernism, Middlebrow and the Literary Canon: The Modern Library Series, 1917–1955* (London: Routledge, 2014).
25. Grimshaw, *A Descriptive Bibliography*, 43.
26. RPW to Max Shulman, July 29, 1963. See Randy Hendricks and James A. Perkins, eds., *Selected Letters of Robert Penn Warren: New Beginnings and New Directions, 1953–1968* (Baton Rouge, LA: Louisiana State University Press, 2008), 386.
27. Grimshaw, *A Descriptive Bibliography*, 47.
28. RPW to T. S. Rosenthal, April 6, 1976. See Randy Hendricks and James A. Perkins, eds. *Selected Letters of Robert Penn Warren: Backward Glances and New Visions, 1969–1979* (Baton Rouge, LA: Louisiana State University Press, 2011), 299.
29. RPW to Katherine Anne Porter, June 15, 197[6]. See Hendricks and Perkins, *Backward Glances and New Visions*, 305.
30. RPW to Allen Tate, July 25, 1976. See Hendricks and Perkins, *Backward Glances and New Visions*, 312.
31. RPW to Allen Tate, July 25, 1976. See Hendricks and Perkins, *Backward Glances and New Visions*, 312.

32. RPW to Louis D. Rubin, Jr., October 8, 1976. See Hendricks and Perkins, *Backward Glances and New Visions*, 328.

33. RPW to Allen Tate, October 10, 1976. See Hendricks and Perkins, *Backward Glances and New Visions*, 330.

34. RPW to Katherine Anne Porter, November 8, 1976. See Hendricks and Perkins, *Backward Glances and New Visions*, 333.

35. All inflation adjustments were made using the Consumer Price Index (CPI) Inflation Calculator, provided by the United States Bureau of Labor Statistics, https://www.bls.gov/data/inflation_calculator.htm.

36. RPW to Donald E. Stanford, February 27, 1981. See Hendricks and Perkins, *Toward Sunset, at a Great Height*, 83.

37. RPW to Cleanth Brooks, March 2, 1981. See Hendricks and Perkins, *Toward Sunset, at a Great Height*, 84–85.

38. Genette, *Paratexts*, 239.

39. Warren, *All the King's Men*, 1981, xiii.

40. Joseph Blotner, *Robert Penn Warren: A Biography* (New York: Random House, 1997), 173.

41. Blotner, *Robert Penn Warren*, 177. The Warrens lived first in Sirmione near Lake Genoa, then Capri and Rome, returning to the United States in June 1940. See Blotner, *Robert Penn Warren*, 176–184.

42. William Bedford Clark, ed. *Selected Letters of Robert Penn Warren: The Southern Review Years, 1935–1942* (Baton Rouge, LA: Louisiana State University Press, 2001), 226.

43. Clark, *The Southern Review Years*, 229.

44. Clark, *The Southern Review Years*, 232.

45. Clark, *The Southern Review Years*, 242.

46. Clark, *The Southern Review Years*, 244.

47. Clark, *The Southern Review Years*, 269.

48. See Blotner, *Robert Penn Warren*, 181.

49. David Madden, "Preface," in *The Legacy of Robert Penn Warren*, ed. David Madden (Baton Rouge, LA: Louisiana State University Press, 2000), xiv.

50. RPW to Kenneth Burke, Fall 1939. Quoted in Blotner, *Robert Penn Warren*, 179.

51. Blotner, *Robert Penn Warren*, 179.

52. Warren, *All the King's Men*, 1953, i.

53. Warren, *All the King's Men*, 1953, ii.

54. Warren, *All the King's Men*, 1953, ii.

55. Warren, *All the King's Men*, 1953, iv.

56. Warren, *All the King's Men*, 1953, iv–v.

57. "Editor's Preface," in Warren, *All the King's Men*, 1963, vii.

58. Genette, *Paratexts*, 224.

59. Warren, *All the King's Men*, 1963, xvi.
60. Warren, *All the King's Men*, 1963, xvi.
61. Warren, *All the King's Men*, 1963, xvi.
62. Warren, *All the King's Men*, 1963, xvii.
63. Warren, *All the King's Men*, 1963, xvii.
64. Warren, *All the King's Men*, 1963, xvii.
65. Warren, *All the King's Men*, 1963, xvii.
66. Gado, "A Conversation with Robert Penn Warren," 39.
67. Warren, *All the King's Men*, 1977, iv.
68. Bill Moyers, "A Conversation with Robert Penn Warren," 1976, in *Conversations with Robert Penn Warren*, eds. Gloria L. Cronin and Ben Siegel (Jackson, MS: University Press of Mississippi, 2005), 93.
69. Warren, *All the King's Men*, 1977, iv.
70. Warren, *All the King's Men*, 1977, iv.
71. Warren, *All the King's Men*, 1953, v.
72. Warren, *All the King's Men*, 1963, xi.
73. Warren, *All the King's Men*, 1963, xiii.
74. Warren, *All the King's Men*, 1977, vi.
75. Warren, *All the King's Men*, 1953, i.
76. Warren, *All the King's Men*, 1963, xvi.
77. Warren, *All the King's Men*, 1977, iv–v.
78. Warren, *All the King's Men*, 1977, vii.
79. Warren, *All the King's Men*, 1977, vii.
80. Warren, *All the King's Men*, 1981, ix.
81. Warren, *All the King's Men*, 1981, ix.
82. Warren, *All the King's Men*, 1981, xiii.
83. Warren, *All the King's Men*, 1953, vi.
84. Warren, *All the King's Men*, 1963, xv.
85. Warren, *All the King's Men*, 1977, v.
86. Warren, *All the King's Men*, 1981, xv.
87. Warren, *All the King's Men*, 1981, xix.
88. Warren, *All the King's Men*, 1981, xv.
89. Warren, *All the King's Men*, 1953, iii.
90. Warren, *All the King's Men*, 1981, xx.
91. Warren, *All the King's Men*, 1981, xx.
92. Warren, *All the King's Men*, 1953, v.
93. Perry, *The Kingfish in Fiction*, 194. For a thorough analysis of Warren's treatment of Long in the introductions, see Perry, *The Kingfish in Fiction*, 186–195.
94. Perry, *The Kingfish in Fiction*, 195.
95. Ladell Payne, "Willie Stark and Huey Long: Atmosphere, Myth, or Suggestion?" in *Twentieth Century Interpretations of* All the King's Men,

ed. Robert H. Chambers (Englewood Cliffs, NJ: Prentice-Hall, Inc., 1977), 100.

96. Payne, "Willie Stark and Huey Long," 115.
97. Perry, *The Kingfish in Fiction*, 208–209.
98. Warren, *All the King's Men*, 1953, v.
99. Perry, *The Kingfish in Fiction*, 209.
100. Perry, *The Kingfish in Fiction*, 221.
101. Hugh Ruppersburg, *Robert Penn Warren and the American Imagination* (Athens, GA: University of Georgia Press, 1990), 11.
102. William Bedford Clark, *The American Vision of Robert Penn Warren* (Lexington, KY: University Press of Kentucky, 1991), 83.
103. Clark, *The American Vision of Robert Penn Warren*, 89.
104. John Burt, *Robert Penn Warren and American Idealism* (New Haven, CT: Yale University Press, 1988), 171.
105. Jonathan S. Cullick, *Robert Penn Warren's* All the King's Men: *A Reader's Companion* (Lexington, KY: University Press of Kentucky, 2018), 35.
106. Perry, *The Kingfish in Fiction*, 228.
107. Charlotte H. Beck, *Robert Penn Warren, Critic* (Knoxville, TN: University of Tennessee Press, 2006), 79.
108. Warren, *All the King's Men*, 1953, v.
109. Warren, *All the King's Men*, 1953, v.
110. Perry, *The Kingfish in Fiction*, 188.
111. Warren, *All the King's Men*, 1953, vi.
112. Warren, *All the King's Men*, 1963, xiii.
113. Warren, *All the King's Men*, 1963, xvi.
114. Warren, *All the King's Men*, 1963, xvii.
115. Perry, *The Kingfish in Fiction*, 193.
116. Warren, *All the King's Men*, 1977, iv.
117. Warren, *All the King's Men*, 1981, ix.
118. Warren, *All the King's Men*, 1977, vi.
119. Warren, *All the King's Men*, 1981, xii.
120. Warren, *All the King's Men*, 1981, xiii.
121. Ruppersburg, *Robert Penn Warren and the American Imagination*, 22.
122. Warren, *All the King's Men*, 1981, xiii.
123. Warren, *All the King's Men*, 1977, vii.
124. Warren, *All the King's Men*, 1963, xvi.
125. Warren, *All the King's Men*, 1953, iii.
126. Perry, *The Kingfish in Fiction*, 209.
127. Warren, *All the King's Men*, 1977, iv.
128. Payne, "Willie Stark and Huey Long," 115.
129. Robert Penn Warren, *All the King's Men*, 1946, ed. Noel Polk (New York: Harcourt, Inc., 2002), 609. This chapter does not address Warren's

initial decision to name his Long character Willie "Talos," after Talus, the black knight of justice in Edmund Spenser's *The Faerie Queen*. The restored edition of *All the King's Men*, edited by Noel Polk and released in 2001, incorporates a number of emendations to the first edition, including Polk's controversial decision to rename Willie Stark back to Willie Talos, citing Warren's initial intentions. When citing passages from the novel, I refer to the restored edition. See Noel Polk, "Editing *All the King's Men*." *Southern Review* 38, no. 3 (2002): 849–860; and "The Text of the 'Restored' Edition of *All the King's Men*." *RWP: An Annual of Robert Penn Warren Studies* 2 (2002): 17–64.

130. Robert Penn Warren, "All the King's Men: Preface to Franklin Library Edition," Typescript, Robert Penn Warren Papers, Beinecke Rare Book and Manuscript Library, Yale University, New Haven, CT.

131. Warren, *All the King's Men*, 1981, x.

132. Warren, *All the King's Men*, 1981, xiii.

133. Randy Hendricks and James A. Perkins, eds. *Selected Letters of Robert Penn Warren: Triumph and Transition, 1943–1952*. Baton Rouge, LA: Louisiana State University Press, 2006. 177. See RPW to Lambert Davis, February 7, 1946, note 1.

134. Grimshaw, *A Descriptive Bibliography*, 35.

135. Hendricks and Perkins, *Triumph and Transition*, 227. See RPW to S. Spencer Scott, December 23, 1946, note 1.

136. C. Van Woodward, "The Uses of History in Fiction," 1968, in *Conversations with Robert Penn Warren*, eds. Gloria L. Cronin and Ben Siegel (Jackson, MS: University Press of Mississippi, 2005), 70.

137. Peter Stitt, "An Interview with Robert Penn Warren," 1977, in *Conversations with Robert Penn Warren*, eds. Gloria L. Cronin and Ben Siegel (Jackson, MS: University Press of Mississippi, 2005), 116.

138. Robert Penn Warren, *All the King's Men*, 1946, ed. Noel Polk (New York: Harcourt, Inc., 2002), 613.

Bibliography

Beck, Charlotte H. *Robert Penn Warren, Critic*. Knoxville, TN: University of Tennessee Press, 2006.

Blotner, Joseph. *Robert Penn Warren: A Biography*. New York: Random House, 1997.

Burt, John. *Robert Penn Warren and American Idealism*. New Haven, CT: Yale University Press, 1988.

Carter, James Earl, Jr. "Crisis of Confidence." July 15, 1979. PBS. https://www.pbs.org/wgbh/americanexperience/features/carter-crisis/.

Chambers, Robert H. "Introduction." In *Twentieth Century Interpretations of* All the King's Men, edited by Robert H. Chambers, 1–16. Englewood Cliffs, NJ: Prentice-Hall, Inc., 1977.

Clark, William Bedford. *The American Vision of Robert Penn Warren.* Lexington, KY: University Press of Kentucky, 1991.

Clark, William Bedford, ed. *Selected Letters of Robert Penn Warren: The* Southern Review *Years, 1935–1942.* Baton Rouge, LA: Louisiana State University Press, 2001

Cullick, Jonathan S. *Robert Penn Warren's* All the King's Men: *A Reader's Companion.* Lexington, KY: University Press of Kentucky, 2018.

Gado, Frank. "A Conversation with Robert Penn Warren." 1966. In *Conversations with Robert Penn Warren,* edited by Gloria L. Cronin and Ben Siegel, 37–51. Jackson, MS: University Press of Mississippi, 2005.

Genette, Gerard. *Paratexts: Thresholds of Interpretation.* 1987. Jane E. Lewin, trans. New York: Cambridge University Press, 1997.

Grimshaw, James A. *Robert Penn Warren: A Descriptive Bibliography, 1922–1979.* Charlottesville, VA: University Press of Virginia, 1981.

Hemingway, Ernest. *Death in the Afternoon.* New York: Charles Scribner's Sons, 1932.

Hendricks, Randy, and James A. Perkins, eds. *Selected Letters of Robert Penn Warren: Backward Glances and New Visions, 1969–1979.* Baton Rouge, LA: Louisiana State University Press, 2011.

———. *Selected Letters of Robert Penn Warren: New Beginnings and New Directions, 1953–1968.* Baton Rouge, LA: Louisiana State University Press, 2008.

———. *Selected Letters of Robert Penn Warren: Toward Sunset, at a Great Height, 1980–1989.* Baton Rouge, LA: Louisiana State University Press, 2013.

———. *Selected Letters of Robert Penn Warren: Triumph and Transition, 1943–1952.* Baton Rouge, LA: Louisiana State University Press, 2006.

Kennedy, William. "Robert Penn Warren: Willie Stark, Politics, and the Novel." 1973. In *Conversations with Robert Penn Warren,* edited by Gloria L. Cronin and Ben Siegel, 84–92. Jackson, MS: University Press of Mississippi, 2005.

Madden, David. "Preface." In *The Legacy of Robert Penn Warren,* edited by David Madden, xi–xv. Baton Rouge, LA: Louisiana State University Press, 2000.

Moyers, Bill. "A Conversation with Robert Penn Warren." 1976. In *Conversations with Robert Penn Warren,* edited by Gloria L. Cronin and Ben Siegel, 93–111. Jackson, MS: University Press of Mississippi, 2005.

Newquist, Roy. "Conversation: Eleanor Clark and Robert Penn Warren." 1967. In *Conversations with Robert Penn Warren,* edited by Gloria L. Cronin and Ben Siegel, 52–63. Jackson, MS: University Press of Mississippi, 2005.

Payne, Ladell. "Willie Stark and Huey Long: Atmosphere, Myth, or Suggestion?" In *Twentieth Century Interpretations of* All the King's Men, edited by Robert H. Chambers, 98–115. Englewood Cliffs, NJ: Prentice-Hall, Inc., 1977.

Perry, Keith. *The Kingfish in Fiction: Huey P. Long and the Modern American Novel.* Baton Rouge, LA: Louisiana State University Press, 2004.

Polk, Noel. "Editing *All the King's Men.*" *Southern Review* 38, no. 3 (2002): 849–860.

———. "The Text of the 'Restored' Edition of *All the King's Men.*" *RWP: An Annual of Robert Penn Warren Studies* 2 (2002): 17–64.

Ruppersburg, Hugh. *Robert Penn Warren and the American Imagination.* Athens, GA: University of Georgia Press, 1990.

Stitt, Peter. "An Interview with Robert Penn Warren." 1977. In *Conversations with Robert Penn Warren,* edited by Gloria L. Cronin and Ben Siegel, 112–122. Jackson, MS: University Press of Mississippi, 2005.

Vitale, Tom. "A Conversation with Robert Penn Warren." 1985. In *Conversations with Robert Penn Warren,* edited by Gloria L. Cronin and Ben Siegel, 218–226. Jackson, MS: University Press of Mississippi, 2005.

Warren, Robert Penn. *All the King's Men.* 1946. Franklin Center, PA: Franklin Library, 1977.

———. *All the King's Men.* 1946. New York: Harcourt Brace Jovanovich, 1981.

———. *All the King's Men.* 1946. New York: Modern Library, 1953.

———. *All the King's Men.* 1946. New York: Time, Inc. 1963.

———. *All the King's Men.* 1946. Noel Polk, ed. New York: Harcourt, 2001.

———. "All the King's Men: Preface to Franklin Library Edition," Typescript. Robert Penn Warren Papers. Beinecke Rare Book and Manuscript Library. Yale University. New Haven, CT.

———. *Brother to Dragons: A Tale in Verse and Voices.* New York: Random House, 1953.

Woodward, C. Van. "The Uses of History in Fiction." 1968. In *Conversations with Robert Penn Warren,* edited by Gloria L. Cronin and Ben Siegel, 64–70. Jackson, MS: University Press of Mississippi, 2005.

CHAPTER 7

Ensuring Presence: Toni Morrison and the Language of Legacy

My choices of language ... are attempts to transfigure the complexity and wealth of Black-American culture into a language worthy of the culture.
—Toni Morrison, Afterword to *The Bluest Eye*[1]

To render enslavement as a personal experience, language must get out of the way.
—Toni Morrison, Foreword to *Beloved*[2]

In her preface to *Playing in the Dark: Whiteness and the Literary Imagination*, Toni Morrison argues that "writing and reading mean being aware of the writer's notions of risk and safety, the serene achievement of, or sweaty fight for, meaning and response-ability."[3] Of all her novels, Morrison fought hardest for her first, *The Bluest Eye*, released by Holt, Rinehart, and Winston to little fanfare and middling reviews in 1970. Alfred A. Knopf released a new edition of the novel, featuring an afterword by the author, after Morrison received the Nobel Prize in 1993. Reprint editions of *Sula*, *Song of Solomon*, and *Tar Baby* would follow, but *The Bluest Eye* was the only reprint to include new material from Morrison. In her afterword she describes how "beauty was not simply something to behold; it was something one could *do*,"[4] and she uses her characterization of protagonist Pecola Breedlove as the metaphor for "racial self-loathing."[5] Morrison focuses on "how something as grotesque as the demonization of an entire race could take root inside the most delicate member of society:

© The Author(s), under exclusive license to Springer Nature Switzerland AG 2021
R. K. Tangedal, *The Preface*, New Directions in Book History,
https://doi.org/10.1007/978-3-030-85151-4_7

a child; the most vulnerable member: a female," while she explores "social and domestic aggression that could cause a child to literally fall apart."[6] She notes the "conspiratorial" nature of an early line in the novel, "Quiet as it's kept." "The conspiracy is both held and withheld, exposed and sustained," she explains. "In some sense it was precisely what the act of writing the book was: a public exposure of a private confidence."[7] She and her readers share in the secret of the line, with "sudden familiarity or instant intimacy,"[8] because Morrison knows "that this is to be a terrible story about things one would rather not know anything about."[9] Her readers are protected and provoked, and finally subsumed into the text: "the book can be seen to open with its close: a speculation on the disruption of 'nature' as being a social disruption with tragic individual consequences in which the reader, as part of the population of the text, is implicated."[10] Her afterword makes clear her willingness to engage in the "serene achievement of, or sweaty fight for" meaning and reader engagement, issues included in much of the public writing she did throughout her career. But her narrative project expanded beyond those issues: "My choices of language (speakerly, aural, colloquial), my reliance for full comprehension on codes embedded in black culture, my effort to effect immediate co-conspiracy and intimacy (without any distancing, explanatory fabric), as well as my attempt to shape a silence while breaking it are attempts to transfigure the complexity and wealth of Black-American culture into a language worthy of the culture."[11] Language, full comprehension, immediate intimacy, shaping and breaking silence, being worthy. In her Nobel address she spoke of language as sublime, generative, making meaning "that secures our difference, our human difference—the way in which we are like no other life," and doing language "may be the measure of our lives."[12] But her first novel, "like Pecola's life," was "dismissed, trivialized, misread. And it has taken twenty-five years to gain for her the respectful publication this edition is," signed "Princeton, New Jersey/ November, 1993."[13]

Morrison reworked the afterword into a foreword for a Vintage reprint in 1999, and again in 2007, much of it still the language she set out in the earlier version. But she clears the way for herself, the successful professional author with the ability to look back, as so many do, "on the problems expressive language presented to me. ... Hearing 'civilized' languages debase humans, watching cultural exorcisms debase literature, seeing oneself preserved in the amber of disqualifying metaphors—I can say that my narrative project is as difficult today as it was then."[14] Though this exact passage is included in the 1993 afterword as the penultimate paragraph, it offers an altogether different meaning in the context of 2007. The "amber of disqualifying metaphors" could mean her possible disquietude with a number of issues: exposure as part of Oprah Winfrey's Book Club; the interviews and public appearances; her role as a public figure; and her desire to be an American writer rather than a "problem to be solved."[15] In 1993, the metaphors were aimed at her first novel, but here the scope has broadened, and the narrative has sharpened to include a public writer's "difficulty" with being Toni Morrison. She told Pam Houston in 2005 that "television is hard, but I feel obliged to do it, to garner readers and to make myself available as much as I can since I am around. And I have a nice readership in universities, which is a big benefit because I can speak in ways there that I couldn't on television. And to have future generations reading my books—*The Bluest Eye* they read in junior high school."[16] The preservation of her life lives in her work, a fact she knew too well. "There is danger inherent in being an artist, always—" she wrote in "The Individual Artist," "the danger of failure, the danger of being misunderstood."[17] But failure and misunderstanding are not always mutually exclusive, another fact Morrison recognizes.

In the previously mentioned response to Houston, Morrison admits to using television to "garner readers" that differ from her "nice readership" at universities, yet the future generations she notes are as young as junior high schoolers, neither television readers nor academic ones. Her forewords for a Vintage reprint series of her novels (2004–2014) stem from her desire to maintain a narrative project rooted in language, though the forewords complicate that project in textual and interpretive ways. Which readers do her forewords speak to? To whom can she help better understand her project, her work, her life? What failures can she turn into victories, and how much control does she exert over the reader? The reworked foreword to *The Bluest Eye* features a sentimental opening, a gift of reassurance that Morrison's targeted readers, clearly young, inexperienced ones, will be able to give her novel a chance: "There can't be anyone, I am sure, who doesn't know what it feels like to be disliked, even rejected, momentarily or for sustained periods of time. … It may even be that some of us know what it is like to be actually hated—hated for things we have no control over and cannot change. When this happens, it is some consolation to know that the dislike or hatred is unjustified—that you don't deserve it."[18] Though this opening was first printed in 1999, its appearance in the 2007 foreword seems to call back to her comment in 2005 about junior high schoolers reading *The Bluest Eye*. She is an usher, a guide, a calm voice, the adult who can level with the children. In her essay, "The Writer Before the Page," she claimed that because her "métier is black, the artistic demands of black culture are such that I cannot patronize, control, or pontificate."[19] Forewords, prefaces, and introductions are, by their very nature, zones of control, transmission, and transaction.[20] They also lend themselves to what Gerard Genette refers to as retrospective (or retroactive) discourse, "of emotional permanence and intellectual curiosity," where readers are either reminded of an author's good works or informed that the author has not changed (when in fact they have).[21] Morrison's foreword to *The Bluest Eye*, and its sentimental opening, may be read as a sincere gesture to less experienced readers, though it has also been read as "a travesty. … It reduces her own work to 'social anthropology.'"[22] If Morrison has changed, as Genette suggests happens with writers who append delayed prefaces to their past work, what effect does that change have on her narrative project? In one of her most famous essays, "Unspeakable Things Unspoken: The Afro-American Presence in American Literature" (1988), Morrison suggests that in her writing, "spaces, which I am filling in, and can fill in because they were planned, can conceivably be filled in with other significances," and "into these spaces should fall the ruminations of the reader and his or her invented or recollected or misunderstood knowingness."[23] At what point are openings to forewords like the one for *The Bluest Eye* going back on, or potentially scuttling, the readers' knowledge of their power?

By 2007, Morrison had removed the parts about her novel being misunderstood like its protagonist. Does Morrison believe she has become "like Pecola: dismissed, trivialized, misread" due to some of the "disqualifying metaphors" lobbed her way—Black writer, radical intellectual, feminist author, classic American writer, difficult to understand, commodified sell-out, Nobel Prize winner? Is the source of her language in the forewords the same language she strives for in her novels? Morrison searches for the language of legacy as much as a language "worthy of the culture,"[24] and her choices can be read as either significant supplements to her texts or textual deterrents. For a writer who referenced readers and reading regularly in her public lectures, interviews, and essays, Morrison uses her forewords as vehicles of explanation and interpretation, not unlike Henry James's prefaces for the New York edition. But the forewords elicit more questions than answers: Was the act of reading still her primary goal, or had the target shifted slightly in the wake of her increased profile due to her Nobel Prize win in the early 1990s and her exposure as part of Oprah's Book Club in the late 1990s and early 2000s? Are Morrison's forewords an extension of her lifelong "narrative project"[25] or a unique authorial act, connected perhaps, but not necessarily a continuation of that project? With particular focus on storytelling, language interrogation, and Black representation, this chapter evaluates Morrison's forewords in the context of her own mission. Are they worthy of the culture, and therefore, worthy of Toni Morrison?

A Public Exposure of a Private Confidence

Morrison's late-career forewords help reestablish the concept of the "uniform edition" in the contemporary literary marketplace. Morrison sets out to further define and advance her narrative project and explicate meanings in her texts. Appending reprints with forewords alters readers' expectations, with authors "reconstituting the genesis of the work,"[26] according to Genette. Henry James assured readers of *The Portrait of a Lady* that "the house of fiction has in short not one window, but a million—a number of possible windows not to be reckoned, rather; every one of which has been pierced, or is still pierceable, in its vast front, by the need of the individual vision and by the pressure of the individual will."[27] Morrison opens some windows and asserts her individual artistic will with her forewords. All told, eight of her eleven published novels have been reprinted as Vintage International editions,[28] featuring seven new forewords and a reworked afterword/foreword. Aside from Tessa Roynon's excellent investigation into these forewords in her essay, "Lobbying the Reader: Toni Morrison's Recent Forwords to Her Novels" (2014), these pieces have received little serious recognition, as academics and popular readers have yet to recognize their value. But Morrison hinted at her intentions in a 12 February 2004 radio interview with Michael Silverblatt for *Bookworm*. "The more familiar [the book] becomes, my hope is that it doesn't become dross, that it's still interesting," she told Silverblatt, "to look in these nooks and crannies, to have that visceral response as well as this sort of cognitive, intellectual response to how this whole thing is put together."[29] Her books deserve to be read, and reread, and she knows how to set that up:

> I mean I, and I'm sure you have, books that you read one year and later on you read them again, and it's a different book or it appears to be. It isn't.

You've changed perhaps or you know more now, or you're looking for something else other than the obvious, other than the *what happens*. And the only other thing I know like that—well I'm sure they're many other things—but the one that comes closest to mind is, in addition to becoming familiar with and interested in a house, is also music in which you hear a song when you're seventeen and then you have a powerful reaction in one way. And you hear it later, and you have another reaction. But what you're reacting to is the same piece of music, perhaps done in different hands, but your memories of it are of the first time you encountered it, as well as what you're thinking now, and so now it's worth listening to again.[30]

Morrison uses her forewords to help readers, at least new readers, recognize the personal importance of her narrative project. She wants us to hear her again, have another reaction, or she wants new readers to feel that first-time experience with her books. She remembers moments with her readers and offers them semi-privately between the covers of her fiction.

As a uniform edition, the reprints move Morrison ahead in age for her back cover portrait. She presents as an older, wiser, and more reflective author—a persona she takes up in her forewords. Her forewords allow for readers and critics to understand her private and public lives simultaneously, as her facts and her fictions lay claim to the same textual space. Morrison told interviewer Ann Hostetler that "a book is a place you can inhabit and return to. When did we get afraid to go back, to reread? … I'd like my books to be read more than once."[31] Her stance on rereading prompts her readers to "circle back into the text,"[32] a similar task she requires of her students. Morrison's reprint forewords offer platforms for literary, pedagogical, and critical exercises from the writer, author, editor, teacher, critic, and reader known professionally as "Toni Morrison." After rereading *The American*, James wished to "woo back such fine hours of precipitation" and feel the romantic instincts of his youth again.[33] Likewise, Morrison uses her forewords to woo her narrative preoccupation with language out into the open for new—and old—readers to appreciate. "Over and over again I am amazed by the treasure trove that American literature is," Morrison wrote in *Playing in the Dark*. "How compelling is the study of those writers who take responsibility for all of the value they bring to their art. How stunning is the achievement of those who have searched for and mined a shareable language for the words to say it."[34] Throughout her forewords, Morrison compels readers to see her language, the language made visible through responsibility and craft.

Of course, the very existence of the Vintage forewords calls into question issues of intention, authorial and otherwise. Many of the forewords feature repurposed portions of earlier essays—in particular "Unspeakable Things Unspoken," where she scrutinizes the first sentences of each of her novels from *The Bluest Eye* (1970) to *Beloved* (1987). If one were to collate the essay against the forewords, one would find several identical passages between the two. Yet repackaged into smaller, emended units, the same passages take on a very different function as parts of forewords than as case studies in a larger academic lecture/essay. Tessa Roynon reminds us that "as often as not, authorial prefaces are indicative of a lack of confidence, and express a desire to achieve what is ultimately impossible: full control over the reception of a text."[35] The number of readers who will read one of her titles with a foreword care of Vintage International far outnumbers those who have read or heard "Unspeakable Things Unspoken." But if Morrison knew that her sound investigation in the longer essay would benefit each text individually, would it not behoove her to place specific portions of that essay into forewords for new printings of those texts? Repurposing older material for "new" prefaces is not new, as we have seen with Ring Lardner earlier in this study, and it does not necessarily suggest indecision or anxiety. In fact, few writers have expressed themselves as confidently in public as Toni Morrison, with scores of public lectures, essays, interviews, and other epitexts that speak directly to her work.[36] In the final years of her life, Morrison saw two collections of essays published in handsome volumes from Harvard University Press (*The Origin of Others*, 2017) and the publisher of her fiction, Alfred A. Knopf (*The Source of Self-Regard*, 2019). Other essay collections include *Goodness and the Literary Imagination* (2019), which featured essays by scholars alongside Morrison's 2012 Ingersoll Lecture at Harvard Divinity School, and *What Moves at the Margin: Selected Nonfiction* (2008), and two volumes of interviews provide a healthy survey of her public engagement: *Toni Morrison: Conversations* (2008) and *Conversations with Toni Morrison* (1994). Few writers, living or dead, revealed as much to the public outside of their narrative texts than Morrison. Released five years after the final Vintage foreword, *The Source of Self-Regard* has the trappings of an omnibus volume, meant to act as the central collection of Morrison's nonfiction. "A writer's life and work are not a gift to mankind," she writes in "Peril," the opening essay, "they are its necessity."[37] The book sets out to remind readers of Morrison's aesthetic and social concerns, a far cry from Stephen King's popular *On Writing: A Memoir of the Craft* (2000). "The individual artist is by nature a questioner and a critic; that's what she does," she writes in "The Individual Artist." "Her questions and criticism are her work, and she is frequently in conflict with the status quo."[38] In "Literature and Public Life," she argues that literature "refuses and disrupts passive or controlled consumption of the spectacle designed to nationalize identity in order to sell us products. Literature allows us—no, demands of us—the experience of ourselves as multidimensional persons."[39] In "The Writer Before the Page," she wants her fiction "to urge the reader into active participation in the nonnarrative, nonliterary experience of the text. And to refuse him makes it difficult for him (the reader) to confine himself to a cool and distant acceptance of data."[40] And in "Unspeakable Things Unspoken," arguably Morrison's finest and most-respected essay, she writes, "Writing is, *after* all, an act of language, its practice. But *first* of all it is an effort of the will to discover."[41] Morrison's multi-year projects to encourage writers and readers to read, to find, to search, and to do language play out time and time again in her essays. She exhibits the confidence to maintain a thorough public life for her work, in a business that requires some mode of privacy—to think, to dream, to compose, to revise. These essays, more so than any of her forewords, are public exposures of private confidences, which Morrison used skillfully for most of her professional writing life.

Even with Morrison's clear self-assurance, displayed frequently in her public essays, Roynon's point about confidence and control is well taken. Henry James's prefaces to the New York edition certainly fit the mold, as do F. Scott Fitzgerald's introduction to the Modern Library edition of *The Great Gatsby* and, to some degree, Robert Penn Warren's introductions to *All the King's Men*. Ernest Hemingway's prefaces on writing and Willa Cather's introduction to *My Ántonia* do not lack confidence, but they most definitely interrogate control. Where, then, do Morrison's forewords land? Are her pieces the result of a lack of confidence in her readers, her skills, her legacy? Does she feel untethered to her books, needing to control their reception? Her forewords in many ways deal with all of these issues, which stem from a particularly popular period in her career. From 1996 to 2002, Morrison had four books selected as part of Oprah Winfrey's Book Club: *Song of Solomon* (1996), *Paradise* (1998), *The Bluest Eye* (2000), and *Sula* (2002), and she appeared with Winfrey on her daytime talk show to discuss her work. John K. Young traces how Morrison was able to enjoy the success that exposure can provide even the most critically acclaimed of writers. She became "the most dramatic example of postmodernism's merger between canonicity and commercialism," for "by embracing Oprah's Book Club, Morrison replaces separate white and black readerships with a single, popular audience."[42] The persona she exhibited on the show played to the strengths of her best essays on craft and reading. In discussing *Paradise*, a difficult novel for even the seasoned reader, Morrison tells viewers "I didn't want to write an essay. … I wanted you to participate in the journey."[43] Cecilia Konchar Farr notes that "Morrison's deferential attitude toward readers is not traditionally professorial." Instead Morrison leans on "*a constant insistence on openness, participation, and involvement,* a decided focus on the social aspects of reading."[44] Viewers are encouraged to "trust your own reading while trusting others to expand that reading in conversation."[45] Winfrey's efforts, bolstered by Morrison's acclaim and cultural clout, represent "the triumph of the social life of literature."[46] Morrison's novels, like other Book Club selections, sold considerably more copies, and those copies were read by more readers (or at least owned by more readers).[47] In an interview with Paul Gray, Morrison was astonished at the success of *Song of Solomon* after the Oprah effect set in. "A million copies of that book sold. … And sales of my other books in paperback jumped about 25%," she told Gray, who notes that "Morrison naturally welcomes the commercial windfalls such recognition brings, but she is not terribly comfortable with being recognized in that way."[48] The terrible discomfort of popularity, and the "windfalls such recognition brings," complicates Pierre Bourdieu's literary economy, where the chief interest of the artist is disinterest.[49] Morrison wrestled publicly with herself, knowing she could be a popular guest on Oprah's talk show *and* the venerated Nobel Laureate championing the demands of literature.

She told Michael Saur in 2004: "My son asked me recently: 'The person who got the Nobel Prize, does she walk behind you or in front of you? Do you like her, or don't you?' I do like her, and she walks ahead of me, so that I can see her and warn her before she does anything foolish."[50] Morrison's recognition, not only of her cultural status but also of her duality—as author and writer, public and private—builds upon the layers of self she spent years developing in her public essays and appearances. "Narrative fiction," she wrote in "Narrating the Other," "provides a controlled wilderness, an opportunity to be and to become the Other. The stranger. With sympathy, clarity, and the risk of self-examination."[51] But there is little if any naïveté on her part as to her position in the academy, the market, or the reading public. Young concludes that "By constructing an audience built through popular, ostensibly low, culture for her serious novels, Morrison explodes the high-low divide that still holds for much of postmodern art. Morrison sells herself and her novels, like jazz, through popular media and thus constructs herself as a self-consciously commodified textual authority."[52] Morrison's textual and economic self-consciousness may have played a role in her forewords, which can be read as compromises between her public essays and her clear willingness to take part in a more commodified space. Depending on the approach taken, Morrison's forewords either add to the narrative texts they preface or detract from those same narrative texts. As Genette argues, "although we do not always know whether [prefaces] are to be regarded as belonging to the text, in any case they surround it, precisely in order to present it, in the usual sense of this verb but also in the strongest sense: to make present, to ensure the text's presence in the world, its 'reception' and consumption in the form (nowadays, at least) of a book."[53] The forewords give Morrison the opportunity to ensure her texts' presence in multiple reading publics—academic, high-brow, low-brow, and commercial—where anyone can contribute to her narrative project. How she feels about those multiple publics is problematic, and her forewords complicate her own historical intentions gleaned from other writings. But one thing that remains are the forewords, with the author's public *and* private presence, "her or his intentions, blindness, and sight,"[54] on full display.

Language Must Get Out of the Way

Toni Morrison never liked being labeled a "politically minded writer."[55] In the foreword to *Sula*, Morrison asks, "What could be so bad about being socially astute, politically aware in literature? Conventional wisdom agrees that political fiction is not art; that such work is less likely to have aesthetic value because politics—all politics—is agenda and therefore its presence taints aesthetic production."[56] This statement speaks directly to her involvement in editing *The Black Book* for Random House, published in 1974 and developed during her composition of *Sula*. Morrison makes the reader aware of the "inordinate burden on African American writers" because of their association with politically motivated works by the end of the 1960s. She argues further, "whether they were politically motivated of any sort, or whether they were politically inclined, aware, or aggressive, the fact of their race or the race of their characters doomed them to a 'political-only' analysis of their work."[57] She claims that "it may be difficult now to imagine how it felt to be seen as a problem to be solved rather than a writer to be read" and cites the "no-win" situation of prominent black writers—like Zora Neale Hurston, Ralph Ellison, James Baldwin, and Richard Wright—being called upon to "write an essay addressing the 'problem' of being a 'Negro' writer."[58] Her forewords are, to an extent, an attempt to subvert that kind of essay. Morrison's goal was "to use folk language, vernacular in a manner neither exotic nor comic, neither minstrelized nor microscopically analyzed. I wanted to redirect, reinvent the political, cultural, and artistic judgments saved for African American writers."[59] Yet, as she outlines in "Unspeakable Things Unspoken," her practice is also "a search for a deliberate posture of vulnerability to those aspects of Afro-American culture that can inform and position my work."[60] There is a strength in admitting her desire to control and her desire to remain vulnerable, both personae appealing to different kinds of readers.

James Weldon Johnson recognized the same duality in Black poets in his preface to *The Book of American Negro Poetry* (1922), where he traces the effects of what he terms "Negro dialect" on Black poets and white readers. Paul Laurence Dunbar told him, "'I've got to write dialect poetry; it's the only way I can get them to listen to me,'"[61] and Johnson calls Dunbar, "the first to rise to a height from which he could take a perspective view of his own race. He was the first to see objectively its humor, its superstitions, its shortcomings; the first to feel sympathetically its heart-wounds, its yearnings, its aspirations, and to voice them all in a purely literary form."[62] Poets, like Dunbar, "are working through a problem not realized by the reader, and, perhaps, by many of these poets themselves not realized consciously. They are trying to break away from, not Negro dialect itself, but the limitations on Negro dialect imposed by the fixing effects of long convention."[63] Morrison spoke and wrote at length about breaking away from the more limiting traditions of language denying entry to narrative potential. Her work, as she outlines in *Playing in the Dark,* requires her "to learn how to maneuver ways to free up the language from its sometimes sinister, frequently lazy, almost always predictable employment of racially informed and determined chains."[64] "Nothing would be more hateful to me," she wrote in "The Writer Before the Page," "than a monolithic prescription for what black literature is or ought to be,"[65] and in her Nobel address she argued that "oppressive language does more than represent violence, it is violence; does more than represent the limits of knowledge, it limits knowledge."[66] In many ways, Morrison's entire oeuvre is an answer to the question that plagued writers like Hurston, Ellison, Baldwin, and Wright; and language, both its peril and its promise, offers her a pathway out of addressing why she is a problem or the result of other writers' problems. Yet, in that continuum of Black writers, whom Johnson cared for by collecting dozens of folktales, poems, and other writings in the early twentieth century, Morrison's project appears to mirror Johnson, who concluded:

> In stating the need for Aframerican poets in the United States to work out a new and distinctive form of expression I do not wish to be understood to hold any theory that they should limit themselves to Negro poetry, to racial themes; the sooner they are able to write *American* poetry spontaneously, the better. Nevertheless, I believe that the richest contribution the Negro poet can make to the American literature of the future will be the fusion into it of his own individual artistic gifts.[67]

Morrison's forewords highlight the fusion of her many concerns—history, folktales, language, family, reading—as part of the long history of Black narrative expression. She seeks to neither escape nor embody any particular persona: a Black writer, a woman writer, a political writer. She is all of these and none of them, within and without the confines that limit Black expression, fusing, as Johnson hoped Black writers could, all elements into an individual authority. *Sula* stretched her "attempts to manipulate language to work credibly and, perhaps, elegantly with a discredited vocabulary," while *Paradise* was "an effort to disrupt the assumptions of racial discourse."[68] Morrison navigates the trials of her authority with language, both its effects and its influence, and she does not shy away from it.

Many of the forewords feature explanations and elaborations, not a radical shift from most prefaces. She explains the various flights throughout *Song of Solomon*, but "unlike most mythical flights, which clearly imply triumph, in the attempt if not the success, Solomon's escape, the insurance man's jump, and Milkman's leap are ambiguous, disturbing."[69] She repurposes the myth of the "tar baby" in the novel of the same name: "the principal relationship is not limited to the rabbit and the farmer; it is also between the rabbit and the tar figure. She snares him; he knows it, yet compounds his entanglement while demanding to be freed."[70] Sethe, her protagonist in *Beloved*, would "represent the unapologetic acceptance of shame and terror; assume the consequences of choosing infanticide; claim her own freedom."[71] "Following *Beloved*'s focus on mother-love," she writes in her foreword to *Jazz*, "I intended to examine couple-love—the reconfiguration of the 'self' in such relationships; the negotiation between individuality and commitment to another. Romantic love seemed to me one of the fingerprints of the twenties, and jazz its engine."[72] Her novel *Paradise* "places an all-black community, one chosen by its inhabitants, next to a raceless one, also chosen by its inhabitants. The grounds for traditional black vs. white hostilities shift to the nature of exclusion, the origins of chauvinism, the sources of oppression, assault, and slaughter."[73] In *Sula*, "Hannah, Nel, Eva, Sula were points of a cross—each one a choice for characters bound by gender and race. The nexus of that cross would be a merging of responsibility and liberty difficult to reach, a battle among women who are understood to be least able to win it."[74] *Love* features "the story of disintegration—of a radical change in conventional relationships and class allegiances that signals both liberation and estrangement," below the surface story "of the successful revolt against a common enemy in the struggle for integration";[75] and "in exploring the social and domestic aggression that could cause a child to literally fall apart," she writes in the foreword to *The Bluest Eye*, "I mounted a series of rejections, some routine, some exceptional, some monstrous, all the while trying hard to avoid complicity in the demonization process Pecola was subjected to."[76] Though the forewords are small, and many deal with subject matter treated earlier in other essays and public writing, Roynon admits that "To hold all the forewords and all the novels simultaneously in play is to apprehend fully the breadth and cohesiveness of the author's project, and the versatility or the suppleness of her intellect."[77] The forewords offer Morrison the space to explain and really teach her novels, yet the opportunity to do so complicates the purposes of language that she spent decades decoding.

Aside from the previously mentioned admission, and another that "as Morrison's sole mode of autobiography thus far, they also have unique value," Roynon provides an effective critique of Morrison's forewords, particularly as they relate to language. Embodying the active and curious reader that Morrison aims for time and again in her essays, Roynon argues that "the ambiguous feel of the editions in which the forewords appear express the precariousness of the 'celebrity radical intellectual' position that she occupies—one in which she is somehow perceived as both too 'difficult' and too 'popular' at the same time."[78] The gulf widens between the academic intellectual of *The Source of Self-Regard* and the more public celebrity book club guest on Oprah Winfrey's television program, as

Morrison asserts "an apparently unchallengeable veracity and authenticity," which could "compromise both the author and her readership."[79] Prefaces, as we have seen in earlier chapters, can be inhibiting signposts, a space where readers can step in or turn back. But they can also be illuminating, ensuring a text's presence in the world by framing the text and, usually, coming as part of a new edition of that text. The issue is not whether Morrison had the right to write prefaces for her books. Of course she did. They were hers after all, and regardless of a reader's expectations, she argued in *Playing in the Dark* that "readers and writers both struggle to interpret and perform within a common language shareable imaginative worlds. And although upon that struggle the positioning of the reader has justifiable claims, the author's presence … is part of the imaginative activity."[80] As that presence, she uses the forewords to introduce herself, not welcome back old readers. But herein lies the problem. Roynon takes issue with Morrison's handling of her readers, the same readers whom Morrison urges into "active participation," since "the experience of looking is deeper that the data accumulated in viewing it."[81] "The prominence and 'forwardness' of these forewords increases authorial authority and decreases that of the reader,"[82] Roynon argues. "The best Morrisonian critique of Morrison provokes rather than closes down controversy and discussion, and often takes the form of a disclosure that morphs into a further strategic concealment or withholding of information."[83] And in what amounts to a lament, she concludes that the forewords "occupy many of the 'spaces' into which we used to be summoned; our status as readers has fallen, and our responsibilities have lessened."[84]

Roynon's treatment of the forewords, as a reader, first and foremost, puts them at odds with so much of what Morrison espoused as integral to her project. Morrison has called for her readers to provide "wisdom"[85] and struggle with the "discomfort and unease"[86] of her prose, experience her books as maps rather than "the authority,"[87] and reimagine or alter her work.[88] Her language is shareable, flexible, fluid, and unpredictable, and readers must travel with her as she makes her way in and out of tradition to arrive at "a kind of truth."[89] At no point does the author's presence disappear. In fact, the opposite is true: by relying so much on the activity of reading, Morrison becomes like her father in the foreword to *Song of Solomon*, "muse, insight, inspiration, 'the dark finger that guides,' 'bright angel.'"[90] In "Invisible Ink: Reading the Writing and Writing the Reading," she claims that her work forces readers "into helping to write the book. … Writing the reading involves seduction—luring the reader into environments outside the pages. Disqualifying the notion of a stable text for one that is dependent on an active and activated reader who is writing the reading—in invisible ink."[91] There are so many examples outside of Morrison's forewords where she analyzes, dissects, defines, and interrogates readers and reading that the forewords become less and less authoritative regarding the practice. So what are we to do with them? Roynon sees Morrison motivated by three distinct issues: "a wish to consolidate her position and the significance of her works; a continuing perception of a political urgency that necessitates her project and its clarification; and a desire to ensure that readers appreciate the scope of her artistry and her vision to the full."[92] To these I would add: a perceived need to explain her work to a new public, most likely a student-centered one; a sincere wish to have the essence of her more complete public essays repackaged as parts of her novels, rather than apart from them; and quite frankly, an opportunity to sell more books in a uniform edition that canonizes her eight novels as a unit with a similar design and layout, as well as the same photograph of her on every back cover.[93] But these are not issues of language, nor are they issues of narrative projects or perceptive readers. Instead, we have returned to the writer as professional, the phenomenon which affected every writer under investigation in this book. Morrison's forewords live in the liminal space between her overall narrative project and the desire to see herself become "worthy of the culture" not only of language and art but also of legacy and cultural capital.

LIKE A GROWN-UP WRITER

Morrison's foreword to *Song of Solomon* begins with a denunciation of "muses" in a literary sense, which is ironic since Robert Gottlieb, her editor at Knopf, encouraged Morrison to go big with *Song of Solomon* and identify as a writer.[94] Morrison initially regards them as "a shield erected by artists to avoid articulating, analyzing, or even knowing the details of their creative process—for fear it would fade away."[95] Consequently, the foreword to *Tar Baby* has the author "on the linoleum floor, breathing through my mouth, rapt, watching the giveaway eyes of the grown-up telling the story," for "all narrative begins for me as listening."[96] *Song of Solomon* would be "all very saga-like. Old-school heroic, but with other meanings,"[97] and *Tar Baby* "a love story, then. Difficult, unresponsive, but seducing woman and clever, anarchic male, each with definitions of independence and domesticity, or safety and danger that clash."[98] Her characters collide into "lore and reality," which creates "a blend that proved heady, even dizzying, but I believed the plotline solid and familiar enough to withhold or contain a reader's sense of vertigo."[99] The myth of the "tar baby" was popularized by Joel Chandler Harris in his Uncle Remus stories, first published in 1881. In the preface to the first volume, Harris assured readers that "each legend has its variants, but in every instance I have retained that particular version which seemed to me to be the most characteristic, and have given it without embellishment and without exaggeration."[100] He claims later on to have found few Black subjects "who will acknowledge to a stranger that they know anything of these legends, and yet to relate one of the stories is the surest road to their confidence and esteem," and because of that he could "collect and verify the folklore" in his book.[101] Whether acknowledged or not, Morrison controls the myth with her novel and the foreword. She is not a collector of folklore but a caretaker of narrative. "The figure of the tar," she writes, "having done its work, falls out of the action of the tale, yet remains not only as its strange, silent center, but also as the sticky mediator between master and peasant, plantation owner and slave. Constructed by the farmer to foil and entrap, it moves beyond trickery to art."[102] More than a variant of Harris's original tale, Morrison's tale—with its "new life"[103]—is concerned more with who tells stories and how they are told and to whom. Morrison had tackled the issue before, writing in "Unspeakable Things Unspoken" that "Folklore may have begun as allegory for natural or social phenomena; it may have been employed as a retreat from contemporary issues in art; but folklore can also contain myths that reactivate themselves endlessly through providers—the people who repeat, reshape, reconstitute, and reinterpret them."[104] And she would later argue in *Playing in the Dark* that "Black slavery enriched the country's creative possibilities. For in that construction of blackness *and* enslavement could be found not only the not-free but also, with the dramatic polarity created by skin color, the projection of the not-me. The result was a playground for the imagination."[105] To a degree, Morrison relies on her reader knowing the myth of the tar baby, yet she needs to recount her version for them in the foreword to ensure its significance. She knows that the result of these tales, among other aspects of racialized rhetoric, was "a fabricated brew of darkness, otherness, alarm, and desire that is uniquely American."[106] But there is a need to define, guide, and delineate that Morrison takes on, a role more pronounced in her public essays and lectures. What troubles readers like Roynon is that Morrison appears to suggest "that it is her own expectations of her readers that have diminished."[107] Readers are not the same as attendees at a lecture, or viewers of Oprah's talk show, or interviewers from *Time*. So, are the forewords further evidence of Morrison's growth from new writer to seasoned writer to successful writer to canonical writer? And if so, are the forewords capable of bridging the gap between the private artist and the professional author, as she too made her way through the zones of authority from 1970 to 2019?

Sula opens with what Morrison calls "a lobby" where a white gaze separates the "black-topic" text from the "diminished expectations of the reader."[108] Quoting from "Unspeakable Things Unspoken," Morrison recasts her "lobby" as an introduction and translation by a "valley man" where she lets "'a stranger in, through whose eyes it can be viewed.' This deference paid to the 'white' gaze was the one time I addressed the 'problem.'"[109] Indeed, rather than thrust the reader into the mind of the suicidal veteran Shadrack, Morrison offers a slight history of "the Bottom" and Medallion, as well as the mythological connotations Sula's name conjures in the community. Morrison reads her lobby as a political move that separates white gaze and black-topic text in order to make light of and situate the "problem" of Black authorship. She defends her revision: "In the revised opening I tried to represent discriminatory, prosecutorial racial oppression as well as the community's efforts to remain stable and healthy: the neighborhood has been almost completely swept away by commercial interests (a golf course), but the remains of what sustained it (music, dancing, craft, religion, irony, wit) are what the 'valley man,' the stranger, sees—or could have seen." Her new space is more suited for readers, "a more inviting embrace than Shadrack's organized public madness—it helps to unify the neighborhood until Sula's anarchy challenges it."[110] It may also unify the reader with the author. Ernest Hemingway never published a preface to *The Sun Also Rises* (1926) where he outlined how we revised his opening chapters. To do so would demystify that which remains mysterious to the public. Morrison's lobby is for her readers, and she tells them so, whether they already knew her meanings and intentions or not. But, as Roynon concludes, "we do not need lobbies or front porches on the homes that she has so painstakingly built."[111] What matters here is the "we," and who is responsible for determining which "we" deserves consideration.

Morrison feels more free in the foreword to *Beloved*, where she relates that "in 1983 I lost my job—or left it. One, the other, or both. In any case, I had been part-time for a while, coming into the publishing house one day a week to do the correspondence-telephoning-meetings that were part of the job; editing manuscripts at home."[112] She left for two reasons: one, "I had written four novels and it seemed clear to everyone that writing was my central work," and two, "the books I had edited were not earning scads of money, even when 'scads' didn't mean what it means now."[113] In a bit of calculated reluctance, she recollects convincing herself "that it was time for me to live like a grown-up writer: off royalties and writing only. I don't know what comic book that notion came from, but I grabbed it."[114] She offers just enough disinterest to assure her more astute readers that making the jump from editor to writer was not purely economic, that being a "grown-up writer" still meant relying on "how language arrives"[115] as much as it meant relying on the royalties and the advances. The passive construction belies her very active process of language-making, and the pose matters since Morrison cannot be seen as being too reliant on the economic aspects of her decision to give up editing as a career. Another important factor is Morrison's transition to teaching, first as the Albert Schweitzer chair (an endowed position) at the University of Albany, SUNY, within a year of leaving Random House. Reading her foreword to *Beloved* without that context gives readers the impression that Morrison cared little for financial stability, even casting it aside so she could write what would become her great American novel. Whether Morrison does this deliberately is difficult to determine, but no other foreword, even those culled partially from other public essays, mentions employment. If *Beloved* is the transition, then the power that came from that transition was as much an economic venture as it was an artistic one.

A year after the publication of *Beloved*, and its accompanying success, Morrison told an interviewer that "there is no suitable memorial or plaque or wreath or wall or park or skyscraper lobby" for slavery and because of that absence "the book had to."[116] Dedicated to "*Sixty million and more*,"[117] *Beloved* is itself a memorial for slavery, and Morrison's self-consciousness surrounding that act, that memorial, is striking. Her foreword mentions her joblessness several times, meaning the time after she left her role as an editor at Random House, not a time spent not writing. She is edgy, rather than calm; nothing was "new or pressing" in her "index of problem areas"; then it hits her: "I was happy, free in a way I had never been, ever. It was the oddest sensation. Not ecstasy, for satisfaction, not a surfeit of pleasure or accomplishment. It was a purer delight, a rogue anticipation with certainty. Enter *Beloved*." A narrative of inspiration, coupled with a sense of what she calls "certainty," is backed up with the more important narrative of researching her subject matter. Again, few of her forewords go into her research methods, though many of them use family stories or anecdotes as "research" more broadly. Morrison, her mother, her grandmother, and her great-grandmother "people the writing of *Tar Baby* as witness, as challenge, as judges intent on the uses to which stories are put and the manner of their telling,"[118] with Morrison "eager for their praise."[119] She casts herself as a girl who spent her time listening rather than as a writer doing field work. In the foreword to *Jazz*, she opens her mother's metal trunk and finds that "right on top of crepe dresses is an evening purse, tiny jeweled with fringe dangled in jet and glass."[120] She "would keep this glimpse" of her mother's world: "It was private. It was glittery. And now, it was mine as well."[121] She concludes that foreword with an anecdote of her mother singing. "How interesting it would be," she exclaims, "to raise the atmosphere, choose the palette, plumb the sounds of her young life, and convert it all to language as seductive, as glittery, as an evening purse tucked away in a trunk!"[122] She reads her family and consumes their dreams and tales; she listens and finds, and sensations direct her purpose, for "language can never live up to life, once and for all," as she noted in her Nobel lecture. "Nor should it. Language can never 'pin down' slavery, genocide, war. Nor should it yearn for the arrogance to able to do so. Its force, its felicity is in its reach toward the ineffable."[123] *Beloved*, then, is not only a memorial for slavery, its effects, and violence, but also a memorial to its maker. No grandfather or mother, no friends or family, just her and her focus, a professional author for the first time.

But the language she describes and wields so fervently presents real issues of control. *Jazz* was meant to showcase "improvisation, originality, change"—the book would "seek to become them"[124] rather than be about them—and "a manifestation of the music's intellect, sensuality, anarchy; its history, its range, and its modernity."[125] It is hard to read these lines as anything other than a sincere metaphor of herself, Morrison struggling to force language and music into a new place, a new song. The book as character concludes the novel speaking to the reader: "If I were able I'd say it. Say make me, remake me. You are free to do it and I am free to let you because look, look. Look where your hands are. Now."[126] Another metaphor emerges, one of remaking and recasting, similar to her many calls for readers to become the kind of people that *do* language which "surges toward knowledge, not its destruction."[127] The book would archive the Jazz Age and become invention, become change, become music. She wanted "to expose and bury the artifice and to take practice beyond the rules. I didn't want simply a musical background, or decorative reference to it," and her final line echoes her intention to write a novel where "structure would *equal* meaning."[128] Few writers would attempt an experiment of this scope without the clout of past success. *Jazz* happened because of *Beloved*, a book that represented freedom beyond the text for Morrison. It "unleashed a host of ideas about how and what one cherishes under the duress and emotional disfigurement that a slave society imposes. One such idea—love as perpetual mourning (haunting)—led me to consider a parallel one: how such relationships were altered, later, in (or by) a certain kind of liberty."[129] The music is a new freedom, and the book must be a memorial to that form of freedom, not unlike her acclaimed memorial for slavery. "Whatever the truth or consequences of individual entanglements and the racial landscape," she asserts in her foreword, "the music insisted that the past might haunt us, but would not entrap us."[130] Her two immediate post-Random House novels are about freedom, and the power and peril that comes from being not only a full-time writer (with endowed professorships first at a public state university and then at Princeton) but also a figure expected to follow one memorial with another, all in service to developing a wide and diverse readership.

And yet, the forewords are not always read as faithful agents of her project, nor should they be. In her foreword to *Beloved*, she claims that "the terrain, slavery, was formidable and pathless. To invite readers (and myself) into the repellant landscape (hidden, but not completely; deliberately buried, but not forgotten) was to pitch a tent in a cemetery inhabited by highly vocal ghosts."[131] The convenient narrative of family inspiring her writing in all of the other forewords, again, is missing here. Instead, the ghosts of the past, what some would call "muses," speak. "There would be no lobby into this house, and there would be no introduction into it or into the novel," she writes. Her readers would be "kidnapped," "snatched," given no "preparation or defense,"[132] for "to render enslavement as a personal experience, language must get out of the way."[133] Roynon sees the obvious irony in Morrison's claim, and the "paradox" it presents: "Without any apparent self-conscious irony, in the foreword itself Morrison stresses the importance of readers' direct, violent and introduction-less encounter with the house on Bluestone Road, and with the history that it embodies. The very presence of the foreword threatens to negate the technique that it describes."[134] She is right. When a writer claims that language must get out of the way, they are in essence negating themselves from the experience they wish to create for readers. Morrison wants language to become something else in *Jazz*, but language cannot come close to representing the experience of slavery in *Beloved*. A similar passage in "Unspeakable Things Unspoken'" is the basis for Morrison's claim about language and slavery: "No compound of houses, no neighborhood, no sculpture, no paint, no time, especially no time because memory, prehistoric memory, has no time. There is just a little music, each other, and the urgency of what is at stake. Which is all they had. For that work, the work of language is to get out of the way."[135] Her other novels up to that point featured ways to "link arms with the reader and facilitate making it one's own," whereas *Beloved* does not.[136] She wanted "the compelling confusion of being there as they (the characters) are; suddenly, without comfort or succor from the 'author,' with only imagination, intelligence, and necessity available for the journey."[137] In the foreword, Morrison tells readers that she will be kidnapping them, snatching them; yet she prepares them it. She tips her hand before the game begins, making some readers question why her most important novel now has a lobby that the author claims it does not need.

It makes sense, then, why Morrison and Oprah Winfrey did not highlight *Beloved* during the former's run on the latter's book club; she had claimed that there was no way in for readers who did not possess imagination or intelligence. Of course this does not mean that Oprah's viewers lack those qualities, or that the host requires comfort from a book in order to read it. But there is a sense that *Beloved* should not have been given a foreword, just like it did not appear on Oprah's Book Club. Morrison chooses, at first, to protect *Beloved* (either consciously or subconsciously) from commodification and exposure on television (though she later allowed the book to be made into a film, starring Oprah Winfrey), yet she repurposes a public lecture that leaves more to the imagination into a foreword that tells readers they should, like Hemingway claimed in his preface to Jerome Bahr's *All Good Americans*, "excuse the preface"[138] and focus on the book. Morrison may have set herself up for the kind of rebuke the foreword to *Beloved* elicits from Roynon, for when one makes language their work, that language can deny and disregard as much as it builds and beckons. But the grown-up writer that Toni Morrison had become, thanks to her flight from Random House and her decision to train her focus on dangers and hauntings, is the story of the foreword. There is no language for the highly vocal ghosts of slavery, but there must be a language for Morrison's freedom. And she needs to give that story to her readers so they can see, really see, what kind of writer it takes to claim that the language she herself is responsible for writing is in fact incapable (even in its sharpness and its focus) of doing what no writing can do: bring back the dead. Yet the book as memorial remains, and the story of Toni Morrison as a freed professional author grows. Again, for Morrison, "a writer's life and work are not a gift to mankind; they are its necessity."[139]

ASSUMING POWER

Paradise, written as a "race-less" experiment and an analysis of contrasting communities, proves even more difficult and narratively complex than Morrison's previous work. She notes in her 2014 foreword (which features reworked portions from her earlier essay, "The Trouble with Paradise") how the violent displacement of Native Americans from the Oklahoma Territory provided "the opportunity to establish black towns," and the rush "was as feverish as the rush for whites to occupy the land. The 'colored' newspapers encouraged the rush and promised a kind of paradise to the newcomers: land, their own government, safety—there were even sustained movements to establish their own state."[140] Upon discovering the communal exclusivity and self-imposed separation between light-skinned and dark-skinned African Americans during the rush, Morrison notes, "I also noticed that the town leaders in the photographs were invariably light-skinned men. Was skin privilege also a feature of the separation? One that replicated the white racism they abhorred?"[141] As an author in her mid-80s, Morrison recollects specific research questions which troubled, haunted, and disrupted her some seventeen years earlier. Her novel seeks to "(1) to examine the definition of paradise, (2) to delve into the power of colorism, (3) to dramatize the conflict between patriarchy and matriarchy, and (4) disrupt racial discourse altogether by signaling then erasing it."[142] Her final item, erasing race in order to disrupt our understanding of paradise and control, cuts deeply into the author's canon, for to her "the idea of paradise is no longer imaginable or, rather, it is overimagined, which amounts to the same thing."[143] Morrison has done her research, and the novel can only be read by attending to these research topics and practices.

Similar to her earlier forewords, Morrison again describes the germination of her first line. She wrestles with her choice to begin *Paradise* with "They shoot the white girl first. With the rest they can take their time."[144]— a line as provocative as any of her openings. "In the Convent race is indeterminate," she writes, "all racial codes are eliminated, deliberately withheld. For some readers this was disturbing and some admitted to being preoccupied with finding out which character was the 'white girl'; others wondered initially and then abandoned the question; some ignored the confusion by reading them all as black." However, in a moment of judgment, she highlights that "the perceptive ones read them as fully realized individuals—whatever their race."[145] To her, "the conflicts are gender-related and generational. They are struggles over history—who will tell and thereby control the story of the past? Who will shape the future? There are conflicts of value. Of personal identity. What is manhood? Womanhood? And finally what is personhood?"[146] Morrison speaks to the need for "freedom and safety; for plentitude, for rest, for beauty; by the search for one's own space, for respect, love, bliss—in short, how to reimagine paradise."[147] She asserts full control over her public and private authority. We see the craft, and we feel the craft. The questions need answers, and she will provide them by working. Somewhat answering for her career-long attention to violence and violent ends, she reminds readers that "the visionary language of the doomed reaches heights of linguistic ardor with which language of the blessed and saved cannot compete."[148] In a way, readers are forced to consider how best to read Toni Morrison as author, since "an open, borderless, come-one-come-all paradise, without dread, minus a nemesis is no paradise at all."[149] For readers to understand her personal and difficult narrative project, they must have access to the professional writer Toni Morrison rather than just the esteemed cultural, public figure. Her research methods are sound and accounted for; her dedication to the subject is considerable, for to challenge the "view of universalism, to exorcise, alter, and de-fang the white/black confrontation and concentrate on the residue of that hostility seemed to me a daunting project and an artistically liberating one. 'They shoot the white girl first. With the rest they can take their time.'"[150] She wants readers to know that the book was more to her than a selection on Oprah's Book Club. Just as *Jazz* followed in the aftermath of *Beloved*, so too does *Paradise*, though this time the language is primary. It need not get out of the way: "I was eager to manipulate, mutate and control imagistic, metaphoric language in order to produce something that could be called race-specific/race-free prose, language that deactivated the power of racially inflected strategies."[151]

The foreword to *Paradise* comes last in the line of Vintage forewords, but it may say the most about the kind of figure she wants readers to find when they open her books. The author's presence, the attention to personal research and work ethic, the highlighting of perceptive readers (and the judgment of the opposite), and the signature at the bottom—"Toni Morrison"—separate Morrison from anything but a professional persona. Her final paragraph returns to a story about her grandfather, Big Papa, who "if he wanted the chair you were in, he stood there, silent, looking at the sitter until you got the message and got up. … Wherever he was … that's where the power and deference were. He didn't exert power; he assumed it. And it was in part from knowing him that I felt I could understand and create the men in Ruby—their easy assumption of uncontested authority."[152] In another example of Morrison's family anecdotes, her tale of Big Papa seems to reverberate into a more contentious present. By 2014, Morrison was nearing the end of her life and career, a time of great conflict for any writer. Unlike the earlier forewords, the last one feels like a conclusion, one tightened by the assurance that its author wants more for *Paradise* (and maybe for all of her novels). Though her novel features a newspaper headline, "Come Prepared or Not at All,"[153] which beckons Black people out West, the foreword highlights one aspect of Morrison's practice over anything else: preparation. Though, like her grandfather, she assumes power and receives deference as Toni Morrison, she recognizes the need to check assumptions of uncontested authority. Readers need not be afraid of being turned away, but they must come prepared. She can question authority while assuming it, and that is the space, ultimately, where her forewords live.

Morrison's experiences with the Nobel Prize, Oprah's Book Club, and public authority, with all their troubles and expectations, are linked to her work on the Vintage forewords. She came prepared, and her forewords make the effort to bring readers into her narrative project, with or without past experience with her work. The language was always a part of the project, yet the forewords promote her role not only as a public figure but also as a professional author in the literary marketplace of the twentieth and twenty-first centuries. Morrison knew that by being who she was she had the opportunity to inspire and create communities of readers and writers, and the forewords speak to that responsibility. The early novels provided a canvas for family, folklore, and Black lives. *Beloved* gave her the opportunity to call writing her focus rather than her side-job, *Jazz* extended that focus into freedom, and both focus and freedom culminated in *Paradise*. We may not know what Morrison thought her forewords would mean to scholars, teachers, students, or readers, but her dual focus on language and professional authorship ensures that we see Toni Morrison's narrative project as one that was worthy of the culture.

NOTES

1. Toni Morrison, *The Bluest Eye*, 1970 (New York: Alfred A. Knopf, 1993), 215–216.
2. Toni Morrison, *Beloved*, 1987 (New York: Vintage International, 2004), xix.
3. Toni Morrison, *Playing in the Dark: Whiteness and the Literary Imagination* (Cambridge, MA: Harvard University Press, 1992), xi.
4. Morrison, *The Bluest Eye*, 1993, 209.
5. Morrison, *The Bluest Eye*, 1993, 210.
6. Morrison, *The Bluest Eye*, 1993, 210.
7. Morrison, *The Bluest Eye*, 1993, 212.
8. Morrison, *The Bluest Eye*, 1993, 212.
9. Morrison, *The Bluest Eye*, 1993, 213.
10. Morrison, *The Bluest Eye*, 1993, 214.
11. Morrison, *The Bluest Eye*, 1993, 215–216.
12. Toni Morrison, "The Nobel Lecture in Literature," in *The Source of Self-Regard: Selected Essays, Speeches, and Meditations* (New York: Alfred A. Knopf, 2019), 106.
13. Morrison, *The Bluest Eye*, 1993, 216.
14. Toni Morrison, *The Bluest Eye*, 1970 (New York: Vintage International, 2007), xiii.
15. Toni Morrison, *Sula*, 1973 (New York: Vintage International, 2004), xii.
16. Pam Houston, "Pam Houston Talks with Toni Morrison," *Other Voices* 18, no. 42 (2005). Reprinted in *Toni Morrison: Conversations*, ed. Carolyn C. Denard (Jackson, MS: University Press of Mississippi, 2008), 242.
17. Toni Morrison, "The Individual Artist," in *The Source of Self-Regard*, 59–60.
18. Morrison, *The Bluest Eye*, 2007, ix.
19. Toni Morrison, "The Writer Before the Page," in *The Source of Self-Regard*, 266–267.
20. Genette, *Paratexts: Thresholds of Interpretation*. 1987, trans. Jane E. Lewin (New York: Cambridge University Press, 1997), 1.
21. Genette, *Paratexts*, 256.
22. Tessa Roynon, "Lobbying the Reader: Toni Morrison's Recent Forwords to Her Novels," *European Journal of American Culture* 33, no. 2 (2014): 92.
23. Toni Morrison, "Unspeakable Things Unspoken: The Afro-American Presence in American Literature," in *The Source of Self-Regard*, 192.
24. Morrison, *The Bluest Eye*, 1993, 215.
25. Morrison, *The Bluest Eye*, 1993, 216.
26. Genette, *Paratexts*, 252.

27. Henry James, "*The Portrait of a Lady*," 1908. *Literary Criticism: French Writers, Other European Writers, The Prefaces to the New York Edition*, ed. Leon Edel (New York: Library of America, 1984), 1075.
28. Her novels *A Mercy* (2008), *Home* (2012), and *God Help the Child* (2015) were not released with forewords.
29. Michael Silverblatt, "Michael Silverblatt Talks with Toni Morrison about *Love*." *Bookworm* on KCRW Radio (12 February 2004). In *Toni Morrison: Conversations*, ed. Carolyn C. Denard (Jackson, MS: University Press of Mississippi, 2008), 222.
30. Silverblatt, "Silverblatt Talks with Toni Morrison," 222–223.
31. Ann Hostetler, "Interview with Toni Morrison: 'The Art of Teaching.'" Previously unpublished (17 April 2002). In *Toni Morrison: Conversations*, ed. Carolyn C. Denard (Jackson, MS: University Press of Mississippi, 2008), 200.
32. Hostetler, "Interview with Toni Morrison," 200.
33. Henry James, "*The American*," 1907. *Literary Criticism: French Writers, Other European Writers, The Prefaces to the New York Edition*, ed. Leon Edel (New York: Library of America, 1984), 1057.
34. Morrison, *Playing in the Dark*, xiii.
35. Roynon, "Lobbying the Reader," 88.
36. Genette defines the epitext as a piece outside of the codex that has the effect of a preface, foreword, or introduction. See Genette, *Paratexts*, 8.
37. Toni Morrison, "Peril," in *The Source of Self-Regard*, ix.
38. Toni Morrison, "The Individual Artist," in *The Source of Self-Regard*, 62.
39. Toni Morrison, "Literature and Public Life," in *The Source of Self-Regard*, 100.
40. Morrison, "The Writer Before the Page," in *The Source of Self-Regard*, 264.
41. Morrison, "Unspeakable Things Unspoken," in *The Source of Self-Regard*, 182.
42. John K. Young, *Black Writers, White Publishers: Marketplace Politics in Twentieth-Century African American Literature* (Jackson, MS: University Press of Mississippi, 2006), 120.
43. Toni Morrison, quoted in Cecilia Konchar Farr, *Reading Oprah: How Oprah's Book Club Changed the Way America Reads* (Albany, NY: State University of New York Press, 2005), 48.
44. Farr, *Reading Oprah*, 48.
45. Farr, *Reading Oprah*, 49.
46. Farr, *Reading Oprah*, 108.
47. For instance, Young notes that "within a week of Winfrey's announcement that *Song of Solomon* would be the club's next selection, Morrison's nineteen-year-old novel had reached the top spot on *Publishers Weekly*'s trade paperback best-seller list." See Young, *Black Writers, White Publishers*, 131.

48. Paul Gray, "Books: Paradise Found," *Time*, January 19, 1998, http://content.time.com/time/subscriber/article/0,33009,987690-6,00.html.

49. Pierre Bourdieu, "The Field of Cultural Production, or: The Economic World Reversed." 1993. In *The Broadview Reader in Book History*, eds. Michelle Levy and Tom Mole (Toronto, ON: Broadview Press, 2015), 337.

50. Michael Saur, "'I Want to Write like a Good Jazz Musician': Interview with Toni Morrison." *Rowohlt Revue* (Fall 2004). Reprinted in *Toni Morrison: Conversations*, ed. Carolyn C. Denard (Jackson, MS: University Press of Mississippi, 2008), 227.

51. Toni Morrison, "Narrating the Other," in *The Origin of Others* (Cambridge, MA: Harvard University Press, 2016), 91.

52. Young, *Black Writers, White Publishers*, 121.

53. Genette, *Paratexts*, 1.

54. Morrison, *Playing in the Dark*, xii.

55. Morrison, *Sula*, 2004, xi.

56. Morrison, *Sula*, 2004, xi.

57. Morrison, *Sula*, 2004, xi.

58. Morrison, *Sula*, 2004, xii.

59. Morrison, *Sula*, 2004, xiv.

60. Morrison, "Unspeakable Things Unspoken," in *The Source of Self-Regard*, 196.

61. James Weldon Johnson, ed. *The Book of American Negro Poetry* (New York: Harcourt, Brace, and Company, 1922), xxxiv.

62. Johnson, *The Book of American Negro Poetry*, xxxiii.

63. Johnson, *The Book of American Negro Poetry*, xl.

64. Morrison, *Playing in the Dark*, xi.

65. Morrison, "The Writer Before the Page," in *The Source of Self-Regard*, 268.

66. Toni Morrison, "The Nobel Lecture in Literature," in *The Source of Self-Regard*, 104.

67. Johnson, *The Book of American Negro Poetry*, xli–xlii.

68. Toni Morrison, *Paradise*, 1997 (New York: Vintage International, 2014), xv.

69. Toni Morrison, *Song of Solomon*, 1977 (New York: Vintage International, 2004), xiv.

70. Toni Morrison, *Tar Baby*, 1981 (New York; Vintage International, 2004), xiii.

71. Morrison, *Beloved*, xvii.

72. Toni Morrison, *Jazz*, 1992 (New York: Vintage International, 2004), xviii.

73. Morrison, *Paradise*, xvi.

74. Morrison, *Sula*, xiii–xiv.

75. Toni Morrison, *Love*, 2003 (New York: Vintage International, 2005), xi.
76. Toni Morrison, *The Bluest Eye*, 1970 (New York: Vintage International, 2007), xii.
77. Roynon, "Lobbying the Reader," 95.
78. Roynon, "Lobbying the Reader," 88.
79. Roynon, "Lobbying the Reader," 89.
80. Morrison, *Playing in the Dark*, xii.
81. Morrison, "The Writer Before the Page," in *The Source of Self-Regard*, 264.
82. Roynon, "Lobbying the Reader," 90.
83. Roynon, "Lobbying the Reader," 91.
84. Roynon, "Lobbying the Reader," 95.
85. Toni Morrison, "The Source of Self-Regard," in *The Source of Self-Regard*, 308.
86. Morrison, "The Writer Before the Page," in *The Source of Self-Regard*, 265.
87. Morrison, "The Writer Before the Page," in *The Source of Self-Regard*, 267.
88. Morrison, "Literature and Public Life," in *The Source of Self-Regard*, 101.
89. Toni Morrison, "The Site of Memory," in *The Source of Self-Regard*, 238.
90. Morrison, *Song of Solomon*, xii.
91. Toni Morrison, "Invisible Ink: Reading the Writing and Writing the Reading," in *The Source of Self-Regard*, 350.
92. Roynon, "Lobbying the Reader," 88.
93. Only *Love* deviates in any way from the design, though there are still enough similarities to consider it part of the set.
94. In a 1980 interview with Kathy Neustadt, Morrison recounted an exchange between her and Gottlieb: "I now think of myself as a writer. I didn't realize it on my own though. It was after *Sula* was published; I was talking to my editor (Robert Gottlieb of Knopf) one day and he said, 'This is what you are going to be when you grow up. This is it.' I said, 'A writer?' He said, 'That's right. Of all those other little things you do, this is it. This is what you are.'" See Kathy Neustadt, "The Visits of the Writers Toni Morrison and Eudora Welty." *Bryn Mawr Alumnae Bulletin* (1980). Reprinted in *Conversations with Toni Morrison*, ed., Danille Taylor-Guthrie (Jackson, MS: University Press of Mississippi, 1994), 88.
95. Morrison, *Song of Solomon*, xi.
96. Morrison, *Tar Baby*, xi.
97. Morrison, *Song of Solomon*, xii.
98. Morrison, *Tar Baby*, xiii. Morrison described the myth in an interview with Charles Ruas as follows: "It's a lump of tar shaped like a baby, with a dress on and a bonnet. It's a sunny day and the tar is melting, and the rabbit is getting stuck and more stuck. It's really quite monstrous. ... Of course, as in most peasant literature, that sort of weak but cunning animal gets out of it by his cleverness. So I just gave these characters parts, Tar

Baby being a black woman and the rabbit a black man. I introduced a white man and remembered the tar." See Charles Ruas, "Toni Morrison." *Conversations with American Writers.* 1984. Reprinted in *Conversations with Toni Morrison,* ed. Danille Taylor-Guthrie (Jackson, MS: University Press of Mississippi, 1994), 102.

99. Morrison, *Tar Baby,* xiii.
100. Joel Chandler Harris, *Uncle Remus: His Songs and Sayings* (New York: D. Appleton and Company, 1886), 3.
101. Harris, *Uncle Remus,* 10.
102. Morrison, *Tar Baby,* xii–xiii.
103. Morrison, *Tar Baby,* xiii.
104. Morrison, "Unspeakable Things Unspoken," in *The Source of Self-Regard,* 193.
105. Morrison, *Playing in the Dark,* 38.
106. Morrison, *Playing in the Dark,* 38.
107. Roynon, "Lobbying the Reader," 92.
108. Morrison, *Sula,* 2004, xv.
109. Morrison, *Sula,* 2004, xvi.
110. Morrison, *Sula,* 2004, xvi. Morrison's passage bears a striking resemblance to the opening of William Faulkner's *The Sound and the Fury,* which has Benjy Compson looking out onto his family's old property— now a golf course. See Faulkner, *The Sound and the Fury* (New York: Cape & Smith, 1929).
111. Roynon, "Lobbying the Reader," 95.
112. Morrison, *Beloved,* xv.
113. Morrison, *Beloved,* xv.
114. Morrison, *Beloved,* xvi.
115. Morrison, *Playing in the Dark,* 17.
116. Toni Morrison, "A Bench by the Road: *Beloved* by Toni Morrison." *The World: The Journal of the Unitarian Universalist Association* (January/ February 1989). Reprinted in *Toni Morrison: Conversations,* ed. Carolyn C. Denard (Jackson, MS: University Press of Mississippi, 2008), 44.
117. Morrison, *Beloved,* xi.
118. Morrison, *Tar Baby,* xiv.
119. Morrison, *Tar Baby,* xiv.
120. Morrison, *Jazz,* xvii.
121. Morrison, *Jazz,* xviii.
122. Morrison, *Jazz,* xix.
123. Morrison, "The Nobel Lecture in Literature," in *The Source of Self-Regard,* 106.
124. Morrison, *Jazz,* xviii.
125. Morrison, *Jazz,* xix.

126. Morrison, *Jazz*, 229.
127. Morrison, "The Nobel Lecture in Literature," in *The Source of Self-Regard*, 106.
128. Morrison, *Jazz*, xix.
129. Morrison, *Jazz*, xvi.
130. Morrison, *Jazz*, xvi.
131. Morrison, *Beloved*, xviii.
132. Morrison, *Beloved*, xviii.
133. Morrison, *Beloved*, xix.
134. Roynon, "Lobbying the Reader," 86.
135. Morrison, "Unspeakable Things Unspoken," in *The Source of Self-Regard*, 196.
136. Morrison, "Unspeakable Things Unspoken," in *The Source of Self-Regard*, 195.
137. Morrison, "Unspeakable Things Unspoken," in *The Source of Self-Regard*, 196.
138. Ernest Hemingway, "Preface." *All Good Americans.* By Jerome Bahr (New York: Charles Scribner's Sons, 1937), viii.
139. Morrison, "Peril," in *The Source of Self-Regard*, ix.
140. Morrison, *Paradise*, xii.
141. Morrison, *Paradise*, xiii.
142. Morrison, *Paradise*, xiii.
143. Morrison, *Paradise*, xiii.
144. Morrison, *Paradise*, 3.
145. Morrison, *Paradise*, xvi.
146. Morrison, *Paradise*, xvi–xvii.
147. Morrison, *Paradise*, xvii.
148. Morrison, *Paradise*, xv.
149. Morrison, *Paradise*, xv.
150. Morrison, *Paradise*, xvi.
151. Morrison, *Paradise*, xv.
152. Morrison, *Paradise*, xvii.
153. Morrison, *Paradise*, 13.

BIBLIOGRAPHY

Bourdieu, Pierre. "The Field of Cultural Production, or: The Economic World Reversed." 1993. In *The Broadview Reader in Book History*, edited by Michelle Levy and Tom Mole, 335–352. Toronto, ON: Broadview Press, 2015.

Farr, Cecilia Konchar. *Reading Oprah: How Oprah's Book Club Changed the Way America Reads.* Albany, NY: State University of New York Press, 2005.

Faulkner, William. *The Sound and the Fury.* New York: Cape & Smith, 1929.

Genette, Gerard. *Paratexts: Thresholds of Interpretation*. 1987. Jane E. Lewin, trans. New York: Cambridge University Press, 1997.

Gray, Paul. "Books: Paradise Found." *Time*, January 19, 1998, http://content. time.com/time/subscriber/article/0,33009,987690-6,00.html.

Harris, Joel Chandler. *Uncle Remus: His Songs and Sayings*. New York: D. Appleton and Company, 1886.

Hemingway, Ernest. "Preface." *All Good Americans*. By Jerome Bahr. vii–viii. New York: Charles Scribner's Sons, 1937.

Hostetler, Ann. "Interview with Toni Morrison: 'The Art of Teaching.'" Unpublished (17 April 2002). In *Toni Morrison: Conversations*. Carolyn C. Denard, ed., 196–205. Jackson, MS: University Press of Mississippi, 2008.

Houston, Pam. "Pam Houston Talks with Toni Morrison." *Other Voices* vol. 18 no. 42 (2005). Reprinted in *Toni Morrison: Conversations*. Carolyn C. Denard, ed., 229–259. Jackson, MS: University Press of Mississippi, 2008.

James, Henry. "*The American*." 1907. *Literary Criticism: French Writers, Other European Writers, The Prefaces to the New York Edition*, Leon Edel, ed., 1053–1069. New York: Library of America, 1984.

———. "*The Portrait of a Lady*." 1908. *Literary Criticism: French Writers, Other European Writers, The Prefaces to the New York Edition*, Leon Edel, ed., 1070–1085. New York: Library of America, 1984.

Johnson, James Weldon, ed. *The Book of American Negro Poetry*. New York: Harcourt, Brace, and Company, 1922.

Morrison, Toni. *Beloved*. 1987. New York: Vintage International, 2004.

———. "A Bench by the Road: *Beloved* by Toni Morrison." *The World: The Journal of the Unitarian Universalist Association* (January/February 1989). Reprinted in *Toni Morrison: Conversations*. Carolyn C. Denard, ed., 44–50. Jackson, MS: University Press of Mississippi, 2008.

———. *The Bluest Eye*. 1970. New York: Alfred A. Knopf, 1993.

———. *The Bluest Eye*. 1970. New York: Vintage, 1999.

———. *The Bluest Eye*. 1970. New York: Vintage International, 2007.

———. *Jazz*. 1992. New York: Vintage International, 2004.

———. *Love*. 2003. New York: Vintage International, 2005.

———. *The Origin of Others*. Cambridge, MA: Harvard University Press, 2016.

———. *Paradise*. 1997. New York: Vintage International, 2014.

———. *Playing in the Dark: Whiteness and the Literary Imagination*. Cambridge, MA: Harvard University Press, 1992.

———. *Song of Solomon*. 1977. New York: Vintage International, 2004.

———. *The Source of Self-Regard: Selected Essays, Speeches, and Meditations*. New York: Alfred A. Knopf, 2019.

———. *Sula*. 1973. New York: Vintage International, 2004.

———. *Tar Baby*. 1981. New York: Vintage International, 2004.

Neustadt, Kathy. "The Visits of the Writers Toni Morrison and Eudora Welty." *Bryn Mawr Alumnae Bulletin* (1980). Reprinted in *Conversations with Toni Morrison*, edited by Danille Taylor-Guthrie, 84–92. (Jackson, MS: University Press of Mississippi, 1994.

Ruas, Charles. "Toni Morrison." *Conversations with American Writers.* 1984. Reprinted in *Conversations with Toni Morrison*, edited by Danille Taylor-Guthrie, 93–118. Jackson, MS: University Press of Mississippi, 1994.

Roynon, Tessa. "Lobbying the Reader: Toni Morrison's Recent Forwords to Her Novels," *European Journal of American Culture* 33, no. 2 (2014): 85–96.

Saur, Michael. "'I Want to Write like a Good Jazz Musician': Interview with Toni Morrison." *Rowohlt Revue* (Fall 2004). Reprinted in *Toni Morrison: Conversations.* Carolyn C. Denard, ed., 224–227. Jackson, MS: University Press of Mississippi, 2008.

Silverblatt, Michael. "Michael Silverblatt Talks with Toni Morrison about *Love.*" *Bookworm* on KCRW Radio (12 February 2004). Reprinted in *Toni Morrison: Conversations,* Carolyn C. Denard, ed., 216–223. Jackson, MS: University Press of Mississippi, 2008.

Young, John K. *Black Writers, White Publishers: Marketplace Politics in Twentieth-Century African American Literature.* Jackson, MS: University Press of Mississippi, 2006.

CHAPTER 8

Coda: Any Given Moment Has Its Value

*After all, any given moment has its value; it can be questioned in the light of
after-events, but the moment remains. The young princes in velvet gathered in
lovely domesticity around the queen amid the hush of rich draperies may
presently grow up to be Pedro the Cruel or Charles the Mad, but the moment
of beauty was there.*
—F. Scott Fitzgerald[1]

My ultimate goal in writing *The Preface: American Authorship in the
Twentieth Century* is to provide a template for continued study of prefaces
and other authorial adornments that live alongside our favorite texts.
Prefaces provide an intriguing gateway into the study of professional
authorship in America. As with any discipline, demonstrating the significance of something proves challenging, and windows are needed to peak
through and eventually open. Luckily, there are more prefaces than one
can count scattered throughout the twentieth century. My investigation
opened many windows, as each preface documented a relationship, a compromise, an evolution, or a reaction. The business of literature contains so
many moving parts that neglecting a piece here or there is not uncom-
mon, but we must strive to learn as much about an author's habits, ideas,
and practices if we are to understand truly the art of literary creation.
Though *The Preface* is by no means exhaustive, the authors under investigation represent the very human side of writing, their prefaces (as well as
their texts) a construct of that humanity.

© The Author(s), under exclusive license to Springer Nature   203
Switzerland AG 2021
R. K. Tangedal, *The Preface*, New Directions in Book History,
https://doi.org/10.1007/978-3-030-85151-4_8

In June 1933, Willa Cather told her friend, fellow writer Dorothy Canfield Fisher, that "As soon as I think of myself as a human figure in that past, in those scenes (Red Cloud, Colorado, New Mexico) the scenes grow rather dim and are spoiled for me. When I remember those places I am not there at all, as a person." Though she was grateful to have "so good a front presented to the public," she was a fiercely private person, not one to go out of her way to promote herself unless it was needed. "I seem to have been a bundle of enthusiasms and physical sensations, but not a person," she continues. "How can anyone really see himself? He can see a kind of shadow he throws, but not the real creature. I have been running away from myself all my life (have you?) and have been happiest when I was running fastest."[2] Writers navigate their public personae by fixating on a moment in their authorial evolution: a place where it all started, who they were when they began to write, what they cared about when they first put pen to paper. Cather's Jim Burden, the narrator of *My Ántonia*, chases the shadows of his past (and the pasts of others) with little to show for it, except the knowledge of "what a little circle man's experience is."[3] Without Cather's introduction to the novel, we may not have understood fully the intensely private business of that chase, and why Cather had to get out of the way so that Jim could see just how far his shadows actually stretched. Her aim, begun in the introduction, was to celebrate someone striving for meaning in an unfulfilled present by recreating an idealized, if not entirely true, past to cling to. Jim's burden, his ultimate tragedy, is being shackled to his own memory, while Cather finds apparent joy in running away from herself, her past selves. Prefaces represent something similar: they are an escape and a return; a tragedy and a triumph. In what follows I discuss, albeit briefly, more writers and their prefaces, moments of value that illuminate the very human business that writing becomes for those who make it their trade.

Robert Frost's preface to his 1939 *Collected Poems*, "The Figure a Poem Makes," was later published in multiple venues as the key to unlocking the mystery of the poet's work. "No tears in the writer, no tears in the reader. No surprise for the writer, no surprise for the reader,"[4] he advises. "Like a piece of ice on a hot stove the poem must ride on its own melting."[5] Earlier that year he had written a preface to an anthology for the Bread Loaf School of English at Middlebury College in Vermont.[6] He argues that "a writer can live by writing to himself alone for days and years. Sooner or later to go on he must be read. It may well be that in appealing to the public he has but added to his own responsibility; for now besides judging himself he must judge his judges. ... All we know is that the crowning mercy for an author is publication in one form or another."[7] There exists a stark divide between these two prefaces, one focused on art, the other on commerce. Of course Frost is right, as he wrangles with the dual roles (writer and author) that began our investigation into prefaces. He mentions "writer" four times in the *Bread Loaf* preface, a teacher offering practical advice to eager young writers. The artist stands out in his preface to the *Collected Poems*: "the happy-sad blend of the drinking song,"[8] "the straight crookedness of a good walking stick,"[9] "the vast chaos of all I have lived through,"[10] "the wild free ways of wit and art."[11] A poem "will forever keep its freshness as a metal keeps its fragrance," and the artist must always have a sense of surprise and craft to operate.[12] He mentions "art," "artist," and "poet" at several points, leaving "writer" only to his now-famous maxim mentioned earlier. Frost realized that writers want to know more about writing, and readers want to know more about artists. Both prefaces serve him well, and both prove crucial to understanding his relationship to the profession he spent his life perfecting.

Similarly, Arna Bontemps recognized the timing of the reissuing of his novel *Black Thunder* (1936) in 1968, hoping that readers would link the events of an 1800 slave revolt in Virginia to the contemporary struggle for civil rights in America.[13] "Time is not a river," he wrote in his introduction to the new printing, "Time is a pendulum."[14] Bontemps, a key figure in the Harlem Renaissance, reads the murder of Dr. Martin Luther King, Jr., as part of a larger "metaphor of turbulence" that engulfs Black men who dare to press out from racist systems.[15] The first edition of his book made back its advance, but Bontemps was convinced that "the theme of self-assertion by black men whose endurance was strained to the breaking point was not one that readers of fiction were prepared to contemplate at the time." Thirty years later, with the novel reprinted at the height of civil rights struggles, Bontemps's cautious optimism belies a truer cynicism: "Now that *Black Thunder* is published again, after more than thirty years, I cannot help wondering if its story will be better understood by Americans, both black and white. However, I am convinced that time is not a river." Earlier in the introduction Bontemps carefully reconstructs his experiences with racism (what he refers to as "quaint hostilities"[16]) while teaching at Oakwood Junior College in Huntsville, Alabama, where the white head of the school demanded he burn many of his books, "a number of which were trash in his estimation anyway, the rest, race-conscious and provocative." He refused, instead relocating back to the Watts neighborhood of Los Angeles, California, with his wife and children to write what became *Black Thunder*, an act of rebellion in its own right. His refusal to "make a clean break with the unrest of the world"[17] at Oakwood reflects the theme of Black self-assertion he saw in Gabriel Prosser's 1800 slave revolt, and in Dr. King's public advocacy for equality prior to his assassination in 1968. Bontemps's act may have been the smallest of the three, but he survived his act of self-assertion, and time has proven that his curatorial efforts kept many texts of the Harlem Renaissance alive and well. For nearly thirty years Bontemps developed considerable collections on Black culture at Fisk University, the University of Illinois, and as curator of the James Weldon Johnson Collection at Yale University. The study of Black literature exists in part because of Bontemps's force of will to curate and catalogue the Black experience in America. Time may be a pendulum, but Bontemps's bibliographical impact assured Black culture a place in reader's hands regardless of its swing.

"No one elected me the boss of the memoir," declares Mary Karr in "Caveat Emptor," her preface to the preface to *The Art of Memoir* (2016). "I speak for no one but myself. Every writer worth her salt is sui generis." Buyer beware, as Karr pulls back the curtain of genre, for "this is no compendium of popular approaches to form,"[18] but rather an investigation into what to do about memory. What she has to offer "may well apply to writing novels or poems or love letters or bank applications or parole board pleas. … But since it's memoir they've paid me for, I'll stick to it," she writes, but her suggestion that every good writer may have the touch of genius weds craft with creation, and legitimacy with authenticity.[19] In her designated preface that follows, "Welcome to My Chew Toy," she maintains that "there's artifice to the relationship between any writer and her reader. Memoir done right is an art, a made thing. It's not just raw reportage flung splat on the page. Most morally ominous: from the second you choose one event over another, you're shaping the past's meaning."[20] She hopes readers recognize their own "divided selves and ever-morphing past." We all have a past, she concludes, "and every past spawns fierce and fiery emotions about what it means."[21] Later in the book she chooses to draw with her "little stick … a line in the dirt for the sake of memoir's authenticity," for ultimately, "you're seeking the truth of memory—your memory and character—not of unbiased history."[22] For Karr there is art to a lived life, truth in memory, and reliability in good storytellers.

In what became a defining memoir of mental illness and recovery, William Styron's *Darkness Visible: A Memoir of Madness* (1990) chronicles the depths of its author's depression. The book features a very practical author's note charting the history of what began as a lecture, then became a piece for *Vanity Fair*, then a nonfiction memoir.[23] While relatively uneventful, the short author's note is followed by Styron's epigraph, a quote from the Biblical Book of Job: "For the thing which/I greatly feared is come upon me,/and that which I was afraid of/Is come unto me./I was not in safety, neither/had I rest, neither was I quiet;/yet trouble came."[24] That Styron survived his depression makes his matter-of-fact note all the more triumphant. He endured the whirlwind, "so mysteriously painful and elusive in the way it becomes known to the self—to the mediating intellect—as to verge close to being beyond description,"[25] and can now write a textual note about the chaos he charts. A simple note becomes a courageous note. Job's fear, unease, and chilling anticipation concludes and begins; its transitory space amplifies the simple note that came before it, and the darkness, now visible, that comes after. To paraphrase Karr, Styron's memoir is, like all others, a "made thing," but his avenue of healing begins, textually, with a short author's note about provenance followed by the fierce and fiery power of Job's suffering.

Of course composition history becomes as much a tale as the work it supposedly results in when writers are given the chance to recount, for themselves, how and why they wrote something. Far from a household name in 1932, William Faulkner had published two of the novels upon which his current reputation rests—*The Sound and the Fury* (1929) and *As I Lay Dying* (1930)—and would release a third, *Light in August*, later that year. In between the three was *Sanctuary*, a sordid tale of the kidnapping and rape of Temple Drake, published in early 1931 and reprinted in the Modern Library series in early 1932. Faulkner wrote a now-famous introduction to the Modern Library edition of *Sanctuary*, claiming the book was "a cheap idea, because it was deliberately conceived to make money."[26] Faulkner's claims in the introduction became the prevailing history of *Sanctuary*, similar to how the table of contents to *Tales of the Jazz Age* (1922) reinforced F. Scott Fitzgerald's supposed cavalier attitude toward writing.[27] A "systematic inversion of the fundamental principles of all ordinary economies" occurs within literary expression, argues Pierre Bourdieu. "The literary and artistic world is so ordered that those who enter it have an interest in disinterestedness," yet when writers amplify either an affinity for economic gain or a stated intention to write less-than-quality literature for the sake of popularity, they buck against any claims of being a legiti-mate artist.[28]

But Faulkner appears to want his cake and eat it too. His books had been "published but not bought" for five years, and he claims to not know "that people got money for them," so he "began to think about making money by writing."[29] "I had just written my guts into *The Sound and the Fury* though I was not aware until the book was published that I had done so, because I had done it for pleasure," he claims. "I believed then that I would never be published again. I had stopped thinking of myself in pub-lishing terms."[30] Down on his luck, Faulkner discovers that his third book, *Sartoris*, was to be published, though a publisher warned him that it would not sell. He sees himself "again as a printed object" and begins "to think of books in terms of possible money," before setting out to write the book he has already told readers he wrote to make money. He "invented the most horrific tale" he could imagine and "wrote it in about three weeks … in the summer of 1929."[31] In reality Faulkner spent several months writ-ing *Sanctuary*, and he revised it meticulously prior to its publication two years later.[32] But given his less-than-flattering composition history in the introduction, Faulkner amplifies *The Sound and the Fury* and *As I Lay Dying* indirectly over *Sanctuary*. He wrote his guts into *The Sound and the Fury*, and he claims to have built the table upon which *As I Lay Dying* was written "out of a wheelbarrow in the coal bunker, just beyond a wall from where a dynamo ran" while working at a power plant. Of the latter novel he told publisher Harrison Smith "that by it I would stand or fall." Having allegedly forgotten about *Sanctuary*, "just as you might forget about any-thing made for an immediate purpose," Faulkner received the galleys for the novel from Smith after the publication of *As I Lay Dying*. "Then I saw that it was so terrible that there were but two things to do: tear it up or rewrite it," he proclaims, figuring it may sell due to its lurid subject mat-ter.[33] He rewrites the book in galleys, "trying to make out of it something which would not shame *The Sound and the Fury* and *As I Lay Dying* too much and I made a fair job and I hope you will buy it and tell your friends and I hope they will buy it too."[34] Much like Fitzgerald's Modern Library introduction to *The Great Gatsby*,[35] Faulkner's introduction to *Sanctuary* is a call for readers to revisit (or discover for the first time) the books he really wants them to read: *The Sound and the Fury* and *As I Lay Dying* (for Fitzgerald, he wanted them to reconsider *Tender Is the Night*). The more people who buy *Sanctuary* and read the introduction the better, since he only wrote it for money. He wrote the other two out of artistic necessity, with a purity of vision and strong "hard-bellied" intentions.[36] While prominent textual scholars like Noel Polk have disproven Faulkner's compositional narrative and apparent disdain for *Sanctuary*,[37] the fog of his introduction still covers the novel, and his preferred books are now the cornerstones of his legacy, just as he'd hoped.

But just as Ring Lardner mastered the craft of sending up the preface as a serious authorial device, other writers have stretched and manipulated our understanding of the preface. Philip Roth's *Operation Shylock: A Confession* (1993) is bookended by a preface at the beginning and a note to the reader at the end. Since doubling and doppelgängers play a major role in the novel, Roth sets up readers with what appears to be a fact-based preface outlining the process by which he has, "for legal reasons," changed some facts throughout the book. "These are minor changes that mainly involve details of identification and locale and are of little significance to the overall story and its verisimilitude." He claims to have created the novel using notebook journals, and "The book is as accurate an account as I am able to give of actual occurrences that I lived through during my middle fifties and that culminated, early in 1988, in my agreeing to undertake an intelligence-gathering operation for Israel's foreign intelligence service, the Mossad."[38] He writes himself into his novel, opening it with the provocative first line, "I learned about the other Philip Roth in January 1988," but he writes himself into the novel in two ways: one as Philip Roth, and one as the "other" Philip Roth, his double. Should a reader's skepticism call into question Roth's claims, they are vindicated with Roth's note to the reader, on the last page of the novel. "This book is a work of fiction," he writes. "Any resemblance to actual events or locales or persons, living or dead, is entirely coincidental. This confession is false."[39] What is and is not Philip Roth's words proves equally puzzling. The preface is signed "P.R. December 1, 1992,"[40] while the note to the reader goes unsigned. Further, there appears to be three Philip Roths: the Philip Roth who wrote the book, the Philip Roth who is the protagonist of the novel, and the Philip Roth who is impersonating the protagonist. Roth had used himself as the narrator in *Deception* (1990) and again in *The Plot Against America* (2004), though with *Shylock* he maintained that the story was true. He had only written the note to the reader to throw readers off the scent.[41] Roth interrogates authorial identity and self-fashioning, his preface and note to the reader zones of postmodern misdirection that question the very structures we have grown accustomed to accepting in books. The story is plausible, and that might have to be enough.

Dave Eggers uses literally every possible space in the front matter to his memoir *A Heartbreaking Work of Staggering Genius* (2000) to forward a postmodern sense of storytelling, critique the "author" as a figure, and represent textually the fraught mind of a grieving son. Instead of a half-title the first page reads: "THIS IS UNCALLED FOR."[42] On the copyright page he repurposes rote legalese to function instead as bursts of looked-over comedy. The "Published in the United States" statement runs eleven lines, lambasting the size and influence of Simon & Schuster and its parent company Viacom. Under the ISBN, Eggers lists his height, weight, eye and hair colors, and "Hands: chubbier than one would expect." The Printer's Key is repurposed as a "sexual-orientation scale, with 1 being perfectly straight, and 10 being perfectly gay"; he circles the three. He concludes the copyright page with a fourteen-line note that claims the book is both fiction and fact: "All events described herein actually happened, though on occasion the author has taken certain, very small, liberties with chronology, because that is his right as an American."[43] Eggers gets the most out of his copyright page, a space most readers gloss over even more so than they do prefaces. The rest of his front matter consists of the following: "Rules and Suggestions for Enjoyment of this Book," "Preface to this Edition," "Contents," "Acknowledgments," and "Incomplete Guide to Symbols and Metaphors."[44] According to Gerard Genette, once a preface or introductory material has been written into a book, the reader "will have to make an effort to circumvent this inhibiting signpost, which won't be that easy to do."[45] With the front matter taken as a single unit, I can think of no greater example of the preface as "inhibiting signpost" than what Eggers has created. One must wade through forty pages before arriving at the first chapter, which tests even the most patient reader. But his pieces are essential in their non-essentiality, simultaneously about everything and nothing, a truly postmodern approach. "The author would also like to acknowledge his propensity to exaggerate. And his propensity to fib in order to make himself look better, or worse, whichever serves his purposes at the time," he notes on the last page of his front matter. "He would also like to acknowledge that no, he is not the only person to ever lose his parents, and that he is also not the only person ever to lose his parents and inherit a youngster. But he would like to point out that he is currently the only such person with a book contract."[46] If the inner workings of trauma mean anything to the reader, they will know why the book begins as it does. Nothing can be harder than writing about the death of one's parents, and the immense responsibility of raising a younger sibling. Eggers's front matter, with its suite of individual, prefatory pieces, acts as a textual representation of the grieving process. Misdirection, obsession with minute details, changing the subject, laughing to stop from crying, showing off, and so on. The breakdowns and regenerations that occur stir more than the narrative; they stir the very structure of how that narrative is displayed to the public. They are, for lack of a better word, heartbreaking.

Our appreciation of literature is amplified if we learn to appreciate the process necessary to create that literature. We have to know where to look, and we have to be willing to look, since writers consciously engage in spaces outside of their narrative texts. If they do this, it stands to reason that they want us to read what they wrote there. I argue not that prefaces take precedence over a narrative proper, but that they have a place at the table due to their very existence in the book. Prefaces help readers experience the profession of authorship in context, since they, at times, portray process, pain, success, failure, inspiration, meaning, aspiration, and ultimately, the life of the writer. "To part is to die a little, it is said (in every language I can read)," writes Katherine Anne Porter in "Go Little Book …" her preface to *The Collected Stories of Katherine Anne Porter* (1965). "But my farewell to these stories is a happy one, a renewal of their life, a prolonging of their time under the sun, which is what any artist most longs for—to be read, and remembered." Her preface is a goodbye, as she parts with the past reception and reputation of her stories in hopes of them finding new lives. They must move out of the house, Porter now the empty nester wishing them well. "Go little book …" she concludes.[47] With sweet sorrow she lays the stories at our feet, hoping that we too will come to love them as much as she does. What else can a writer ask for? Read me. Remember me. Go little book.

Notes

1. F. Scott Fitzgerald, *The Notebooks of F. Scott Fitzgerald*, ed. Matthew J. Bruccoli (New York: Harcourt Brace Jovanovich/Bruccoli Clark, 1972), 192.
2. Willa Cather, "#1186: Willa Cather to Dorothy Canfield Fisher, June 22 [1933]," in *The Complete Letters of Willa Cather*, eds. the Willa Cather Archive team. The Willa Cather Archive, 2018. Accessed April 8, 2021, https://cather.unl.edu/writings/letters/let1186.

3. Willa Cather, *My Ántonia*, 1918, eds. Charles Mignon and Kari A. Ronning (Lincoln, NE: University of Nebraska Press, 1994), 360.

4. Robert Frost, "The Figure a Poem Makes." 1939. In *The Collected Prose of Robert Frost*, ed. Mark Richardson (Cambridge, MA: Harvard University Press, 2007), 132.

5. Frost, "The Figure a Poem Makes," 133.

6. W. Storrs Lee, ed., *The Bread Loaf Anthology*, with a preface by Robert Frost (Middlebury, VT: Middlebury College Press, 1939). The preface was titled "The Doctrine of Excursions."

7. Robert Frost, "The Doctrine of Excursions." 1939. In *The Collected Prose of Robert Frost*, 129.

8. Frost, "The Figure a Poem Makes," 132.

9. Frost, "The Figure a Poem Makes," 132.

10. Frost, "The Figure a Poem Makes," 132.

11. Frost, "The Figure a Poem Makes," 133.

12. Frost, "The Figure a Poem Makes," 133.

13. Arnold Rampersad claims that the novel "arose out of what might be seen as a set of concentric circles of despair and disaster, with Bontemps himself at the center." See Rampersad's "Introduction to the 1992 Edition," in *Black Thunder*, 1936 (Boston, MA: Beacon Hill Press, 1992), vii.

14. Arna Bontemps, "Introduction to the 1968 Edition." In *Black Thunder*, 1936 (Boston, MA: Beacon Hill Press, 1992), xxi.

15. Bontemps, "Introduction to the 1968 Edition," xxii.

16. Bontemps, "Introduction to the 1968 Edition," xxvii.

17. Bontemps, "Introduction to the 1968 Edition," xxviii.

18. Mary Karr, *The Art of Memoir* (New York: Harper, 2016), xi.

19. Karr, *The Art of Memoir*, xii.

20. Karr, *The Art of Memoir*, xvii.

21. Karr, *The Art of Memoir*, xxiii.

22. Karr, *The Art of Memoir*, 11.

23. William Styron, *Darkness Visible: A Memoir of Madness* (New York: Random House, 1990), ix.

24. Styron, *Darkness Visible*, 1.

25. Styron, *Darkness Visible*, 7.

26. William Faulkner, "Introduction." In *Sanctuary*, 1931 (New York: Modern Library, 1932), v.

27. See F. Scott Fitzgerald, "Table of Contents," *Tales of the Jazz Age*, 1922, ed. James L. W. West III (New York: Cambridge University Press, 2002), 5–9.

28. Pierre Bourdieu, "The Field of Cultural Production, or: The Economic World Reversed," in *The Broadview Reader in Book History*, eds. Michelle Levy and Tom Mole (Toronto, ON: Broadview Press, 2015), 341.

29. Faulkner, "Introduction," v. By 1929, Faulkner had published *Soldier's Pay* (1926), *Mosquitos* (1927), *Sartoris* (1929), and *The Sound and the Fury* (1929).
30. Faulkner, "Introduction," vi.
31. Faulkner, "Introduction," vi.
32. Noel Polk calls the introduction "infamous and deliberately misleading," since the textual evidence proves that Faulkner worked much harder on the novel than he cared to admit. "Clearly *Sanctuary* cost him a great deal to write," Polk claims, "—much more, the evidence of the manuscript suggests, in the original writing than in the revising; just as clearly, the materials of *Sanctuary* were far more significant to him than his smart-aleck indictment of it ... allows." See Noel Polk, "Children of the Dark House," in *Children of the Dark House: Text and Context in Faulkner* (Jackson, MS: University Press of Mississippi, 1996), 40; 44.
33. Faulkner, "Introduction," vii.
34. Faulkner, "Introduction," vii–viii.
35. The preface to the Modern Library edition is reprinted in F. Scott Fitzgerald, *The Great Gatsby*, 1925, ed. Matthew J. Bruccoli (New York: Cambridge University Press, 1991), 222–225.
36. Faulkner, "Introduction," v.
37. See note 32.
38. Philip Roth, *Operation Shylock: A Confession* (New York: Simon & Schuster, 1993), 13.
39. Roth, *Operation Shylock*, 399.
40. Roth, *Operation Shylock*, 14.
41. See Esther B. Fein, "Philip Roth Sees Double. And Maybe Triple, Too," *New York Times*, March 9, 1993, sec. C. Roth claims: "When I wrote 'Portnoy's Complaint,' everybody was sure it was me, but I told them it wasn't. When I wrote the 'Ghost Writer' everybody was sure it was me, but I said none of these things ever happened to me. I never met a girl who looked like Anne Frank. I didn't have some nice writer take me into his house. I made it all up. And now when I tell the truth, they all insist that I made it up. I tell them, 'Well, how can I make it up since you've always said I am incapable of making anything up?' I can't win!"
42. Dave Eggers, *A Heartbreaking Work of Staggering Genius* (New York: Simon & Schuster, 2000), i.
43. Eggers, *A Heartbreaking Work of Staggering Genius*, iv.
44. Eggers, *A Heartbreaking Work of Staggering Genius*, vii–xl.
45. Gerard Genette, *Paratexts: Thresholds of Interpretation*, 1987, trans. Jane E. Lewin (New York: Cambridge University Press, 1997), 224.
46. Eggers, *A Heartbreaking Work of Staggering Genius*, xxxix.
47. Katherine Anne Porter, "Go Little Book ..." In *The Collected Stories of Katherine Anne Porter* (New York: Harcourt, Inc., 1965), vi.

BIBLIOGRAPHY

Bontemps, Arna. "Introduction to the 1968 Edition," *Black Thunder*. 1936, xxi–xxix. Boston, MA: Beacon Hill Press, 1992.

Bourdieu, Pierre. "The Field of Cultural Production, or: The Economic World Reversed." 1993. In *The Broadview Reader in Book History*, edited by Michelle Levy and Tom Mole, 335–352. Toronto, ON: Broadview Press, 2015.

Cather, Willa. *My Ántonia*. 1918. Charles Mignon and Kari A. Ronning, eds. Lincoln, NE: University of Nebraska Press, 1994.

Eggers, Dave. *A Heartbreaking Work of Staggering Genius*. New York: Simon & Schuster, 2000.

Faulkner, William. "Introduction." In *Sanctuary*. 1931, v–viii. New York: Modern Library, 1932.

Fein, Esther B. "Philip Roth Sees Double. And Maybe Triple, Too." *New York Times*, March 9, 1993, sec. C.

Fitzgerald, F. Scott. *The Great Gatsby*. 1925. Matthew J. Bruccoli, ed. New York: Cambridge University Press, 1991.

———. *The Notebooks of F. Scott Fitzgerald*. Matthew J. Bruccoli, ed. New York: Harcourt Brace Jovanovich/Bruccoli Clark, 1972.

———. *Tales of the Jazz Age*. 1922. James L. W. West III, ed. New York: Cambridge University Press, 2002.

Frost, Robert. "The Doctrine of Excursions." 1939. In *The Collected Prose of Robert Frost*, Mark Richardson, ed., 129–130. Cambridge, MA: Harvard University Press, 2007.

———. "The Figure a Poem Makes." 1939. In *The Collected Prose of Robert Frost*, 131–133.

Genette, Gerard. *Paratexts: Thresholds of Interpretation*. 1987. Jane E. Lewin, trans. New York: Cambridge University Press, 1997.

Karr, Mary. *The Art of Memoir*. New York: Harper, 2016.

Lee, W. Storrs, ed. *The Bread Loaf Anthology*, with a preface by Robert Frost. Middlebury, VT: Middlebury College Press, 1939.

Polk, Noel. "Children of the Dark House." In *Children of the Dark House: Text and Context in Faulkner*, 22–98. Jackson, MS: University Press of Mississippi, 1996.

Porter, Katherine Anne. "Go Little Book…" In *The Collected Stories of Katherine Anne Porter*, v–vi. New York: Harcourt, Inc., 1965.

Rampersad, Arnold. "Introduction to the 1992 Edition." In Arna Bontemps, *Black Thunder*. 1936, vii–xx. Boston, MA: Beacon Hill Press, 1992.

Roth, Philip. *Operation Shylock: A Confession*. New York: Simon & Schuster, 1993.

Styron, William. *Darkness Visible: A Memoir of Madness*. New York: Random House, 1990.

The Willa Cather Archive team, eds. *The Complete Letters of Willa Cather*. The Willa Cather Archive, 2018. Accessed April 8, 2021. https://cather.unl.edu/writings/letters.

INDEX[1]

[1] Note: Page numbers followed by 'n' refer to notes.

© The Author(s), under exclusive license to Springer Nature Switzerland AG 2021

R. K. Tangedal, *The Preface*, New Directions in Book History, https://doi.org/10.1007/978-3-030-85151-4_8

Printed by Printforce, the Netherlands